THE
A GUIDE FOR

THE CHURCH:
A GUIDE FOR THE PERPLEXED

MATT JENSON

AND

DAVID E. WILHITE

t&t clark

Published by T&T Clark International
A Continuum Imprint
The Tower Building, 11 York Road, London SE1 7NX
80 Maiden Lane, Suite 704, New York, NY 10038

www.continuumbooks.com

British Library Cataloguing-in-Publication Data
A catalogue record for this book is available from the British Library.

ISBN 13: 9780567033369 (Hardback)
          9780567033376 (Paperback)

Typeset by Newgen Imaging Systems Pvt Ltd, Chennai, India
Printed and bound in Great Britain by the MPG Books Group

CONTENTS

CONTENTS

ACKNOWLEDGEMENTS

In the last few years, we each have moved to new cities for new jobs. We thank God for the churches that ministered to us and formed us during this transition: Trinity Church of the Nazarene in Kansas City, Kansas; First Free Methodist Church in Seattle, Washington; Fountain of Life Covenant Church in Long Beach, California and University Baptist Church in Waco, Texas. These congregations serve as cities set on a hill and we dedicate this book to them in gratitude and hope.

We would also like to credit the people who helped bring this project together. Thanks to Tom Kraft, utterly professional and always friendly, an author's editor, and for the various folks at T&T Clark who shepherd the publishing process and oversee the *Guides for the Perplexed*. Marc Cortez graciously gave of his time in the nick of time and offered invaluable insights on our first draft. Any unconvincing item in this book is probably a result of our ignoring one of his suggestions. Suzanne Holsomback took on the Herculean task of editing a co-authored project and helping us bring our manuscript and our ideas into some sort of coherence. Her long hours and her careful eye deserve much of the credit for the current state of the project. Any shortcomings remaining in this work are entirely our own (even though I tried to convince David to change them).

Matt would like to thank the Torrey Honors Institute and Biola University for affording me time and space for research and writing. To be graced with such support in research at a teaching school in a core humanities programme is a unique gift. I love where I work and, as glad as I've been for time to read and write, it is good to be back with such generous colleagues and students. (Thanks, too, to all those students who have talked church with me in these last few years.) Thanks to Greg and Kirstin Johnson (in Beckwith, Ontario) and Ron and Mary Jenson (in San Diego, California) for carving out room in their lives and homes and affording me much-needed friendship and nurture while on leave. My parents, sister and a lavish supply of friends make life good.

David would like to thank the George W. Truett Theological Seminary of Baylor University for the institutional support given in resources and sabbaticals which enabled this project to come to fruition. I would especially like to thank the assistant dean (and for much of this project the interim dean), Dennis Tucker, who was so supportive of this work, as well as the rest of my colleagues at Truett whose encouragement kept me going. Most of all I thank the love of my life, Amber, for having the patience of Job, the dedication of Ruth, the wisdom of Solomon and the good looks of Esther. She sacrificed as much if not more than anyone for this book.

We hope this is more than a book about the church; we pray it is a service to the church, the people of God, the body of Christ, the fellowship of the Spirit. *Soli Deo Gloria.*

INTRODUCTION

We begin with a prayer and a vision. The prayer is Jesus' last one for the church:

> I ask not only on behalf of these, but also on behalf of those who will believe in me through their word, that they may all be one. As you, Father, are in me and I am in you, may they also be in us, so that the world may believe that you have sent me. (Jn 17.20–21)

The vision is of the church as the heavenly Jerusalem:

> Then one of the seven angels who had the seven bowls full of the seven last plagues came and said to me, 'Come, I will show you the bride, the wife of the Lamb.' And in the spirit he carried me away to a great, high mountain and showed me the holy city Jerusalem coming down out of heaven from God. It has the glory of God and a radiance like a very rare jewel, like jasper, clear as crystal. . . . The wall is built of jasper, while the city is pure gold, clear as glass. . . . And the twelve gates are twelve pearls, each of the gates is a single pearl, and the street of the city is pure gold, transparent as glass. (Rev. 21.9–11, 18, 21)

Lofty thoughts, these. Jesus envisions a church enfolded in the life of God, united with the Father and the Son even as they are with one another. John sees a church of almost unspeakable beauty and radiance, filled as it is with the glory of God. We begin here not to assert an ideal vision of the church – an ideal which, when tested by experience, would quickly deteriorate into an impossibly crushing moral standard or a blueprint utterly abstracted from the experiences

1

of Christians in their local church.[1] No, we begin here because most of us do not recognize the church in Jesus' prayer and John's vision. We do not recognize that the company of people who have been brought into *koinonia* – into fellowship, into communion – with the Father and the Son by the Spirit is none other than that contentious, immature, lackadaisical collection of individuals brought incongruously together on Sunday mornings. And yet, this company of people – and no other – is the people of God, the body of Christ, the fellowship of the Holy Spirit. Paul can even call a church whose members included a man sleeping with his stepmother 'the church of God' and 'those who have been sanctified in Christ Jesus' (1 Cor. 1.2). This does not excuse sin. If anything, it should agitate a complacent church, in view of its position between the prayers of Jesus and the hope of the new Jerusalem.

* * *

Ecclesiology dominated the twentieth-century theological scene as Christians in the pew, pulpit and classroom sought to consider the implications of new realities within the church (such as Pentecostalism and ecumenism) and outwith the church (such as secularism and religious pluralism). Much has been written, and it is difficult to navigate between breezy generalities on the one hand and arcane specificities on the other. This is, in part, a function of the very real perplexities that plague – or, as the case may be, enrich – a full-orbed understanding of the church.

This book serves as a rigorously comprehensive (though not exhaustive) introduction to the doctrine of the church by taking the tack of walking readers through the internal logic of ecclesiology. Rather than simply offering a compendium of perspectives on each issue that arises, we seek to teach and model thinking theologically, with the grain of scripture and ecclesial reflection, about the church. The chapters are written with an eye to comprehension, if not always to the depth which a longer book might afford. The overall structure is roughly systematic. Instead of a historical half followed by a constructive one, we will take a broadly systematic approach that richly integrates insights, challenges and concerns from the history of the church. While we initially considered halving the book into historical and theological sections, we realized quickly that that would do a disservice to both. It would invite us to think of history as mere prolegomena – interesting, perhaps, but only ornamental, not the real stuff of ecclesiology. It would invite us to think of theology as unresponsible and incline us to equate the novel with the significant and, worse, the faithful. The chapters are peppered with excurses in which we pause to consider a particularly pertinent issue that arises from the doctrine's development or contemporary concerns. While the overall tone and content of the book articulates and invites discussion on the problematics of ecclesiology, these excurses will provide ample opportunity to examine and (where appropriate) untangle ecclesiological knots.

The four main chapters revolve around a set of macro-issues which invite immediate controversy and confusion. The first chapter critically examines the recent turn to defining and locating the church with reference to models. This chapter is an exercise in ground-clearing, as we note again and again the ambiguity of the models and the insufficiency of any one model as an account of what the church is. The ambiguity of these models in themselves invites us to ask after the location of the church, and in Chapter 2 we ask where the church is with reference to the classical marks attributed to the church (one, holy, catholic and apostolic). A concern for the visibility of the church occupies our search, but it is matched by a growing sense of the only partial and often contested nature of this visibility. In the third chapter, we turn to the question of ecclesial mediation, considering the means of grace appointed as avenues along which the triune God gives himself to the church. Finally, in considering the church's mission we turn to an oft-neglected aspect of ecclesiology, situating mission in relation to the mission of God to establish his kingdom on earth. We discern the shape of mission in the church's ministry of reconciliation and the scope of mission in ecumenism and the church's relation to Israel and other religions.

Three brief treatments of ascension, Pentecost and parousia serve as frames for the book, intended to remind readers of the place of the church in the economy of salvation and to tether ecclesiology to the history of the triune God's redemptive ways with the world. A present danger in ecclesiology is to abstract the doctrine of the church from the economy of salvation and from the triune God who saves. But the church – and this is no mark against it – lives only and ever on borrowed resources, on gifts it has received from Israel, from Christ and the Spirit, even from the world.

METHODOLOGY

As for our methodology, the reader should be aware of the following aspects of our work in order to appreciate what we are (and are not) doing.

(1) As co-authors, we have attempted to hold many points in tension. Jenson is a systematic theologian and Wilhite is a historical theologian. Now we both cringe at being labelled, but this is on the whole a fair assessment of where we are each most comfortable. Beyond our disciplinary differences we could list a whole array of tensions, such as Augustinian/Thomistic, Reformed/Wesleyan and Barthian/Tillichian. These labels do not adequately represent our theology or how we might answer any particular theological question, but they do illustrate how we approach a theological matter often, but not always, in different ways. But enough about us; all of this is to say that in co-authoring this monograph, we have sought to harmonize our two voices, with all the baggage and benefits that accompany dual authorship.

(2) We work under the authority of scripture while admitting that our interpretation is guided by tradition (including the present tradition, that is, our context). We desire to be biblical, yet we hope to avoid making the Bible say what we want it to say. Therefore, we have taken into account good historical critical scholarship of the original context (*Sitz im Leben*), the canonical trajectory of the early church up to our times (*Wirkungsgeschichte*) and the need for our doctrine to be contextualized to the current situation (*aggiornamento*).

(3) We are striving for catholicity in our theology, and yet we begin from a sectarian vantage point. We write *from* our own traditions and experiences, but in what follows we strive to write *for* and even *with* the historic and ecumenical Christian church. That having been said, we make no claims to pure objectivity. We will interact with a wide array of voices who represent many Christian traditions, yet we always read these interlocutors with lenses shaped by specific questions that arise out of our own traditions. We believe that what follows is a fair representation of the current state of theological discourse on the doctrine of the church. We respond to the discourse, however, by offering our own evaluation that includes both appreciation and criticism, as well as a few suggestions of our own. We have tried to be clear and state when we are going beyond the views of the theologians we cite, but there is no escaping the fact that we cite them

and present their views in a way we deem most appropriate. There-fore, the bias will be evident where we are unconvinced, but it will be moderated throughout the discussion in a way that still allows other voices to be heard.

(4) We are not being exhaustive. We are being suggestive. In other words, we often times offer 'ways forward' in many of the sub-categories of ecclesiology. When doing so, we do not expect or even desire to convince the reader of all of our ideas, but we do hope to contribute to the discussion by pressing certain aspects we find to be helpful. We humbly submit these points as discussion starters, and we admit – nay, insist! – that much more thought and attention is needed for any one point raised in this book.

But even before we begin, we must ask after the very legitimacy of ecclesiology, in light of a question arising from the turn to history in the biblical scholarship of the last two centuries about whether Jesus ever intended to found a church.

EXCURSUS: DID JESUS ESTABLISH THE CHURCH?

One's assumptions about Jesus' intentions for the church shape one's ecclesiology. Confessionally, if one is a Roman Catholic who believes Jesus handed papal keys to Peter, then one's ecclesiology is Petrine in focus.[2] Whereas, if one is a congregationalist, then the church's essence is found in Jesus' presence amidst any gathering of two or three in his name. In a different vein of thought, one's ideological reading of Jesus will also affect how the church is understood: left-leaning social gospelites (but not only left-leaning social gospelites) will find Jesus and the Jesus community to be revolutionary commun(al)ists, while political conservatives (but not only right-wingers) who find Jesus to teach an inward spirituality distinct from one's outward political allegiances will see Jesus and his earliest followers as proclaimers of repentance from personal sins but with little to say to societal structures. In recognition of this phenomenon, we would do better to try to cross the chasm from the Christ of faith to the historical Jesus, despite how treacherous this path has proven in the past. Better to admit our assumptions than to pretend our route takes us away from this landscape when all along our path is dangerously on the precipice of one side of this canyon. This excursus is provided as a survey of the current scholarly opinions about Jesus' intentions for the church. Such a discussion is important for the purposes of this book for obvious reasons, but it needs to be stated that the church is not merely an afterthought to the life and work of Christ. In order to build on this premise, let us begin with a brief survey of historical Jesus studies, and then attempt to provide a constructive way forward.

The current state of New Testament studies in general and historical Jesus research in particular allows for no single item of discussion to be declared a 'consensus'.[3] Scholars and commentators that are as wide-ranging in their views as Bart Ehrman, N. T. Wright and Lee Strobel can all claim the validity of their approach and conclusions while simultaneously decrying the others as representatives of misguided assumptions.[4] Bart Ehrman is an agnostic who denies the deity and resurrection of Christ via a 'historical approach' that claims to know the first century facts of the Jesus tradition which later became legends believed only by the church. Wright is an Anglican bishop who also claims a 'historical approach', but who still finds the Christian tradition to be a faithful recounting of Jesus who was in fact the divine Son of God who rose from the dead. Lee Strobel is a journalist turned biblical commentator who believes that the evidence alone would convince any jury/readership of Christ's resurrection. The fact that all three can do this simultaneously and all three can claim wide acceptance of their views and at the same time all three nullify each other's approaches illustrates the difficulty of attempting to discern what really happened to Jesus and the earliest Christians. And this is within the self-defined boundaries of what is available to a historian (as opposed to someone who simply believes the apostolic witness as found in the scripture and preserved in the church). Will the real Jesus scholar please stand up?!

The following quest for what the historical Jesus said about the church will proceed by surveying representative views from academic scholars, specifically academic scholars who attempt to find an answer through historical evidence.[5] The reason for this approach is not necessarily because we advocate this method as the most productive, or for that matter even necessary, but because this is the current state of the question – both among academically recognized scholars and in the wider culture that tunes into the History Channel.

Within the fields of New Testament studies, Christian origins, and historical Jesus research, what can be said about Jesus' intentions for the church? The quest for the historical Jesus is typically said to have begun with Hermann Samuel Reimarus, who belongs to the broader Enlightenment shift from faith to reason – to oversimplify just a bit. From this point, scholars begin to approach Jesus in a 'scientific' way: what does the evidence prove? The immediate obstacle for such an approach is the fact that there is no direct evidence – no DNA samples, to use an anachronistic example – but only circumstantial evidence – witness or hearsay, depending on how you look at it. To use Rudolph Bultmann's term, scholars demythologize the accounts of Jesus. Any accounts of supernatural phenomena may be dismissed as remnants of ancient, unenlightened superstition; any accounts of lingering Judaisms may be dismissed as historical dust that should be shaken off after the Christ event; and any claim to Jesus' lordship may be dismissed as embellishments of an early church who needed to divinize its (by then gone) charismatic leader.[6] This last point is especially relevant for the present discussion.

Albert Schweitzer soon points out how, after these supposed layers of tradition are pealed back, the only remaining core claimed as the historical Jesus turns out to look remarkably similar to a modern liberal German scholar.[7] These historians have looked down the long well of history, only to find their own image staring back at them.[8]

The second (and maybe third) quest is now more willing to admit that Jesus may have been a radical who believed the sky was falling.[9] Perhaps, he went about preaching repentance, because he believed that God was approaching the judge's seat ready to dole out retribution to the righteous and the wicked. When Jesus was gone, however, his followers faced a dilemma: they could either go back to life as normal, or they could assume the judgment was still coming 'sooner or later' (or later, or later, or later, etc.). Those who chose the latter formed the church, which was never the intention of Jesus himself.[10]

This somewhat cynical account of the Jesus of history is meant to illustrate how acutely the quest(s) for the historical Jesus affects the subject of ecclesiology. In reality the type of conclusions offered above, which would be more representative of Ehrman, is counterbalanced by just as many historians who find the apostolic witness to Jesus to be exactly that, historically reliable witness, which would be more representative of Wright.[11] Moreover, lest we paint too bleak a picture, James D. G. Dunn and Scott McKnight helpfully articulate how the quest for the historical Jesus is best understood, not as the attempts of skeptics to discredit Christian faith, but as sincere attempts to rediscover the humanity of Jesus which had been eclipsed by the church's portrayals of the heavy-handed Pantocrator and by Michaelangelo's unbending Judge.[12]

We began this excursus by stating that one's assumptions about Jesus' intentions for the church shape one's ecclesiology. It needs to be reiterated at this point that all our facts (the so-called historical as well as the so-called confessional) are assumptions. Nothing is proven about the historical Jesus; we all believe what we believe about Jesus, and it is exactly that – belief, or faith. As to relying ('trusting' or 'believing') on the New Testament sources, James D. G. Dunn has reminded scholars that the Jesus of history has always been the Christ of faith.[13] There is no way around the Jesus of scripture to a historical Jesus. Once this is acknowledged by all sides, we can then proceed to our ecclesiology with full disclosure. In our postmodern condition, our ecclesiology is on no more *nor less* a historical foundation than any doctrine or practice.

That having been said, even within the current state of the question, there are specific matters about Jesus' intentions for the church which are widely accepted by all sides. Our point is that even if one did try to out-flank the Jesus of scripture, almost every portrayal of Jesus includes the following matters that pertain to Jesus and his church: a Jesus who calls, gathers and commissions. In other words, Jesus established a church that was structured, ritualized and transformative.

One aspect of the historical Jesus which is widely accepted by scholars and at the same time which causes wide-ranging speculation about its meaning is Jesus' call for a renewal or redefining of Israel.[14] In some way Jesus' message and mission is largely to 'the lost sheep of Israel' and largely about restoring the Kingdom of Heaven/God, which was once typified in David's reign but has been lost to other empires (the Babylonian, Persian, Greek and, finally, Roman). Scholars widely agree that Jesus took over this motif from John the Baptist, who called all to repentance, not just 'the tax-collectors and sinners'. The renewal that John and then Jesus demanded was an inner repentance, distinct from (though not necessarily opposed to) the outer cult of the temple – a circumcision of the heart, a sacrifice of thanksgiving and an ethic of righteousness. Similar to the acceptance of Jesus' relationship to John the Baptist, Jesus' encounter with the moneychangers in the temple is largely uncontested. While the event's meaning is much disputed by scholars, its occurrence and its interpretation by the religious officials of the time as revolutionary are unquestioned. Jesus called for a people to repent from unethical lives, and he proclaimed a new era for those who do so. This was an era in which the old temple may be destroyed but a new, unconquerable body would be raised up. As to the structure of this new body, scholars disagree as to whether or not Jesus was (a) restoring a political kingdom for Israel in the vein of Judas Maccabeas,[15] (b) calling for Israel's righteous remnant to retreat and await God's intervention like the Qumran community, (c) establishing a new institution which would be hierarchically built on the twelve as judges/bishops, per the Roman Catholic and Eastern Orthodox traditions or (d) calling for a mission-driven movement to carry forth his call to righteousness in diasporic communities, modelled after the synagogues and championed by the free church traditions. Each of these points has biblical support, and none of them can claim to be proven historically. What they all have in common, and what almost all portrayals of the historical Jesus admit, is that Jesus did issue a call for people to join a structured body, only the definition of this body (especially in relation to Israel) and nature of its structure (especially in terms of hierarchical vs. egalitarian) is in debate. In other words, Jesus did intend to found a renewed community, or (if the dictum be true, 'a rose by any other name . . .') a church.

Granted, this new body/renewed Israel is, although widely accepted, still ill-defined.[16] If the notion that Jesus intended to establish a body can be as wide-ranging in its interpretation as the four options listed in the previous paragraph, then it seems we have yet to really establish *what* we mean when we say Jesus established a body. That being said, there is another point about Jesus and the church that enjoys wide acceptance: Jesus instituted a ritualized meal.[17] That many scenes deemed 'authentically Jesus' by scholars include a meal is telling. Jesus eats with tax-collectors and sinners. Jesus is seen as a miracle worker who provides enough food for everyone. Jesus commands that his followers live a kingdom ethic where there is plenty of food to go around. Jesus finds the Passover to be all about his mission and message, and this celebration of new life for the new community is to be celebrated in his name – the (prophetic?, priestly?, kingly?) founder of the new community.[18] 'This is my body'.[19] Did Jesus refer to the bread? The folks sharing it? Both? The (re)new(ed) body instituted by Jesus re-presents itself and its founder/-ing. The ritualized meal establishes the community and simultaneously establishes the community's self-awareness. Whether or not Jesus intended that this meal would become a sacramental ritual with elaborate formulae, Jesus certainly provided a means of ritually embodying his followers.

At this point, we have discussed two aspects of the historical Jesus' actions that relate to the founding of the church which are undisputed in the scholarly discourse. First, Jesus called for a following and these followers were initiated into a community via baptism. Second, Jesus gathered those who answered this call into an embodied fellowship via a ritualized meal. Did Jesus intend to found a 'church'? At the very least, one can confidently affirm that Jesus founded a sacramental community. This sacramental community, otherwise known as the church, is also to be a sacred community.

The third aspect that we must mention here relates to Jesus' followers as a redemptive and transformative body. While the notion of a redemptive community is more ambiguous and therefore less historically verifiable than the previous two points, there is something that can be said about Jesus' called and gathered body of followers other than their initiation and identification rituals. These rituals manifest and nurture the community of Jesus followers, but the renewed body that becomes the church is called by Jesus to live 'in the kingdom'. In other words, those who have answered Jesus' call, become his followers and gathered in his community are expected to live out his message and mission.[20] While we once again have to admit that the particulars of this message and mission are much debated historically, doctrinally, and ideologically, there is nevertheless a broad recognition that Jesus asked his new body of disciples to follow his example and his teachings. That Jesus' *ipsissimus vox* was delivered in person to his earliest followers is uncontested; what the *ipsissimus verba* were depends on who you ask (and in the case of the Jesus Seminar, if you have all your marbles).

What did Jesus call his disciples to do/be? This question depends on one's interpretation of the first point made here, that Jesus called for a renewal of Israel. Those who answer Jesus' call – whatever one thinks that was – will live according to the values of the kingdom as taught by Jesus – however one interprets them. Jesus' call to 'repent for the kingdom is at hand' results in followers who now proceed with a new set of allegiances. Whatever these followers have turned *from* (this could be the temple, Pharisaic legalism, Roman oppression, Hellenistic moral laxity, etc.), they have now turned *to* Jesus' examples and teachings. These can be called ethics, although we should be careful not to limit what we mean by this. After all, an ethical life *for the purpose of* glorifying God might be categorized as worship. But whatever the classification of this third aspect of Jesus' intentions for the church, whatever the content and meaning of Jesus' expectations, and whatever the interpretation and application of Jesus' teachings, there are few who would deny that Jesus established a body of followers whom he expected to do just that: follow. Did Jesus establish a 'church'? He initiated followers into a body. He gathered followers as members of the body via partaking of the body. And finally he commissioned this body of followers to embody teachings not only ritually but practically. In short, yes, Jesus founded the church.

One example of Jesus' teaching that few have questioned is his call to justice. Scholars as diverse as (in no particular order) John Piper, Wright, Bruce Longenecker, Richard Horsley,[21] John Dominic Crossan and Marcus Borg,[22] all agree that Jesus insisted on caring for the poor and oppressed and that his earliest followers understood this to be central to Jesus' teaching. Therefore, Jesus called a body, and he called them to embody his life and teachings both ritually and socially. In other words Jesus founded a transformative community, better known as the church.

Before completing this excursus, let us take stock of how much (or how little) can be said about the Jesus of history and his intentions for the church. Then, let us evaluate the benefit (or lack thereof) gained from such an endeavour. First, while we cannot claim to have established a 'consensus view', it is clear that despite the wide range of scholarly opinions about the historical Jesus, there is an overwhelming number of scholars representative of both left-leaning, right-leaning and centrist viewpoints, who understand Jesus as calling, gathering and commissioning his body of disciples. Jesus founded the church. The only matter to be determined (and it is a complex one) is how Jesus envisioned this church. At this point we offer our evaluation of the benefit of the quest for the historical Jesus: the scholarship establishes the validity of our pursuit of ecclesiology, but it provides little assistance in that pursuit. This is quite a benefit in our postmodern and incredulous age when many shy away from established religion: it would be easy to dismiss the church as an invention of early that is not true to the ideals of Christ himself. Such a dismissive stance, however, ignores genera-tions of modern scholars – many of whom would readily affirm such a conclusion, if only the evidence allowed. That the church's origin is grounded in the life and work of Jesus himself should be recognized as an uncontested starting point for ecclesiology. The first step towards a sound doctrine of the church can thus be claimed. But then again, a first step is all that has been made.

To claim more information about the historical Jesus' intentions for his church via the historical method is highly dubious. We do not oppose scholars' rights to do so. Nor do we wish them to abandon their life's work. But the arguments put forth by historians *qua* historians will inevitably always be hypothetical. The current climate of historical Jesus studies permits virtually any scholar to forward virtually any hypothesis. And all the theologian is left with is one individual's hypothesis over against an array of other individuals' hypotheses. Therefore, we concur with Dunn, who has outlined the way in which the current historical method is no longer sufficient in a postmodern milieu – at least in any attempt to construct doctrine and practice. Instead, we must return to a Ricoeurian second naiveté (which is vastly different from simple naiveté), and listen to the voice of the church.[23]

Yes, this is becoming frighteningly circular. The church is telling us about her founder, so he can tell us about his church. But, as we said at the beginning of this excursus, better to admit our path rather than pretend there is another way around the problem. Perhaps, our journey will be more a hermeneutic spiral than circular reasoning. But whatever we call it and however we chart it, we certainly admit our (now historically viable) dialectical dependence on the church to tell us about Jesus and on Jesus to tell us about the church.

ASCENSION AND ECCLESIA[1]

It is the final week of Jesus' life. Up to this point, the Lord and his disciples have shared life together. Jesus called, the disciples followed, and then they watched, learned and began to share in Christ's ministry. In the days leading up to his death, though, Jesus had alluded to and increasingly spoken plainly of his departure. He was going to his death; then, he would return to his Father.

> But now I am going to him who sent me; yet none of you asks me, 'Where are you going?' But because I have said these things to you, sorrow has filled your hearts. Nevertheless I tell you the truth: it is to your advantage that I go away, for if I do not go away, the Advocate will not come to you; but if I go, I will send him to you. (Jn 16.5–7)

The disciples will be forgiven if they wondered quite how and whether it was to their advantage that Jesus went away. Jesus, after all, was the one by and in whom the messianic kingdom had come. Fulfilling the prophetic voice of Israel as the long-expected 'prophet like Moses',[2] Jesus transcended the prophetic message in that he *was* the message.[3] He was, in Origen's striking phrase, the *autobasileia*, the 'kingdom-in-person'.[4] That his departure might encourage the disciples seems to sit oddly with the manifest, manifold blessings of his presence. Of course, Jesus promises another presence, that of 'the Advocate'; and we will later turn to the gift of the Holy Spirit as a partial fulfilment of Jesus promise to 'not leave you orphaned; I am coming to you' (Jn 14.18).

But first, we must take seriously his departure. In the ascension, we are faced with Christ's absence. The church's time begins with Jesus' ascension and ends with his return and so is throughout marked by this very real absence. This is the time of the no longer and the not yet, one in which the church lives between remembrance and hope. We remember his death. We proclaim his resurrection. We await his coming in glory. This waiting is hopeful, to be sure, but it is also strained. It is the vigilant, spartan waiting of people whose home is elsewhere – 'where Christ is, seated at right hand of God' (Col. 3.1; see Phil. 3.20). It is the ambiguous waiting of people who live on promises, of a church whose life too often seems all expectation and no fulfilment. And it is a long waiting, long enough that many in the church have been tempted to abandon hope, and still more have neglected to watch and pray. The church knows, at times acutely, painfully, that 'friendship with the world is enmity with God' (Jas 4.4). It knows, too, that 'while we are at home in the body we are away from the Lord' (2 Cor. 5.6).

Still, the church's waiting is no meagre asceticism. Only the confident joy of the resurrection could prompt the disciples' response at Jesus' departure. Consider the concluding scene of Luke's gospel:

> Then he led them out as far as Bethany, and, lifting up his hands, he blessed them. While he was blessing them, he withdrew from them and was carried up into heaven. And they worshiped him, and returned to Jerusalem with great joy; and they were continually in the temple blessing God. (Lk. 24.50–53)

This is not the response of the despairing, and it could not be more different than the disciples' response on the night of Jesus' death. Then, they had scattered in fear; now, the resurrected Jesus has gathered them together and their very lives have become doxologies. So, while we must take seriously Jesus' absence, and all the ambiguity, suffering and longing it brings, we do so in the hope of resurrection.

Where has Jesus gone? What is he doing? He has ascended to the right hand of the Father, where he ministers as high priest in the heavenlies, speaks as prophet to the church and the world and reigns as king over all. For while ascension means Jesus' departure for the church, it also means his instalment as king following his vindication in the resurrection. Christ has not retired, but has begun the work of reigning as Lord of all.

> God has gone up with a shout, the Lord with the sound of a trumpet.

Sing praises to God, sing praises; sing praises to our King, sing
praises.
For God is the king of all the earth; sing praises with a psalm.
God is king over the nations; God sits on his holy throne.
(Ps. 43.5–8)

We, too, 'hav[ing] been raised with Christ', have ascended with
him; indeed our 'life is hidden with Christ in God' (Col. 3.4). But
far from inviting the church to complacency, our bi-locality in the
church prompts a holy dissatisfaction in the world. We are agitated
by hope, living uncomfortably in the face of an absent – often enough,
we worry, an absentee – Lord and under the conditions of death and
decay. The church that remembers his death, proclaims his resurrection
and ascension and awaits his coming in glory cannot rest content with
the violence and manipulation, the lying and laziness, the pride and
cowardice that seem to be just the way things are. This is *not* the way
things are, the church protests, even though its own faltering life will
frequently beg to differ. Christ has set up his church – this faltering
church – in the world as a sign of his resurrection, a sign that new
creation is the way things are, in the time between his two advents.

CHAPTER 1

MODELS

What is the church? This chapter aims to construct a definition of church, of what the church *is*. Such a task, however, has usually been undertaken in theological discourse more by way of analogy, by what the church is *like*. In this chapter we will survey the significant metaphors and models that have been utilized to define the church. In so doing, however, we do not wish to simply retrace what those who have gone before us have already done. We hope to build on their work by applying a strict analysis to each major metaphor of the church.

Although we are comfortable within a phenomenological approach and we would love nothing more than to launch into an eloquent rant about semiotics and deconstruction, we elect instead to leave the more technical discussion about symbols to the side. We humbly admit that metaphors are exactly that, metaphors; they tell us something but not everything about that which they describe. In the following chapter we will undertake the following steps in discussing the church in terms of models. Namely, we will briefly acknowledge the wide array of 'images' found in scripture for the church, but then devote an extended analysis of 'models' used by theologians about the church, and then finally attempt to summarize a particularly helpful 'understanding' of the church. Before surveying and analysing these metaphors, however, we need to turn to one dominant form of ecclesiology that became especially prominent in the Roman Catholic Vatican II council. This form, known as communion ecclesiology, shaped the way in which all such metaphors for the church are now used.

EXCURSUS: COMMUNION ECCLESIOLOGY AND VATICAN II

On 25 January 1959, Pope John XXIII announced a forthcoming ecumenical council, Vatican II. One might assume that a brief history of what happened at this council could be easily written. In fact, historians and theologians, especially Roman Catholic historians and theologians, strongly debate each other over the event that happened just five decades ago. Let us begin by sketching the events themselves before considering their theological implications – although such a distinction admittedly is problematic.

The Roman Catholic Church held its twenty-first ecumenical council in four sessions which occurred over 4 years (from 11 October 1962 to 8 December 1965). Pope John XXIII intended for this council to modernize the church ('aggiornamento', or 'updating', being a slogan of the council) and also to be pastoral (rather than doctrinal). It was the largest gathering of its kind with around 2,500 'fathers' (cardinals and bishops) participating, and it was the most open council known in the modern era with non-Catholic 'observers' in attendance. The original statements prepared by the cardinals for the council fathers were quickly rejected, and the reports from the council proceedings told of sensational and sweeping reforms. The council produced four constitutions, three declarations, and nine decrees.[1]

The implications of the council are where the debate begins.[2] For example, two recent works have come out that claim to tell the story of Vatican II, and yet the two accounts have little in common. In his book *What Happened at Vatican II*, John W. O'Malley tells of what is commonly called 'the spirit of the council' which demanded radical change in the Catholic Church.[3] However, in the essays found in *Vatican II: Renewal within Tradition*, the various contributors examine the documents from the council to find a striking continuity with previous Catholic teaching.[4] To put it simply, this history of continuity or discontinuity is what separates 'conservative' and 'liberal' Catholics. The former interpret Vatican II to say nothing different or contrary to previous dogma, while the latter believe the council called for a modified church to serve a new age. It should also be noted that there is a third option: traditionalist Catholics who believe that the entire council was a mistake and/or see a 'pastoral' (vs. 'doctrinal') council as ill-defined and non-binding.[5]

In the immediate aftermath of Vatican II three specific effects resulted. First, liturgical reforms swept through the church. The Tridentine Mass was dropped, and the local vernacular became the norm for Catholic worship. Second, a movement of liberal Catholics marked the first major interpretive phase after the council: this party established the journal, *Concilio*, which provided a forum for explicating further implementation of the council. The liberal party has steadily lost ground, however, to the conservative interpretations of the council, which were supported by Pope John Paul II and now Benedict XVI, and which were given voice in the journal *Communio*. The very name of this journal, *Communio*, illustrates a theme in post-Vatican II ecclesiology, which leads us to our third and last result from Vatican II. The most pertinent impact of Vatican II to the present discussion is that of the Roman Catholic thinkers' shift in the focus of their ecclesiology. We do not suggest that the council was *only* about the church, but the nature and function of the church itself took centre stage.[6] The ecclesiology that emerged in Vatican II is known as 'communion ecclesiology' (henceforth = CE).[7]

CE in a formal sense began prior to Vatican II with the work of Roman Catholic thinkers such as Yves Congar and Henri de Lubac. It was then succinctly articulated by J.-M. R. Tillard.[8] What became known as the *nouvelle théologie* urged for *ressourcement*, an appeal to re-read the early church (especially the pre-Thomistic sources) and accommodate its thinking in modern theology. When these sentiments became codified at Vatican II, the whole of Roman Catholic ecclesiology shifted its language from the juridical and institutional elements. The juridical and institutional elements were not omitted from Catholic dogma, but they were subordinated to other concerns. The shift of emphasis *from* these elements is undisputed. What exactly CE shifts the emphasis *to*, however, is heavily debated.

Generally speaking, the church is now seen as the communion of the saints with each other and with the triune God, seen especially in the shared participation in the sacraments. In such broad terms CE is *the* ecclesiological paradigm of the late twentieth and early twenty-first centuries. Not only is CE centralized in Roman Catholic thought under the influence of Vatican II, the fact that it stems from the aim toward *ressourcement* suggests that CE could easily correspond to, if not aptly describe, Eastern Orthodox ecclesiology as well, with that tradition's famous emphasis on its antiquity.[9] Likewise, since *ressourcement* is akin to the Humanist and Protestant principle of *ad fontes*, Protestants (both mainline and free church) have also been able to claim CE as their own.[10]

Since CE readily suited so many Christian traditions, many theologians believed it to be a promising way forward for both the ecumenical movement and constructive theology. After decades of discussion, however, CE may be losing its prominence. On the one hand CE is still the only viable framework for interdenominational dialogue about ecclesiology, and the centrality of the *communio/koi-nonia* motif in theological discourse on the church is still dominant.[11] Yet on the other hand, the very fact that theologians from various traditions can all employ CE while at the same time disagreeing about the implications of CE offers little hope for future progress.

Our conclusion here about CE is not meant to demoralize those who advocate it. We simultaneously wish to recognize how much CE has formed the present state of ecclesiological discourse and how much more needs be said beyond the ecumenical consensus about CE.[12] Examples of the latter include how to understand the nature of the church itself: Is the church the people? the sacramental union of the people? the sacramental union of the people via the oversight of the clergy? Free church theologians can affirm CE yet differ in their view of the necessity of the sacraments. Theologians from episcopally governed churches can disagree over the necessity of the clergy and the nature of apostolic succession. Any of these specific items fit within (or without) a CE framework, and yet they point to the still disputed matter of what constitutes the church's *esse* ('being'), as opposed to those items that might belong to the church's *bene esse* ('well-being'). The rest of this chapter and the next, therefore, will further interact with communion ecclesiology as part of a broader discussion of various metaphors for the church. In the succeeding chapter we will return to the question of characteristics or marks of the church. At the present, our primary concern is with the church's *esse*, what the church *is*, or what it means to *be* church.

TYPOLOGY OF MODELS

The title of this section intentionally shifts from our preferred term 'metaphor' to the more popular term 'model'. Paul S. Minear famously identified ninety-six images for the church found in the New Testament.[13] Minear, however, admitted that most of these were 'minor images', and he instead devoted four chapters to the 'major' and 'decisive' images for the church found in the Christian scriptures: the people of God, the new creation, the fellowship in faith, and the body of Christ.[14] Seeing the calling of the people of God (i.e. Israel) and the creation of a new humanity (i.e. the nations) as one act of the Father, one can then frame Minear's images into a trinitarian framework, a common move.[15] But before assuming that the earliest Christian sources systematically align in their ecclesiology, one needs to recognize a more pronounced diversity in the New Testament itself.[16] Any particular image may mean something different to different New Testament authors or even be used in different ways by the same author.[17] Any trinitarian framework, therefore, while appropriate for constructing a doctrine of the church, needs to be recognized as a construction built upon one's interpretation of New Testament images that speak to the nature and essence of the church. In order to address these assumptions directly, theologians often analyse the primary models used to define church.

In 1974 Jesuit and cardinal-to-be Avery Dulles outlined five ways of understanding what the church is: institution, mystical communion, sacrament, herald, and servant.[18] The church *is* a 'mystery', Dulles insisted, but the church can be understood in terms of 'models'. By acknowledging that there are many images for the church available to theologians which could be clustered under specific models, Dulles both incorporated scripture and tradition's diversity and avoided essentializing any one model or image. '[N]o good ecclesiologist', he contended, 'is committed to a single model of the Church'.[19] This sentence represents to us the most promising aspect of Dulles' introduction. While Dulles' typological approach (itself 'modelled' after Niebuhr's *Christ and Culture*) is appealing, it also requires incessant qualification.

We will now address all five models with an aim to update Dulles' discussion with contemporary voices. In doing so we also place Dulles' admission ('No good ecclesiologist is committed to a single model') to the forefront, and thereby analyse theologians who champion a particular emphasis that could be caricatured by one of Dulles' models.

First model: institution

When speaking of the church as institution, we are modelling the church on a 'political society',[20] strong examples of which would be a nation-state while softer examples would be a school or hospital. In all cases the institutional model of the church emphasizes the authority held in the church and the submissive role of the members of the church: as head of state is to citizen, teacher is to pupil and doctor is to patient, so the officer of the church is to the member of the church.

The institutional model is negatively defined by contrasting it with a communal understanding of the church (see next section), which relies on the dichotomy between society and community.[21] This, of course, is a false dichotomy in the sense that all 'communities' have institutional elements, and all 'societies' are structured communities. For our purposes, however, the following points need to be clarified: (1) all churches and all sustained theological reflection on ecclesiology will include institutional elements and (2) there is little to indicate when an ecclesiological framework can be described as 'institutional'.

First, to illustrate how this 'model' is inescapable let us give two examples. The magisterial Reformers, such as Luther and Calvin, in effect rejected such an emphasis by claiming that the pope could hold the correct office but teach an incorrect gospel. However, when faced with a more 'communal' (*Gemeinschaft*) emphasis from the radical Reformers, Luther and Calvin insisted on the institutional elements.[22] Another helpful example is the churches of the Anabaptist movement: all of them (until the Quakers under the influence of Deist thinking) retained some sort of clerical roles.

Secondly, to deem a certain ecclesiological framework as 'institutional' is really to assert one's own value on the level of emphasis placed on authoritative office. In other words, any claim that a particular church or ecclesiology is institutional is relative to one's own level of ecclesiological institutionalism: that church is institutional because it is *more* institutional than my own. Since all ecclesiologies have institutional elements, the only question remaining is how much or how little weight should be given to these elements.

The quintessential example of rampant institutionalism in ecclesiology is usually said to be the Roman Catholic Church of Vatican I. After all, say the detractors, this council replaced the spiritual and mystical authority of Christ and established the pope as 'head of the whole Church' (*Pastor Aeternus* 3.1), 'the supreme judge of the faithful . . . than which there is no higher authority' (3.8). A more sympathetic read, however, will note that, while the institutional

model of patriarchal household and school does arise in this council
(e.g. pope as 'father and teacher of all Christian people' [3.1]), the
church itself is implicitly defined as 'the faithful [people] throughout
the world' (2.4), the 'Christian people' themselves (3.1), which is
inclusive of 'the pastors and the faithful' (3.9). This implicit definition, therefore, is in continuity with the later statements of Vatican
II's explicit definition of the church as the whole people of God
(see esp. *Lumen Gentium*). The Vatican I Dogmatic Constitution of
the Church is carefully articulated in such a way that the church is
implicitly defined as the people of God united in Christ, but the
statement is an emphatic clarification on the *necessity* of Petrine
primacy. The church is one thing, but the church is 'founded on' Peter
(note the consistency with the Roman Catholic interpretation of
Mt. 16.18). The church is not defined by the pope, but the pope – with
full juridical authority – is necessary (*sine qua non*) for the church.

On the one hand Vatican I cannot be aptly described as defining
an 'institutional model' for the church, but on the other hand the
institutional elements of concern to this council (i.e. the infallible
papacy) are emphasized (for contextual concerns) and even required
(for doctrinal reasons). In light of this, we wonder: if one's ecclesiological discourse *requires* the authoritative office of the institutional
model but does not *emphasize* the authoritative office of the institutional model, can that ecclesiology appropriately be described as
'institutional'? But then, we have already admitted all ecclesiological
paradigms will include institutional elements. Let us take the case of
John Zizioulas, whose book *Being as Communion* has influenced
much of current ecclesiology. As an Eastern Orthodox theologian,
Zizioulas rejects any tie of the church's authoritative office to a single
office in Rome and sees the church's authority equally dispersed
among all of its bishops. Nevertheless, the institutional element
is still required: while the church, Zizioulas ardently contends, is *constituted* as a communion of persons, the church is *conditioned* by its
submission to the bishop (and his apostolic succession to the first
bishops and conciliarity with all current bishops). The 'conditioned
by' clause makes the episcopacy at large a *sine qua non* of the church.
Should we then label Zizioulas' famous communion ecclesiology as
'institutional'? Is every necessitating of ecclesial office a sign of an
institutional ecclesiology?

The structural union formed through the communion of bishops
is said to be the guarantor of both catholic unity and apostolic

continuity. This model or emphasis, however, is inadequate since ecumenically sensitive theologians have been unable to substantiate the claims of episcopal necessity and infallibility: many episcopally governed churches have not remained united in their polity and have not remained apostolic in their teaching.[23] Taken to an extreme conclusion, affirming the institutional model leads one to insist that the institutional elements (e.g. episcopal hierarchy, seven sacraments, dogma, etc.) stem entirely and completely from Jesus himself – tenets which Dulles stipulates 'scholarly criticism could not demonstrate'.[24] More commonly, according to Dulles, the shortfall of institutional ecclesiology is to treat the institutional elements of the church as primary.[25] Whether by 'primary' Dulles has in mind the emphasis or the requirement of authoritative office is unclear. Another unclear matter is the fact that such a model fails to provide guidelines for dissent (as MacIntyre would have it).[26] Does all institutionalism need critique as an oppressive assertion of power (as Foucault would contend)?[27] In light of such problems, the institutional officers themselves are not only slow to offer possibilities, but these offices in themselves tell us little about what the church *is*: the church is governed by, guided by, and/or guarded by ecclesial authorities, but the church *itself* is yet to be defined. And so we look to the model of the church as mystical communion.

Second model: mystical communion

An immediate weakness with the mystical communion model of the church lies in the slippery notion of both the term 'mystical' and the term 'communion', that is to say that the mystical community is ill-defined to the point of detriment. What makes a certain community a church? Can a chat-room of fellow-believers be considered a church? 'To say that "communion" is a necessary model of the church is to say remarkably little, since the model can be used in conflicting ways and have conflicting theological meanings, depending upon its context'.[28] While this ill-defined nature leaves much to be desired, it does not mean we can dismiss the model altogether, especially given how much widespread agreement can be found on the fundamental definition of the church as the called people of God, the spiritual body of Christ, and the fellowship of the Holy Spirit.

Any analysis of the church in terms of mystical communion must address the problem of specificity: to what is the church being compared? Dulles specifies 'face-to-face' groups, such as families and neighbourhoods.[29] We think it also appropriate to draw an analogy to ancient Greek and Roman societies, social groups such as artisan gilds. A third concrete comparison would be diasporic Jewish synagogues. None of these, of course, was appropriated *in toto* by the earliest Christians. The church was in a sense a kinship (family analogy) that was bound not by descent and marriage but by vocation (*societas* analogy), and which gathered to practice a common faith (synagogue analogy). The church is modelled after, or at least analogous to, these social groups, but advocates of the mystical communion model differentiate the church from any one of these comparative entities in light of the mystical nature of the communion.

The mystical communion model of church lends itself to being uncircumscribable. Attempting to draw a boundary around what church *is* inevitably fails because the church is mysterious, a matter of faith. The focus of this model is not at the boundary (where a shepherd/overseer/bishop/pope is guarding who's in and who's out). The focus is at the centre, with the communion (of people) mystically united to God in Christ through the Holy Spirit. The mystical descriptor encourages a certain amount of slippage in our vocabulary: the church is a communion, that is a communion of persons, a *communio* (Greek = *koinonia*). Not just any communion of persons, but a mystical, mysterious, divine communion of persons – and communion of divine persons. God who is mystically three persons in *communio*, creates a mystical *communio* of persons known as the church.

If the mystical communion model of church sound a great deal like communion ecclesiology, then this model/emphasis begs the question: since the church is a mystery, has not Dulles betrayed his belief that this model is not so much a model, but a primary understanding of the church? Similarly, since Dulles' 1987 revision of his book did in fact argue for the priority of one particular model, 'Community of Disciples', and since the notion of community of disciples in Dulles' description sounds suspiciously close to 'mystical communion', has not Dulles in fact prioritized this model as more than a model, but as the definition of church itself?

On the other hand, who does not claim that the church is a mystical communion of people? Also, everyone seems to insist that the church is a mystical communion, but then simultaneously insist that the church is more than a mystical communion. So how helpful is this model? Is the church mystical and therefore *not* permitted or intended to entail some institutional elements? If institutional elements are part of the church, are these parts of what the church *is* or part of what the church needs to survive? Here, we turn to the ecclesiological thinking of Leonardo Boff, the Brazilian liberation theologian and celebrity of Brazilian university campuses.

In his book *Ecclesiogenesis*, Boff contends that the modern church needs to re-envision its own nature. Writing within the bounds of Roman Catholicism and from the perspective of liberation theology, Boff addresses what seems to him to be a context where the institutional model needs correcting. He begins by quoting Yves Congar: 'Think of the church as a huge organization, controlled by a hierarchy, with subordinates whose only task it is to keep the rules and follow the practices. Would this be a caricature? Scarcely!'[30] Boff's contextual concern is that the church is not adequate for the gross displays of poverty in Latin America. In particular, there are not enough priests to govern the high numbers of church members. As an only alternative these members have formed grassroots communities, known as base ecclesial communities, that are typically small, characterized by a sense of belonging, and promote solidarity among their members. Since these base ecclesial communities also gather regularly for worship, prayer, ministry, and even the Lord's Supper (bottom up), but since these communities have not been provided with a priest who can perform the Roman Catholic Mass (top down), the question arises as to whether or not these communities should be recognized as churches – in other words whether they should be granted 'full ecclesial status'.

It should be noted that Boff does not intend to eradicate all institutional elements. 'Nor is it possible for community to exist in a pure state. Concretely, there is always a power structure . . .'[31] Boff does, however, intend to restore the communal element over the institutional; the former holds 'primacy' over the latter.[32] In so doing, Boff has required that the church be understood in very mystical terms, 'not restricted to the visible limits of church'.[33] The distinction is important because '[t]he hierarchy has the sacramental function of organizing and serving a reality that it has not created but discovered, and within which it finds itself'.[34] The hierarchy is not the church; it shepherds the church. Therefore, these mystical communities will certainly have some leader or shepherd figure, but – and here is where Boff rejects the essentialization of institutional elements in the church – these base ecclesial community leaders need not be ordained priests (much less bishops) for the base ecclesial communities to be truly church. Base ecclesial communities are not some sort of 'movement in the church . . . These are church itself'.[35]

Boff, coming from a Roman Catholic Church with what appears to him to be an overly institutionalized ecclesiology, offers a compelling case for the mystical communal model of church. While Boff desires to remain under episcopal oversight (see the previous model), and while he insists that these 'ecclesial communities'/churches should be celebrating the full sacramental expressions of what it means to *be* church (see the next model), neither of these are essential (*sine qua non*) for the church. The base ecclesial communities already *are* church without these institutional and sacramental elements that visibly manifest them as church. Instead, these communities exist *mystically*. Thus, Boff's mystical communion model of the church, like what was stated above, seems to us more than simply a model. Boff embraces the 'model' language, but only so that the mystical communion model can de-centre the institutional model.[36] It would be more accurate to say that Boff believes the institutional elements are a secondary overlay to what the church actually *is*.

And so we return to our previously stated suspicion that mystical communion describes not so much what the church is *like*, but what the church *is*. The church is (primarily) a mystical communion, but the church should (secondarily) be governed institutionally. Perhaps, we should hold these first two models in a dialectical tension. Perhaps, the church is a mystical communion, but since this does very little to ensure the survival of the church, the church must also include institutional elements.[37] If we recognize that these two elements perennially deconstruct each other, and that the church is never without these two elements, then we both traverse the aporias of each model taken on its own and we guard our ecclesiology from settling into simplistic extremes. Yes, the church, according to ecumenical consensus, is a mystical communion, but not all communions are mystical. Such a dialectic requires that we turn the focus now to how the 'two or three' that constitute a church must do something that defines them as church: they must be gathered in Christ's name. Therefore, our appreciation for the dialectical tension between institution and communion that *is* the church needs to be triangulated in light of other models for the church.

Before turning to the other three models, there remains one unresolved matter between the institutional and communal models:

the necessity of institutional elements in general and the requirement of a bishop in particular. Our discussion of this debate needs to be informed historically as much as it needs to be treated systematically, and so we trace the development of the episcopal office in the early centuries of Christianity in order to appreciate the possibilities for the bishopric today.

EXCURSUS: DEVELOPMENT OF THE EPISCOPACY

One of the most notable impasses in current ecumenical dialogue is the question of the necessity of a bishop (*episkopos*) and the episcopal office. Understanding the historical development of this office, while in no way solving the ecumenical debate, helps to sharpen the focus of where the varying traditions agree and disagree. The history of the episcopate stems from the New Testament itself, but includes a few key moments in early Christian centuries.

When looking to the New Testament, we do not find *the* ecclesiology of the early church but the ecclesiolog*ies* of the early churches. Walter Bauer has championed the notion that groups which would later become known as 'heretics' were often the only expression of Christianity known at the time in that particular place. In other words, the earliest era of church history must be understood in terms of the wide diversity among Christian churches.[38] Not long after Bauer, James Dunn contended that the New Testament documents must be read in this Bauerian light: the different texts represent different viewpoints, including diverse ecclesiologies.[39]

In this work, we leave aside the debate about whether the early churches even had an 'office' (understood as a judicially authoritative position) or simply operated by *charismata* (spiritual gifts).[40] Suffice it to say that some sort of 'office', understood in the very least as a role or function undertaken by certain individuals, existed in New Testament churches. No evidence exists to suggest otherwise.

The two primary examples of church types in the New Testament are the assembly, akin to a Jewish synagogue, and the house church, akin to the Greek *oikos*. It is possible the Jewish–Christian assembly church actually met in synagogues, at least for a time, and the office of 'elder' seems to be a carryover from Judaism. The house church may have taken up not only Greek architectural space but Greek domestic structures, including a steward or overseer (*episkopos*) and servants or deacons (*diaconoi*). The elder-led assembly can be found in the catholic epistles, Revelation, and the Jerusalem church of Acts 15. The house church with overseers and deacons can be found especially in the Pauline letters, but also in the Gentile churches of the last half of Acts.[41] Many scholars believe that Acts and the Pastoral epistles depict a hybridization of these two forms.[42] If this is the case, than it is unclear if 'bishop' and 'elder' came to be synonymous.[43] Would any given congregation include more than one 'bishop', that is, many 'elders'?[44] Would 'elders' be inclusive of all older/honoured ones, irregardless of office, possibly including deacons?[45] New Testament scholars have reached no consensus on these issues. The transition from canonical evidence to other ancient Christian writings entails answering questions about the dating of the canonical texts themselves. In what follows, we will outline the historical stages of the episcopacy as they are often depicted in the secondary literature.

Phase one: presbyter-bishops

As mentioned for canonical texts and in the case of first and early second century texts on the whole, church historians understand 'presbyter' and 'bishop' to be largely synonymous in the earliest phase of Christianity. Scholars disagree as to whether presbyter-bishops should be understood in terms of (a) a single house church, wherein a college of presbyters would 'oversee' the congregation or (b) multiple house-churches, each headed by a 'bishop', the collective of house-church bishops being referred to as the 'presbyters'. The *Didache*, *1 Clement*, the *Shepherd of Hermas* and Polycarp's letter to the Philippians would all be representative of this stage.

Phase two: monarchical bishops

Unique among the early second-century sources, Ignatius of Antioch assumes that there is one bishop in each church who presides over the elders and deacons – the three-fold office of the church. The shift is from a college of presbyters to a single ruling (i.e. *mono-arche*) bishop over the other presbyters. Historians struggle to explain how Ignatius' church in Antioch developed such a structure. Traditionally, the earlier texts from phase one, including the New Testament itself, would be reinterpreted: none explicitly deny monepiscopacy, so they must (albeit ambiguously) implicitly affirm it.[46] More critically,

Ignatius' view of the bishop is dismissed: early Protestants could claim his letters were forgeries, and more recent scholars can assume that Ignatius intentionally re-structured the clerical offices. More sympathetically, Ignatius simply represents development in the early churches: either (option [a] in the previous paragraph) an egalitarian college of presbyters selected one from among them to preside over the church or (option [b] in the previous paragraph) the independent house church leaders recognized the need to have a 'spokesperson' or 'over-seer' to unite all the house churches in each city.[47] While Ignatius is unique in the early second century, by the late second and early third century the monarchical episcopacy is the norm, as seen in writers such as Irenaeus and Cyprian.

Phase three: diocesan bishops

If we understand the previous phase in terms of option (b), then there is practically no difference between the monarchical bishop and the diocesan bishop. We differentiate the two in order to be consistent with the possibility held by many scholars about option (a) for the monarchical episcopacy, and because the diocesan bishop developed further to oversee not only the multiple congregations/ parishes in each city but also the many parishes from the surrounding area. In this framework, which is still the norm in traditions governed by an episcopal structure, the diocese is the fundamental unit of the church, and the bishop himself is the primary authority in his see. If one accepts that there was a substantial difference between phase two and the current phase, then Cyprian can be read as evidence of this kind of episcopal authority.

Phase four: metropolitan bishops

Like the previous phases, scholars disagree as to whether or not this should be understood as a chronological phase or simply a geo-graphical accommodation in the development of the episcopacy. A metropolitan bishop is one that presides as a diocesan bishop in the largest and most influential city in the region. Other diocesan bishops would, if not submit to his jurisdiction, then acknowledge his status as first among equals. The metropolitan presides over local synods, and in many traditions functions as the next level between bishops and archbishops. We choose not to separate another phase for Patriarchs, as these essentially function in the same manner: they are the senior bishop in terms of the region's most ancient and venerated see. At the Council of Nicaea (325) the role of the metropolitans were defined (canon 4), and the sees of Rome, Antioch and Alexandria are given what seems to be patriarchal status (canon 6). Like the traditional reading of bishops mentioned above in the discussion about monarchical bishops, apologists of episcopal structure once assumed that the ancient church had always been organized by a hierarchy of bishops answering to metropolitans and archbishops and patriarchs. Ignatius' reference to himself as the 'bishop of Syria' has been read this way. Again, the *Didache*, and even certain statements in Ignatius' letters, make this assumption more dubious.

Phase five: the papacy

While Roman Catholics still affirm Peter as the first pope via the keys to the kingdom (Mt. 16.18), most Catholic scholars today will also admit that many generations passed before the bishop of Rome functioned as the supreme head of the church on earth. The process slowly developed (see Hippolytus), was contested (see Cyprian), became more accepted (see Gregory the Great and then Innocent III), and finally clarified (see Vatican I). While this is most generally accepted as a historical phase (even by Roman Catholics), it is most vehemently debated as a theological tenet (especially by the Eastern Orthodox).

Future discussion of the episcopacy

Many questions have been left unaddressed about each phase listed above, including the proper understanding of the development – even whether or not there was development or if a particular phase did or did not exist. Nevertheless, as a survey of the development of the episcopacy, this schema illustrates what is available to us in the documents of the ancient church and its interpretation by later Christians. What remains is to formulate how this historical information affects our contemporary understanding of the church. In order, therefore, to constructively analyse and appropriate the evidence of the early Christian centuries regarding the episcopacy, we will here follow the theory of one scholar in particular: Kallistos Ware.[48]

We do so because (1) Ware intentionally and skilfully represents the consensus of both academic scholars and ecumenical theologians on this issue and (2) Ware belongs to a tradition that has highly valued the episcopal office – he is an Orthodox metropolitan himself – which neither of us can claim to adequately represent.

Ware picks up his explication of the episcopate at the point where the New Testament diversity is said to develop into a 'second stage'.[49] Whereas Ware assumes a two-fold ministry of presbyter-bishops and deacons in the apostolic era, he quickly turns to the letters of Ignatius of Antioch who promotes a three-fold ministry of bishop, elders and deacons in each congregation. How this shift occurred, however, is 'far from clear . . . The three-fold pattern, so it seems, was by no means universal in Ignatius' day, and perhaps did not come to prevail generally until the end of the second century'.[50] He acknowledges how other second century witnesses, such as *1 Clement,* the *Didache,* and even Polycarp, offer no evidence of the 'monarchical' episcopate, that is one presiding bishop, but instead they suggest the churches were governed by a collegial body of presbyters.

What is significant for Ware about Ignatius' argument is not the singular authoritative office of the monarchical bishop, but the 'unifying ministry he exercises'.[51] Since there is one loaf which unites one body (cf. 1 Cor. 10.16–7), Ignatius sees the bishop's role 'not imposed upon us from without by some exterior authority, but created from within by our common participation in the Holy Mysteries'.[52] Ignatius places the bishop in harmony with the presbyters, deacons and congregants: 'there is a co-responsibility, not autocracy', as seen in Ignatius' advice to Polycarp to have the congregation elect a messenger. It is not Polycarp's role, as bishop of Smyrna, to act otherwise.[53] Ware deduces that the church should reclaim Ignatius' teaching on the bishop as eucharistic celebrant, with the church defined as those who gather around this table fellowship: 'Ignatius was writing at a time when, to use anachronistic terminology, the bishop's diocese consisted of but a single parish. There was at this time no more than one eucharistic assembly in each city'.[54] Of course, Ware does not expect the church to return to this practice entirely: 'It is scarcely practicable for us today to revert to the second-century pattern whereby the bishop had charge of no more than a single worshipping community'.[55] But Ware does hope that Orthodox churches will re-orient their structures to a more Ignatian intimacy between the pastor and his flock.

The second major development in the episcopal office for Ware is found in Irenaeus. If for Ignatius the bishop is the one who unites the local church eucharistically, then for Irenaeus the bishop links the orthodox churches doctrinally. Ware still finds a eucharistic theology in Irenaeus, but the emphasis in his writings is that the bishop 'is *par excellence* the one who teaches the truth'.[56] Irenaeus champions the notion of apostolic succession, but this phenomenon is a succession of apostolic *teaching* that is located in the succession of apostolic churches. The bishop is the appointed teacher, a point which must be emphasized for two reasons.

First, Irenaeus from time to time betrays 'an interesting survival of the primitive New Testament usage' of the terms presbyters and bishops – that is, that they are interchangeable.[57] The monarchical bishop, therefore, need not be emphasized in one's ecclesiology so long as the 'inward continuity in apostolic faith' be retained by the teaching-elder/bishop.[58] The second important aspect Ware finds in Irenaeus' emphasis on the bishop's teaching role has to do with the validity of any particular church's episcopacy. The question is not so much who consecrated whom in the apostolic succession, but to what local church does the bishop belong and whether that church's doctrine is apostolic.[59]

The third significant moment in the development in the episcopacy comes in the ministry of Cyprian of Carthage. Whereas the Ignatian bishop unites members of the local church, and the Irenaean bishop links the local church with the ancient church, the Cyprianic bishop 'bonds the local church and the Church universal'.[60] The local bishop represents the local church in a synod or council, and each individual bishop shares in the universal church's 'one episcopacy' (*episcopatus unus est*).[61] The individual bishop, however, presides in his individual church, not the council of bishops: for Cyprian, 'no compulsion should be brought to bear upon the dissident bishop or bishops. The Church, while still preserving unity, will be obliged to live for a time with the fact of this disagreement'.[62] In other words, 'each particular church – by which Cyprian still means, as Ignatius does, each local eucharistic assembly – is endowed with autonomy'.[63]

Much like the Ignatian model of one local pastor of one local flock, Ware assumes that a Cyprianic model will be 'dismissed as unworkable'.[64] But unlike later episcopal developments – wherein episcopal dioceses expanded to include multiple eucharistic assemblies, and came to be governed by metropolitans, archbishops, and patriarchs – Ware believes that the church can return to Cyprian's model of collegiality. In fact, because juridical structures that can enforce a conciliar decision on the local bishop and congregation require 'an allegiance between Church and state', and because we now live in 'a "post-Constantinian" context', Ware argues that the church must return to Cyprian's model.

Ware's treatment of 'patterns' of episcopacy should be understood as his attempt to hold two concerns together. First, Ware must acknowledge that the ancient church's structures are not perfectly replicated today. Second, without denying the validity of the later development of an episcopal hierarchy which performs practical governance, Ware hopes to reframe the current episcopal practices in light of the ancient witnesses to the bishop's essential roles. The later historical development of the episcopate is a complicated set of phenomena that leads either to collegial autocephelous communions (the Eastern Orthodox and Anglican understanding) or to a streamlined hierarchy under the universal jurisdiction of one bishop (the Roman Catholic understanding). Which is preferable? The debate as to whether churches should return to autonomous local congregations headed by a bishop/pastor (the free church understanding) or a teaching-elder and elder board (the Reformed understanding) has yet to be resolved in ecumenical dialogue. But for future discussion, we suggest the following as starting points.

First, the 'necessity' of a 'bishop' should be affirmed. This statement may come as a shock to our readers since both of the current authors come from a free church tradition. Of course, we have qualified our statement with the tell-tale quotation marks. To take the items in reverse, we qualify the term bishop because the term bishop is already qualified by *all* ecclesiological traditions. More agreement is needed about what a 'bishop' is today. Ware's local eucharistic presider is structurally indistinguishable from a Baptist 'pastor' and Reformed 'teaching elder'. Also, we qualify 'necessity' because it too is often an ill-defined term in theological discourse. By 'necessary' we (a) recognize the wide-spread consensus on the bishop's office and function both ecumenically and traditionally, and we (b) believe God calls someone to act *in persona Christi* in a shepherding or overseeing role in the church, but we also (c) refer to the etymological significance of necessity (Lat. = *ne-* + *-cedere*) as unavoidable or inescapable – and yet not automatic, nor absolute in its third-century expression. All traditions agree that exceptions arise, such as when a bishop is martyred.[65] Nevertheless, God calls someone to substitute and function *in persona Christi*, that is, as the shepherd/elder/overseer in the church when the church acts as church. (For Christ is 'the great shepherd of the sheep' [Heb. 13.20].) We believe much consensus can be built around this important starting point: even in elder-led churches, the elders/ministers can be understood to function both *in persona Christi* corporately when acting jointly as a supervisory body and *in persona Christi* individually when one of them performs any sort of teaching or sacramental role.

Secondly, members relate to the church through the bishop, and this relating refers both intra-congregationally and inter-congregationally. Within each congregation, each member is connected to the body mystically, but this visible expression is by the ordering under a head. While we do not envision this headship/oversight to be autocratic or one of 'lording it over others', we find the bishop to be the proper means of visibly expressing the unity of the local church. This can be seen especially in the teaching and sacramental functions of the bishop. Between congregations, the mystical unity we share in Christ through the Holy Spirit has always sought expression in the church, whether through the avid letter writing of first- and second-century Christians or in ecumenical councils of later Christian churches. The church has always sought to manifest its intra-congregational commun[icat]ion in a catholic way, and the bishop has always been the proper means to do so. Here again we find that exceptions have always been made, such as when the bishop of Rome sent his emissaries to ecumenical councils.[66] Nevertheless, affirming the bishop's unifying role for both the local and the universal church is the most productive way forward for any ecclesiology that wishes to avoid parochialism and to participate in ecumenism.

Finally, the episcopate must be placed within the larger framework of the priesthood of all believers, and they both must be understood as a sharing in Christ's shepherding and sacrificial work. On the one hand the clerical offices are not simply accepted as dogma because they were declared as such canonically, and on the other hand these are not merely functions that are left entirely to contextualization. The office of the bishop as a unique role and the priesthood of the believer as a universal vocation derive their necessity and their efficacy from Christ by the will of the Father and in the power of the Holy Spirit. This theological acknowledgment can guide our discussion about the church toward a more robust articulation and can guide ecumenical dialogue toward a more hopeful future. At the same time the contextualization of ecclesiology and episcopacy is in no way barred, because the contextual development of the episcopacy itself is taken into account and because the priesthood of every believer lends itself to an ecclesiology and an episcopacy 'from below'.

With this appreciation of the 'necessity' of a 'bishop', we can now return to our discussion of various models for the church. Just as Vatican I represented the institutional model – but in no way denied the mystical communion of the church, and just as Boff championed the communal model – but in no way denied the importance of the bishop, so now we will analyse the sacramental model of the church while keeping other concerns in view.

* * *

Third model: sacrament

To model the church after the notion of 'sacrament' is to liken the church to the Christian rituals of baptism, communion, and perhaps other practices of the church. This model then immediately begs the question, What is a sacrament? We will return to the sacraments in a later chapter, but for now we need a working definition. The Anglican Book of Common Prayer provides a general definition that represents ecumenical consensus: 'The sacraments are outward and visible signs of an inward and spiritual Grace, given by Christ as sure and certain means by which we receive that grace'.[67] The ecumenical consensus breaks down when one attempts to clarify (1) what is meant in the phrase 'certain means by which receive' the grace; that is, the causal/effectual role of the sacraments, at which point Zwinglians leave the table, and (2) the nature of the 'presence' of grace; that is, what kind of presence, at which point Reform, Lutheran, Catholic and Orthodox part ways. Despite these differences, and even in light of the reluctance of some traditions to use the term sacrament, there is a broad agreement on the notion that God chooses certain elements and rituals as 'outward signs' of 'inward grace'.[68]

To claim that the church *is* a sacrament, is first to prioritize the 'inward grace' that is church – that is, mystical communion, and second to insist that 'outward signs' are nevertheless requisite.[69] Thus far, the sacramental model of church fulfils our stated preference for a dialectical tension between the institutional and the communal models of church. But when this model is invoked by theologians, it must be admitted that the emphasis falls clearly on the outward/visible/institutional side of the analogy. A leading advocate of a sacramental ecclesiology, who illustrates this emphasis on the visible, is Pope Benedict XVI (formerly Cardinal Ratzinger).

While Pope Benedict's ecclesiology has certainly developed from the early thought of Joseph Ratzinger, we may still look to certain statements made by then Cardinal Ratzinger as indicative of his understanding of the church as sacrament. Ratzinger attended and participated in Vatican II, wherein the church, quoting Cyprian, was said to be 'the sacrament of salvation' and 'the sacrament of unity'.[70] Moreover, the undisputed ecclesiological framework leading into and coming out of that council was 'communion ecclesiology'. After some time as the Prefect for the Congregation for the Doctrine of the Faith, Ratzinger issued 'A Letter to the Bishops of the Catholic Church on Some Aspects of the Church Understood as Communion'.[71] While communion ecclesiology is affirmed, Ratzinger writes a correction to the direction some have taken under this banner: '[S]ome approaches to ecclesiology suffer from a clearly inadequate awareness of the Church as a mystery of communion, especially . . . [in regards] to the relationship between the Church as *communion* and the church as *sacrament*'.[72] The church as *communio* or *koinonia* must be supplemented with the sacramental model of church.

Ratzinger is quick to admit that the notion of mystical communion 'is very suitable for expressing the core of the Mystery of the Church', and he quotes Pope John Paul II to say, 'communion lies "at the heart of the Church's self-understanding"'.[73] In so doing, Ratzinger at first seems to equate mystical communion with the *esse* of the church to which the institutional elements, defined as 'suitable means for its visible and social union', could be seen as part of the *bene esse*.[74] This understanding, however, is unacceptable in light of Ratzinger's next axiom: 'Ecclesial communion is at the same time both invisible and visible'.[75] This equating of the visible and invisible, which corresponds with our earlier definition of sacrament in terms of outward-and-spiritual, is a strict application of the sacramental model. Indeed, one could make a strong argument that such a move *cannot* be made within the sacramental model. If you conflate the sign with the thing signified, it is difficult to see how that can still be called sacramental.

By insisting on the visible being as equally essential as the invisible, Ratzinger counters any who would 'weaken the concept of the unity of the Church at the visible and institutional level'.[76] Of course, as one who must uphold Roman Catholic dogma inclusive of Vatican I and Vatican II, Ratzinger here is especially concerned with 'regulations regarding juridical dependence' – which is to say Petrine primacy.[77] In so doing, the prefect is explicitly opposing three related errors which represent three theological schools of thought: (1) those who would claim that 'the totality of the mystery of the Church would be made present in such a way as to render any other principle of unity [i.e. other than the papacy] or universality non-essential' – which is the Eastern Orthodox view; (2) those who represent 'an even more radical form, going as far as to hold that gathering together in the name of Jesus is the same as generating the Church' – which is the Protestant free church view and (3) any who might link the church with the pope but not essentially so and say the church 'would arise "from base level"' – Leonardo Boff's view.[78] Each of these are errors, according to Ratzinger, but the latter two are errors that deny the sacramentality of the church. The first only denies the correct outward sign of the mystical communion that is church.[79] To be 'fully church' Ratzinger's framework requires full communion with the Bishop of Rome.[80] The outward sign is necessary. This is because in the sacramental model the visible sign – in this case the pope – is as much one of the 'constituents' of the church as the spiritual grace.[81] In this understanding the outward sign is not merely a manifestation or an indicator of the spiritual reality; it too constitutes what the church *is*.

Since Ratzinger is countering Boff and others who have downplayed the essentiality of the visible aspects of the church, it is no surprise that Boff disagrees with this current pope and his ecclesiology. What may be surprising, however, is the fact that Ratzinger's letter has conflicted not just with liberation, Orthodox and Protestant theologians, but it even goes beyond previous Vatican statements. In our above discussion on the institutional model of the church, we outlined how Vatican I explicitly emphasizes the infallibility and universal jurisdiction of the pope; but it implicitly defines the church as the people of God (*esse*) who should be governed by Peter's successor (*bene esse*) – an implicit distinction that Ratzinger has now dismissed. Vatican II, a growing number of interpreters claim, stands in continuity with Vatican I. In this more recent council, the Roman

Catholic Church declared, '[T]he pre-eminent manifestation of the Church consists in the full active participation of all God's holy people in these liturgical celebrations, especially in the same eucharist, in a single prayer, at one altar, at which there presides the bishop surrounded by his college of priests and by his ministers'.[82] Here, the church *is* the people of God, but the visible 'manifestation' – nay, the 'pre-eminent [but not exclusive] manifestation' – of the invisible church is found in the eucharistic celebration under the bishop. To be church may not require the visible institution, but to be the visible church does.

Because the sacramental model of the church holds together the tension between institution and communion (as well as between visible/invisible, physical/spiritual, outward/inward), we find this model beneficial and promising. When the sacramental model *equates* these two elements rather than *unites* them – as Ratzinger seems to have done – we find the model to be misapplied and misleading. It is worth noting that since his election to the papacy, Benedict has not reiterated this equation of the visible and the invisible.[83] It must also be appreciated that Ratzinger attempts to see the sacramental model through to its logical conclusion: if the visible structure of the church is a sign of the people of God as the invisible grace, the former must be an *efficacious* sign.[84] Many in the ecumenical movement and many who are impacted by Benedict's ecclesiology hope this pope will return to the sentiments of his early career which viewed ecclesial communities outside of Rome's jurisdiction as valid churches.[85] To fully equate the spiritual and the physical, the outward sign with the inward grace, is reductionistic. Such could not be analogously applied to the hypostatic union of Christ – wherein the two natures are united but not equated, and such a move need not be made for the sacramental model of the church.

The sacramental model of the church can be taken in two directions: a model of worship (which describes what the church *does*) or a model of mystical union (which embraces the previous dialectical tension between institution and mystical communion). Let us take each direction in turn and then come back to our journey through these models by analysing the model itself.

A model of what the church does (signifies salvation, worships its Head, etc.) is helpful on one level, but on another level this model compares apples and oranges, at least in regards to the first two models. With the next two models, however, the sacrament model for church aligns neatly, as they too seem to describe what the church *is* by what the church *does*. The functional description of the church proves helpful in seeing the church in terms of agency, but we have yet to define the church in terms of essence. If the essence of the church is indefinable, then we have capitulated to the mystical communion model. Dulles as much as admits this when he avers, 'In principle, [the sacramental] theory seems to allow for a strong, even a primary, emphasis on the interior and spiritual aspects of the church'.[86] The recent statement by the World Council of Churches' Faith and Order Commission, *The Nature and Mission of the Church* (2005), represents an ecumenical consensus that recognizes this distinction between form and function as a helpful pattern. The very title of the document is suggestive: the 'nature' of the church is distinguishable from the 'mission' of the church.[87] Ratzinger himself has invoked the distinction between essence and function for other doctrinal topics, and while we do not wish to set up a structural dichotomy between being and doing, the distinction is an important one when attempting to come to a consensus on definition.[88]

We will return to the function of the church in the next two models and in the conclusion to this chapter. But for now, let us note that worship is an essential aspect of the church, and this tells us something about what the church *is*. Church that does not celebrate the sacred is not church. That having been said, we need to press further than celebration of the sacred in order to do justice to the sacramental model: we need to embody the sacred; church that does not embody the sacred is not church. Sacred embodiment by any other name is sacramentalism, which now brings us to the second direction of this model of church as sacrament.

To say that the church *is* a sacrament is to utilize the outward/inward, visible/invisible, spiritual/physical distinctions only for the purpose of reuniting each side of the binary opposition. The conjoining of, for example, the outward/inward in the sacrament illustrates how the church as sacrament unites outward/inward aspects of its existence. The church is the dialectical tension between physical and spiritual, the heavenly and the earthly. The two things are brought together via the church, and the bringing together of the two *is* the church.

Perhaps, we should better understand this model of church as sacrament to be the dialectical tension of the institutional (outward) and communal (inward) models – Vatican II's understanding. There is more held in tension, however, than the simple visible/invisible dichotomy, for in the sacramental model the church *as* sacrament also holds in tension what the church *is* and what the church *does* – a theme to which we will return in the following two sections. On the one hand, we have once again prioritized the mystical communion model of the church because this in fact tells us what the church *is*. On the other hand, we have prevented the mystical communion model from becoming the single model of church by insisting that the church *be* embodied and *become* manifested.[89] Before attempting to proceed with this appreciation for the holistic tendency in the sacramental model, let us first recognize that there are other essential functions for the church as seen in the next two models.

Fourth model: herald

Dulles' fourth model of the church is that 'of the herald of a king who comes to proclaim a royal decree in a public square'.[90] Champions of this model, such as Luther and Barth, insist that the proclamation of the gospel is primary to what makes the church church. Luther defended the doctrine of justification as 'the article on which the church stands or falls'.[91] There is a noteworthy homology between the Roman Catholic understanding of the church as 'founded' upon Peter (understood as Petrine primacy) and Luther's understanding of the church as 'standing' on the gospel (understood as *sola gratia, sola fide*).[92]

In Dulles' telling this model is a functional model of the church, and the model itself, 'herald', describes the entity by what it *does*. Luther and Barth, however, offered a more robust understanding: the focus is not simply on the church as a herald, but on the heralding itself; it is an 'evangelical ecclesiology'. To unpack what this means, we turn to a recent defence of this understanding of the church by John Webster.

Webster sets out 'to describe the relation between the gospel and the church'.[93] The primary question is, 'Are the gospel and the church extrinsically or internally related?'[94] If extrinsically, then the preaching of the gospel is what the church *does*; if intrinsically, the gospel somehow determines what the church *is*. An evangelical ecclesiology, for both Luther and Webster, is initially a reaction against institutionalism: an institutionally sound church with an evangelically unsound doctrine is problematic. Luther liked to refer to the leader of such a church as 'Antichrist'; Webster is more ecumenically sensitive and is more directly concerned with this problem in terms of 'ecclesiological hypertrophy', that is, ecclesiology which subsumes every other doctrine.[95] If an ecclesiology were hypertrophic, as Webster fears to be inevitable in the institutional and sacramental models, then one's theology-proper loses proper distinctions, especially 'the distinction between God and creatures'.[96] Any institutional linkage between Christ and the church (as found in Vatican I) or any overstated 'participation' of the church in Christ (as found in Ratzinger's sacramental model) results in ontological obfuscation.

The sacramental model allows for a distinction between Christ and Christ's body/church, and yet these two distinct entities are united – to use Chalcedonian terminology. In Webster's view, however, once the hypostatic union becomes the paradigm for the church, the alleged distinction entails no more than lip-service. Chalcedonian Christology defined two 'natures' in one 'person' (Greek = *hypostasis*, thus 'hypostatic' union). Sacramental ecclesiology defines the two hypostases, Christ and Christ's church, as united bodily through the one earthly nature.[97] Where then does Christ stop and the church begin? While certain metaphors – such as body of Christ and bride of Christ – encourage this type of thinking, these metaphors can be pressed too far: although there is a mystical union between Christ and his body/bride, the two are also different. The bride is not the groom; and the body is not the head. The church is not Christ. Christ, while calling, raising and embracing the church, is always *other than* the church.[98] Does Webster then return to the mystical communion model of the church?

Webster admits to the priority of the mystical communion aspect of the church to the institutional: the former is the church's *esse*, the latter the *bene esse*. The ontological clarification needs to be reinserted into ecclesiological discourse, and Christ and the church constitute 'a relation-in-distinction, that is to say, [a] *covenant fellowship*'.[99] While this initially appears to be a return to the mystical communion model, the difference lies in the emphasis, which falls even prior to the church's being as mystical communion. The church *becomes* a mystical communion in response to God's action in sending forth his Word by the Spirit, and the proclamation of this Word is what creates the church. '[T]he gospel and church exist in a strict and irreversible order, one in which the gospel precedes and the church follows'. Webster's church is 'evangelical' (having to do

41

with the gospel) before it is a 'herald' (proclaiming the gospel) because it is the gospel that establishes the church as a communion of saints or mystical communion. This ecclesiological framework, however, while answering Webster's doctrinal concerns, does not adequately exhaust what needs to be said about church, as seen in Webster's practical concerns.

Webster devotes the second half of his essay on 'Evangelical Ecclesiology' to the church's visibility. While we will explicate the visible/invisible distinction more fully in the next chapter, we find it important to follow Webster's argument here in order to understand his definition of the church itself. In a disclaimer that he need not follow the current trend of giving 'primacy to the church's visibility', Webster nevertheless insists on the church's visibility.[100] His stipulation, however, in which his evangelical ecclesiology is quintessentially evangelical (i.e. of the *euangelion*), is to give preference to 'the notion of witness [as one which] tries to express the permanently derivative character of the work of the church'.[101] The concept of witness is the preferred term for expressing what aspect of the church constitutes it as visible, and this is so because it corresponds to God's constituting the church in the proclamation of the Word by the power of the Spirit. Just as the proclamation of the Word constitutes the church, so the church is recognizable when the church proclaims the Word.

Webster's visible church is not equated with the invisible, yet the proper understanding of the church as herald, especially in Reformed thought, rightly orders God's speech to the church and the church's witness to God's speech. God's speech to the church is the vocation of the church into being; the church's witness to God's speech is the vocation of the church's being. While it would be tempting to claim that the church *is* a result of the gospel and the church *should* proclaim the gospel, Webster's high view of sovereignty pre-empts this depiction. Webster does not equate the invisible called church with the visibly witnessing church (as Ratzinger does); he reverses Ratzinger's order by necessitating the visible as a response to the invisible. If the church is truly church, it will witness to the gospel. The strength of Webster's articulation is that he relentlessly focuses the discussion on the action of God in his Word, and not merely on human works. To slip back into sacramental language, however, God's invisible grace must become manifested in visible signs. Although Webster does not utilize the concept, we think his ecclesiology can be aptly described in Zizioulas' terms of what constitutes and what conditions. God's Word constitutes the church; but the condition by which we know (i.e. visibly see) the church is in the church's proclamation of the Word.

Webster's example of evangelical ecclesiology is a helpful clarification of Dulles' herald model of the church. From his presentation, we can draw several important points. First, the herald model (robustly understood) is not simply a reiteration of the mystical communion model only with the stipulation that this community *should* witness. Evangelical ecclesiology is one that believes the church *is* a gospel-formed mystical community and a gospel-proclaiming visible community. Second, in order to hold to the constitutionality of witness for the church's *esse*, one must hold to a high view of divine sovereignty. Any allowance of a church truly being an evangelically called church of God yet not witnessing to the Word of God because of a synergistic framework that permits resistance is to revert to the mystical communion model. Such an allowance in fact defines the church as a (called) mystical community, and defines proclamation as something extrinisic to the church – something it should *do*, not something the church *is*. Third, it is worth noting that the herald model does not exclude the sacramental model altogether. Instead, the herald model requires the 'sacrament' in the sacramental model be defined in a more evangelical way. If by sacrament, one only means a sign of grace (and not an effecter of grace, or 'efficacious sign'), then the church is a sacrament in that it 'signifies' (i.e. non-verbally 'proclaims') Christ. But in so doing, we have once again slipped away from what the church *is*, and defined what the church *does* (signify, proclaim, etc.). Therefore, the kerygmatic understanding of the church, while not necessarily antithetical to it, resists the sacramental model. After all, the Word proclaimed is what calls the church into being, and therefore the church *is* constituted by proclamation. The sacramental understanding somehow articulates a 'manifestation of' but not a 'constitution of' the church. Fourth, we believe that this model offers a proper correction to any ecclesiology that devalues Christian witness as intrinsic to the church. Miroslav Volf has asked the question pointedly: 'Should, for example, a Catholic or Orthodox diocese whose members are inclined more to superstition than to faith and who identify with the church more for nationalistic reasons – should such a diocese be viewed as a church, while a Baptist congregation that has preserved the faith through the crucible of persecution *not* be considered such?'[102] Doyle, a Roman

Catholic who knows and defends his tradition's ecclesiology, responds by defending Volf's sentiments: 'This is not just a matter of emotional persuasion but one of substance. True witness to the gospel can be argued to be as much an essential element of the Church as is any particular structure'.[103] These four points summarize the strengths of evangelical ecclesiology; these strengths, however, must be seen in light of the inadequacy of this model.

Even with Webster's stress on the *ordo salutis*, the herald model is a functional model that defines what the church *is* by what the church *does*, and so our appreciation for evangelical ecclesiology, which we wish to stress, needs to be matched by an appreciation for other functional aspects of the church's being, such as the sacramental functions mentioned in the last model and the diaconal functions that will be discussed in the next. The evangelical critique of communion and sacramental ecclesiologies only provides an alternate emphasis on what constitutes and conditions the church *as* a communion; it does not in fact deny the church to *be* a communion. The church is church because the proclamation of the Word has called (Greek *kaleo*; cf. *ek-klesia*) a people together. That truism having been stated, proponents of the herald-model of church can rest at ease and return to the ecumenical consensus on the church as being a fellowship of (called) persons in Christ. We do not intend to overlook the contributions made from this emphasis; we simply need to clarify the categorical distinction: Webster's (and Barth's) model of the church as herald is an emphasis on what the church *does* but does not differ in what the church *is* (even if Webster's appeal to sovereignty suggests a difference in how the church becomes a mystical communion). The church *is* a communion of persons; the church *does* gather in response to, and – in turn – issue the call of, the gospel of Jesus Christ. If the church is evangelical because this is what the church necessarily *does*, then we must still define what the church *is* and thus return to the communal; if the church is evangelical because the church *becomes* church in the proclamation of the Word, then this model is a return to the sacramental. Either way, the emphasis, while helpfully reorienting the discussion to divine action, must be supplemented with further elaboration on the human response, which includes but is not limited to proclamation. The next step, then, is to inquire as to other functional models of the church, such as the servant model.

Fifth model: servant

If Barth is the great champion of the herald model for the church, then Bonhoeffer is the champion of the servant model of the church, or diaconal ecclesiology.[104] The church is of the Word and thus proclaims the Word, but the Word became flesh and dwelt among us and so should the church. When one sees Christ's mission and ministry as kenotic (cf. Phil. 2.6), then Christ's church must surely follow suit.

Dulles betrays much less sympathy for the servant model than he does for any of the other four. One reason may be that Dulles wrote in the era when the Social Gospel, with its overly optimistic ecclesiology, was widely denounced as a failed endeavour. Another more immediate factor for Dulles' critique is that liberation theology was still relatively new when he first wrote his book, and he and the rest of the North Atlantic Roman Catholic community were still leery of this movement and its Marxist leanings. Fast forward a few decades to our day and it is safe to say that liberation theology has had such an influence on the wider Christian discourse, that even explicit opponents of this movement have better articulated their solidarity with the poor. Dulles' unsympathetic reading of the servant model may have been unduly suspicious, and the model may now be seen as on par with the herald model.[105] After all, the major strength of this model is the credentials of its proponents: Bonhoeffer and liberation theologians have taken their stand of martyrdom and earned confessor status.[106] When these theologians declare that the church is not an institution, but a servant, and that the church should sell all its assets and serve those in need, few wish to snatch away the bullhorn, cross the picket line, and oppose the least of these among us.

On the other hand, our challenge has been to find a recent proponent of the servant model. Boff, a liberation theologian, agrees that the church *should* serve, but Boff and most liberation theologians, and for that matter most ecclesiologists in general, are reluctant to say the church *is* a servant but not a herald.[107] Rather than thinking of diaconal ecclesiology as a model, we must instead look to proponents of a service-for-the-world emphasis.

In order to interact with Dulles' fifth model we must force a few square pegs into some round holes. We beg the reader's patience at this point: what follows is not so much a 'bad fit', but it is a reframing of Dulles' original description of the model in order for proponents of the servant emphasis to be heard. Of course we have said from the beginning that Dulles' typology hinders as well as helps, and so this fifth model is simply the most painfully obvious example of what we already knew.

We will discuss the servant model, or diaconal ecclesiology, by discussing the church's service to the world, or its 'mission'. For our present purposes, 'mission' will be a loaded synonym for 'service'. This is permissible because (1) the concept of 'mission' is analogous to Dulles' articulation of this model's emphasis on ecstatic, world-oriented ecclesiology and (2) it is now the norm in missiological discourse to speak of 'mission' as involving as much 'deed' or 'service' as it does 'word' and 'proclamation'. While we will return to a more thorough analysis of the church's mission in chapter four, we now turn to the church's essence as a servant to the world, or to diaconal/missional ecclesiology.

The champion of missional ecclesiology is the missionary, bishop, ecumenist and theologian, Lesslie Newbigin. Ironically, for the most underrepresented model of the church, we have selected the least systematic theologian of our representatives to articulate this emphasis. 'Newbigin's theology is first and foremost *ad hoc* and contextual. He never accepted the title of a scholar but viewed himself as a pastor who wanted to bring the light of the gospel to bear on the urgent issues of the day. Any examination of Newbigin's ecclesiology, therefore, must pay attention to the historical context in which his view of the church developed'.[108] The responsive nature of Newbigin's writings means that his ecclesiology (1) developed throughout his career and (2) was never expressed in a final, systematic form. Therefore, our interaction with Newbigin will (a) primarily, but not exclusively, draw from a chapter entitled, 'Does Society Still Need a Parish Church?', in his 1994 work, *A Word in Season*, which represents the 'mature' Newbigin, if not the whole of Newbigin's thought and (b) rely more heavily on secondary commentators than our interaction with champions from previous models.[109]

Newbigin's experience as a missionary in South India shaped his understanding of the nature of the church. As a missionary who returned to the Western world, he contended that the church in the West must reclaim its proper posture to the world by becoming 'missional'. The late Protestant dichotomy between church and mission must be abandoned because the church is missional, or it is a failed church. Of course, his context did not erase his doctrinal allegiances, as seen in his relentless emphasis on election, which he learned from his Church of Scotland heritage. The wedding of these two emphases – God's calling and the church's mission – provided the framework for Newbigin to promote an externally focused ecclesiology that was internally rooted in the triune God.

The church is 'summoned', and this summons has been issued by God – a dictum that can be deduced from the New Testament concept of the *ekklesia*, the called out assembly.[110] In accordance with his Reformed heritage, therefore, Newbigin defines the church by its election, but then in accordance with his missionary sensibilities he also stipulates another definitive aspect of the church: 'the *ekklesia theou* [is] defined simply by the place where they meet, and any other definition is ruled out'.[111] In other words the church in New Testament language is the church 'of' God and the church 'for' a specific locale, such as Jerusalem, Corinth or Thessalonica.

From this observation Newbigin concludes that the institutional structures of the church must conform to the needs of the locale. There is no essential office, structure or size for the institutional aspect of the church; instead the only essential aspect of the church's institutional form is that it serve the locale 'for' which it exists:

[T]he structural forms of the Church are determined by the secular reality, and not by the internal needs of the Church; and I think that is true to Scripture. The relation between the Church in a 'place' and the secular reality of that 'place' is intrinsic, not extrinsic. It's not just that it happens to be located in that spot on the map. It is the Church of God *for that place*, and that is because the Church does not exist for itself but for God and for the world that Jesus came to serve.[112]

The church, therefore, must be understood as in between, or 'provisional', because it stands between God and the world; it is called by God and serves the world.[113]

Newbigin sees the *missio Dei* as normative for the church.[114] The church was born out of God's mission in Christ and the Spirit, and the church participates in that same mission of reconciling the world to God. Here we must note Newbigin's differences from Dulles' depiction of the servant model wherein the church exists for the world. While Newbigin's ecclesiology ends there, it begins with the church's call from God.[115] Newbigin, therefore, does say that the church is 'for' the world, but he must also declare that church 'against' the world. He finds this to be revealed in Christ's atoning work:

> . . . Christ on his cross is in one sense totally identified with the world, but in another sense totally separated from the world. The cross is the total identification of Jesus with the world in all its sin, but in that identification the cross is the judgment of the world, that which shows the gulf between God and his world. We must always, it seems to me, in every situation, be wrestling with both sides of this reality: that the Church is for the world against the world. The Church is against the world for the world. The Church is for the human community in that place, that village, that city, that nation, in the sense that Christ is for the world. And that must be the determining criterion at every point.[116]

Just as the *missio Dei* revealed in Christ included Christ's suffering for the world, so the church must participate in God's mission by being 'marked by the scars of the Passion'.[117] Christ's passion is paradigmatic for the church, which also must exist as an ecstatic kenosis; the church gives its life for others.[118]

Newbigin's missional ecclesiology is comparable to Webster's articulation of evangelical ecclesiology. Whereas Webster defined the church as being formed by the gospel and therefore functioning as a herald of the gospel, Newbigin likewise has defined the church as being formed by the mission of God and therefore functioning to further God's mission to the world. Webster focuses on the Word of God who founded the church and the church's proclamation of the Word. Newbigin avoids any confinement of 'witness' and 'proclamation' to verbal communication: 'If you see the mission of the Church in that sense [i.e. the *missio Dei*], then all the futile discussion between evangelism and social action disappears. It is an irrelevant discussion'.[119] While any tension between evangelism and social action may disappear for Newbigin, the distinction does not – nor does the proper order of the two. Newbigin understands the 'preaching' of the gospel to follow and explain social 'action'.[120] The reason for this is Newbigin's understanding of the church's mission as one of service to the world.

Newbigin's understanding of the church always remains carefully balanced, and so his emphasis on service or mission does not fully and adequately define the church. In fact, he clarifies that we should not allow the focus on mission to define the church 'in merely functional terms'.[121] As discussed above, the church 'for' the world is the church 'of' God. Therefore, as opposed to mere functional definitions, 'The Church is defined by what it is. It is already a sharing in the life of God'.[122] While it may appear that Newbigin has reverted to the mystical communion model of church, Newbigin attempts to hold the church 'of' God in tension with the church 'for' the world, which is the church's instrumental purpose, or function.

In terms of communion Newbigin acknowledges that the church's *koinonia* or *communio* with God is one of *arrabon* (Greek = foretaste; see 2 Cor. 1.22; Eph. 1.14). And 'insofar as the Church is a foretaste, it can also be an instrument'.[123] Newbigin provides a definition of what the church *does* beyond a definition of what the church *is*.[124] Mission in particular constitutes the church's visible nature: the church is visible when it functions to carry out the *missio Dei* by serving the world. In contrast to the opposition of 'church' and 'mission' (which Newbigin suggests is a phenomenon unique to post-Christendom), Newbigin can claim that 'the church *is* the mission'.[125] The church *is* the mission because this is the *to what* for which the church is called (Greek *kaleo* = to call, from whence comes *ekklesia*), and it is the primary vehicle of the Spirit's activity in this world. God did not establish another body apart from the church to carry out God's mission. In sum, the church truly embodying its vocation manifests a foretaste of God's kingdom on earth, and this is the *missio Dei* – the church in this sense is the mission. The church is a mystical communion, but in Newbigin's Reformed framework (cf. Webster above), God's calling together of this mystical communion inevitably results in the church's mission. Therefore, mission is intrinsic to the church's *esse*.

Newbigin offers a personal anecdote from his time in Kanchipuram, India, to illustrate the church as mission. The city knew him and his church's mission because of the church's schools for children, and how it helped 'their village people to do something about their desperate poverty, and are involved in attempts to make a more just society'.[126] This concrete example aligns with what Newbigin has articulated elsewhere in more theoretical terms: '[T]he most important contribution which the Church can make to a new social order is to be itself a new social order'.[127] Newbigin speaks of a new social order as the church's mission because in such a visible display the church manifests the *missio Dei*.

The visible church, as the provisional in-between-ness of God and the world's reconciliation to God, signifies that which is invisible: the coming kingdom of God.[128] The church, of course, does not simply 'proclaim' a coming kingdom. Its witness is one of word and deed, in 'attempts to make a more just society. . . . In other words, the words without the deeds lack authority'.[129] On the other hand, these deeds or acts of service for the world are not attempts in and of themselves to establish God's reign on earth:

> We do not offer, nor do we compete with all the other agencies in the world that are offering, solutions to human problems here and now. We are not offering utopian illusions. We are pointing people to a reality that lies beyond history, beyond death. But we are erecting in this world, here and now, signs – credible signs – that make it possible for people to believe that that is the great reality and to join us in going that way.[130]

The church, which is invisibly the communion of the saints with the triune Deity, is made visible when it participates in the *missio Dei*.

In sum, Newbigin does not wish to define the church as service or mission in terms of ontology; the church is the communion of believers with the triune God. On the one hand the church's essence is analogous to the divine essence: being as communion. It is noteworthy that God's essence is not to be confused with God's mission; the same must be said of the church. On the other hand the church's mission is not a structural correspondence with God's mission; instead, the church's mission is a faithful response to the Lord's vocation. Therefore, since the church is formed out of the *missio Dei*, this church's instrumental purpose is to further the *missio Dei*. In this latter sense the church is mission – the *visible* church is mission. Once again we find a particular model or emphasis held in tension. Newbigin's missional ecclesiology attempts to hold to a mystical communion definition of what the church *is* while simultaneously necessitating the church's visible manifestation of service to the world. Mission is not simply the *bene esse*; it is 'intrinsic' to the church, a *sine qua non* of the church. Mystical communion describes that which constitutes the church, while mission is conditional for the church. Even more precisely for Newbigin, the church's acts of service operate as 'signs' (see above quote) of the church's being.

Conclusions: beyond models

In the above survey of Dulles' five 'models' of the church, we have interacted with champions of each emphasis. To conclude this discussion we will attempt to pull together some recurring motifs. These represent a consensus of what must be said about the nature of the church. We would then like to suggest ways forward for future discussion of the church's *esse*.

While we do not claim to have captured the foundational definition of the church, and while we do not claim that any one metaphor, model, or meta-model can be constructed to encapsulate all that should be said about the church's nature, we find that the following points must be included in any ecclesiological framework.

1. The church *is* a mystical communion. All of the primary metaphors of the church and all Christian traditions point to a church of the people – the people are the church, the church is the people of God, or more specifically, the people called of God and united in Christ by the Holy Spirit. Furthermore, this people cannot simply be captured through sociological description. This is a *sui generis* society of those whose citizenship is in heaven and who live in fellowship with the Father, Son and Holy Spirit. All ecclesiological traditions and all of the above surveyed theological voices agree on this point.
2. The church inevitably will be, in practice needs to be, and theologically ought to be structured and ordered. Institutional elements are here to stay for the church. A critique of institutionalism *qua* institutionalism is unhelpful. A more clear rationale for criticism is needed: when are the institutional elements of the church no longer in accordance with the intrinsic nature of the church (see Boff, Webster, and Newbigin)?
3. The church must be externally focused. Any church turned in on itself (*incurvatus in se*) is a failed and sinful church. The external focus of the church is mission. While Webster and Newbigin disagree on the order of the two, both admit that the church not only *should*, but *will* be doing both proclamation and service. The dichotomy between word and deed in Christian witness is a false one, and to be church is to participate in the *missio Dei* which proclaims Good News to the world in both word and deed.

4. The church must be visibly manifested. Whether the visibility of the church is connected to its institutional elements, sacramental practices, evangelical proclamation or missional deeds, the church is only known as church visibly. The mystical communion model of the church fits within each of the other models or emphases in that the church is a mystical communion manifested by each respective emphasis. But more must be said of the church: this invisible *koinonia/communio* must be manifested visibly to be the church. In the formulations of Vatican I and Ratzinger, the church's visible expression is a guarantor of its ecclesiality: *opere ex operato*. In Webster's and Newbigin's Reformed view of God's sovereignty, the will of God for the church results in the church's visible manifestation of the church being necessary and intrinsic. We point out here that without a dogmatized rationale for the efficacious grace of the sacraments or a Reformed view of irresistible grace, the church's manifestation and its fulfilment of vocation can imply what the church *should* do, and not necessarily what the church *will* do. In either framework, however, and for that matter even without such mechanisms, all parties today agree that the church is called to be manifested in the church's practices, and any church that does not respond to its vocation is a failed church.

5. The church is local. We admit that this fifth and last conclusion is controversial and favours free church ecclesiology, but we contend that all of the above surveyed voices, none of which are officially free church, have in fact defined the church only as local. The church is a mystical communion which is manifested through its practices. Whether we speak of the invisible reality of the church (mystical communion) or the visible manifestation of the church (institutional, sacramental, evangelical, missional), we speak of the church as local. Every manifestation of the visible church is a local manifestation, and so to somehow ignore this fact in order to shift the focus to universal terms is to ignore how church is always defined in such a way as to be manifested locally. The mystical communion on the other hand – which all of the above representatives hold as primary – may seem like a diffusion of the church into a nebulous and unknowable reality, but the actual explications of the church as *communio* in fact define the church in local terms. First, the 'face to face' relationships defined both in Dulles' account and in Boff's base

ecclesial communities are themselves local manifestations via intimate group relationships. But even at a more abstract theological level, the church defined as mystical communion is said to be 'in Christ'. In other words, it is gathered around Christ himself who is locally at the right hand of God the Father. We who are 'in Christ' know Christ 'face-to-face' as will be fully realized in the eschatological assembly/*ekklesia* around the throne of Christ.

Suggestions

In saying that the church is local we do not necessarily offer an *apologia* for free church ecclesiology (although it must be admitted that too little attention has been given to this area in most systematic and ecumenical circles). Instead, we suggest that an appropriate starting point for ecclesiology is the local manifestation of the one body of Christ. From there we can debate how, when, and why the church must operate in cooperation with itself as it is manifested in other locales. We will return to these questions in our last chapter, when we discuss ecumenism.

For now we think it is helpful to compare the possibilities for ecclesiology from below with trinitarian theology and Christology. In trinitarian theology it is perfectly acceptable to begin with God's oneness or God's threeness, so long as both are fully embraced. So with Christology, one's understanding of Christ can begin with his divinity or his humanity, but both must be fully affirmed. Analogously, our ecclesiology can be 'from above' or 'from below': there is one church in Christ and yet the church is manifested globally in specific churches in specific localities. On the one hand the free church has failed to articulate how the churches relate; on the other hand too many ecclesiological discussions have suffered from the hegemony of a hierarchy that never embraces the church as local. In his theological framework and ecclesiological definitions, the recent work of Reinhard Hütter strikes us as helpful in suggesting a way forward.

In *Suffering Divine Things: Theology as Church Practice*, Hütter attempts to reframe Protestant theological methodology by reinstituting the church as authoritative.[131] (It should be noted: Hütter has since become Roman Catholic.) The most provocative argument in his book and the one most pertinent to our discussion is Hütter's embrace of the *dynamic* nature of the church's existence, something which appears poietic, but which is in fact 'pathic'. The church need not be reified into static terms; instead, the church (i.e. the invisible, not-yet-manifested-church) *becomes* the church (the visible, yet-not-perfected-church) *in the movement* from God's action in our midst to our response to God in our practices.[132] The church's practices – be they worship, proclamation, or service – play a central role in both creating and recreating, making and manifesting, the church as church. In these practices, through what the church *does*, the church becomes what the church *is*.[133] While not limited to the sacramental practices themselves, we find that Hütter's understanding is a helpful analysis of the church as sacrament and therefore is a promising way of holding together the dialectical tensions found in the above survey of ecclesiological emphases: institution/communion, being/function, etc. Just as Christ's body which *is* at the right hand of God the Father in the love of the Spirit but which also *becomes* (whether 'physically', 'spiritually', or 'symbolically') present in the pastoral invocation, especially at the Lord's table; so also Christ's body *is* mystically united by the call of the Father in the power of the Spirit but also *becomes* visibly united by the pastoral invocation especially at the Lord's table.

We find Hütter's dynamic understanding of the church especially helpful for the tensions outlined above in these five models/emphases. While the church *is* a mystical communion with(in) the triune God, the church is only known as such visibly to the world through its acts of worship, proclamation and service. While Boff's definition of the church is one of mystical communion, he nevertheless agrees that the church *should* be manifested structurally, liturgically, and politically. Ratzinger insists that the church not only *should* but *must* be manifested sacramentally and hierarchically. Newbigin's in-between-ness shares much in common with Hütter's framework mentioned above, only Hütter's use of 'practice' is much more broad and sacramental than Newbigin's. Unlike Hütter, however, Newbigin is not attempting to define what the church *is* by what the church *becomes*, but is instead focused on the church's mission, which is service to the world.[134] Aside from the indicative/imperative dichotomy that divides theologians in regards to the relationship of external manifestation of the church to the intrinsic nature of the church, we suggest that both agree at a Hütterian/pragmatic level: the church *is* only known as such as the church *becomes* the church visibly.

As already stated, Hütter's project is broader than ecclesiology, but he attempts to ground his project within this ecclesiological understanding. Hütter mourns the loss of the church as a 'public' in (post-)modernity. He believes that doctrine, defined as binding teaching, must be reclaimed in order for the church to be church. And yet (at the time of his writing) Hütter does not think the Roman Catholic magisterium is the only solution to this problem. Luther's understanding of the 'keys to the kingdom', Calvin's understanding of church discipline, and the Amish concept of *Ordnung* all shape Hütter's understanding of the church as a public with a binding norm. And yet the binding norm of the church is part of what it means to be church only as it is one of the many practices of the church. The church, manifested in its practices, *becomes* church, and this must be confessed to be a pathic act, that is a suffering/experiencing of the Holy Spirit's re-/creation of the church as church. The church must be confessed as such because mere (and modernistic) sociological explanations are insufficient.[135] On the other hand the theological explication of the church itself would be insufficient because the church is not simply an abstract concept but a reality manifested via its practices. Of course, what the church does includes not only its Spirit-filled faithfulness but also its too-frequent faithlessness in these practices, and so we must speak of the church as *simul iustus et peccator* ('at once righteous and sinful') – a problematic which we will discuss in the next chapter.[136] But in terms of metaphor, model, and understanding, the tension between what the church *is* and what the church *does* can be held together in Hütter's dynamic understanding. Where Hütter has yet to convince his critics, however, is in his understanding of doctrine as public.

Hütter accommodates Lindbeck's understanding of doctrine in order to provide a third way for Protestantism. While one could return to Rome and find a clear sense of binding doctrine, the Protestant church seems to slip inevitably into congregationalism, as witnessed by the debate between Adolph von Harnack and Erik Peterson.[137] Since congregationalism is ruled out as a valid option (for unstated reasons), and since the church now exists in a post-Christian and pluralistic era, Protestantism is left without a true public nature; religion is entirely a private matter. Therefore, Hütter must construct a theological paradigm that leans heavily on Barth and Lindbeck but is supplemented with a stronger ecclesiology and pneumatology. Whether Hütter's project succeeds or fails is not at issue here (although critics can certainly be found[138] and his own turn to Catholicism would suggest as much); what is of concern is the central question of the church as public in Hütter's paradigm.

While Hütter hoped to establish the church as a public in what seems to be a quasi-Constantinian way, we believe that Hütter's approach can work just as well in an ecclesiology from below. In other words every local church is a public for that locale. Here is where Hütter meets Newbigin (who is curiously absent in Hütter's bibliography). Newbigin defines the church as public because it is missional.[139] Hütter clearly appreciates the church as local: for the church to be local it must, among other things, encourage 'concrete communities that practice "life together" in such a way that they become challenges for all Christians (base communities, *integrierte Gemeinde*, Taizé et al.)'[140] In fact, all of Hütter's practices – in which the church *becomes* the church – are localized practices.[141]

To re-establish the church as a public with binding doctrine Hütter must transcend the doctrine/praxis divide. In so doing, however, the emphasis falls on the manifestation of the church locally: 'The core practices embody and enact bindingly and normatively various specific aspects of God's *oikonomia*. The doctrine and practices are interrelated insofar as doctrine also bindingly teaches about these core practices, while the core practices enact church doctrine'.[142] Practice as manifested doctrine must be 'embodied' or, in Ratizinger's framework from Vatican II, 'sacramental'. Earlier, we expressed our appreciation for the sacramental model of the church in that it can encompass the tensions inherent in ecclesiology (institution/ community; being/function, etc.). Hütter's approach, when carried to its end point, is a sacramental ecclesiology, and this emphasis offers a great deal to the current debate over ecclesiology.

The church is a mystical community, but the church is only known as church when manifested, embodied sacramentally. Such a formula must intend 'sacrament' in its most ancient and ecumenical usage: an earthly sign of a heavenly reality (all questions of efficacy aside for the moment). Therein, the church as sacrament is a signifying church. The church signifies the gospel, and this signification is a sacred embodiment through both word and deed. The debate could get bogged down in the necessity of certain 'signs' (e.g. episcopacy), and yet we find that a shift to a Hütterian-sacramental framework offers a way to transcend at least the essence/function dichotomy and possibly the indicative (*esse*) vs. imperative (*bene esse*) dichotomy. This shift also allows the discussion to move forward into more helpful sub-categories of ecclesiology, namely the 'marks' of the church, 'signs' and 'manifestations' of the church. As Hütter states, 'These practices are themselves dogmatic in the sense that they are constitutive of the church. They identify, or mark, the church as the space of God's *oikonomia*'.[143] It is to these 'marks' of the church that we now turn our attention.

CHAPTER 2

MARKS

THE CHURCH IN-/VISIBLE

Where is the church? This question is another way of getting at the 'essence' of the church discussed in the previous chapter: instead of 'what?', we are now asking 'where?' In place of textbook definition ('The church is . . . [this or that]'), we are giving an ostensive definition ('Look! The church is . . . [here or there]'). While this sounds promising, we are faced with similar problems in any attempt to point ('. . . there') at church. Are we pointing at *a* church? *the* church? Or should we say church*es*? Before identifying where the church is, or what 'marks' the church, we need to see how theologians use the categories of visible and invisible to define their ecclesiology.

In our discourse on the in-/visible church we must first establish some parameters. First, when speaking of the visible church it is unhelpful to retreat into denominational or confessional structures. Second, when speaking about the visible church it is unhelpful to reduce the discussion to individual soteriology. The first allows for theological provincialism, and the second ignores the corporate nature of ecclesiology which stands in tension to any individualistic understanding of salvation. Let us take each in turn.

Whenever the complexity of what church 'is' becomes too great, we can simply reply that it is invisible (read 'indefinable', 'ineffable', 'mysterious', etc.) On the other hand, whenever we need to be pragmatic and talk about the church, we can point to where the church is (read 'where *our* church is') and call it the church visible. For example the Roman Catholic Church stated its ecclesiology at Vatican II in a document called *Lumen Gentium*. In that statement, the Roman Catholic Church admitted that *the* church is intangible and mysterious, that is, the church invisible. On the other hand, the council still claimed that the only place to find this mysterious church was the Roman Catholic Church, that is, the church visible. Similar examples can be found in Protestant denominations. Most agree that the church is mysterious and indefinable and so *the* church is invisible. Yet many denominations, for practical purposes, speak of their own membership as *the* church – again, the church visible. The Presbyterian Church (U.S.A.) is in fact not *the* church but a denomination. The same can be said of the Anglican Church, the Evangelical Lutheran Church of America and any other denomination with the word 'church' in its title. We do not list these denominations in order to criticize them – their representatives would agree with us here – but in order to illustrate the practical need to point to a visible church (read 'our church') while recognizing that the church is much more complex and mysterious than our denominational boundaries.

A slightly different approach is found in the congregational or free church tradition. The most common critique of these ecclesiologies is that the church universal, the body of Christ, the one body talked about in Ephesians and elsewhere in the New Testament, is rarely talked about at all in free church circles. This weakness too often opens the door to narrow mindedness and exclusivism: 'We are the only Christians who matter'. The flip side of this ecclesiological coin is that free church practitioners are very strong on the local church. This plays out in the in-/visible debate in claims that, because the church is mysterious and indefinable, its only manifestation is *a* local church/congregation. In other words *the* invisible church made up of all Christians in all places at all times is only manifested in *a* visible church at a particular place at a particular time – the local congregation (thus we have 'congregationalism').

Up to this point, we have been discussing the categories of visible and invisible mostly in terms of the relation between the church and churches – let us call this the institutional level. The visible/invisible distinction also helps us speak about the relation between the church and Christians – let us call this the individual level. Sneak a peek over the shoulder of any minister in any denomination on any given Sunday and take a good account of who is sitting in the pews (or standing, if you are Orthodox). You may see a mixture of all sorts of people – ethnicities, classes, genders, etc. (which is good, according to Paul; see Gal. 3.28). You might also notice a diversity of lifestyles. (Augustine said we would see drunks, adulterers, gamblers, sorcerers, etc.[1]) Whether or not this is also laudable is a point of contention.

Should good, praying, pious Christians be seated in the same pews as thieves, adulterers, and murderers? Perhaps a better question is whether a person can be both. These types of questions raise the issue of who [or what] is a Christian, a question tied to soteriology. However, it is necessary for ecclesiology because in attempting to point to where the church is, we inevitably find a group of people claiming to be (members of) the church, or at least attending it. Is every person sitting in every pew part of the church? Obviously, we all suspect some 'Christians' to be wolves in sheep's clothing, hypocrites who use the church more as a club than a communion. In such instances theologians can stipulate that not everyone in the visible church belongs to the invisible church – they may be registered on the institutional level and yet not truly belong on the individual level.

We could also look at it from another angle: we suspect that there are some people who, for whatever reason, seem to be 'Christians' yet do not belong to any congregation or institutional church. Do they belong to *the* church? One could argue that such a 'Christian' is united to Christ, and thereby unto Christ's mystical body, and therefore belongs to the invisible church, even though they never are 'seen' in the church visible. Here the individual level is simply outside of any institutional level; the 'Christian' in this case has no institutional membership, but she does belong to the church individually. Once we have allowed this move on the individual level, we can tie our discussion back to the institutional level.

If we can say that a Christian who belongs to no local church or denomination can belong to the church invisible, then can we not also expand this to a trans-denominational definition of the church? In other words,

(a) all 'Christians' belong to the invisible church on the individual level,
(b) and not all members of the visible church on the institutional level belong to the invisible church on the individual level (i.e. 'the wolves in . . .'), so,
(c) therefore, the invisible church is more truly church than the visible.

This conclusion, while helpful in one sense, cannot be the final word because it creates as many problems as it solves.

While an exhaustive treatment of the strengths and pitfalls of these two categories cannot be undertaken here, we do wish to stipulate that the points given (a, b, and c) are only helpful to a certain extent and only then in a certain conceptual framework. Few of us would claim a God's-eye-view when it comes to discerning the true church from the false. Therefore, we must navigate a path between two extremes: on the one hand we cannot allow the church's mixed demographic ('saints and sinners'; in/visible) to render the church unmanifestable – the church can be marked, as we will see below; on the other hand we cannot reify the boundaries of the visible church ('our church'; sectarianism) to the point of denominational reductionism – the church's marks signify something which is both local and which is beyond our human horizons.

We certainly do not claim the individual level to have no place in soteriology and ecclesiology – Jesus' message certainly had an individual aspect (see Mt. 10.37). Nevertheless, prioritizing the individual in ecclesiology becomes problematic, as it can quickly lead to a total eclipse of the church, which remains 'a public phenomenon'.[2] Bonhoeffer has made this plain: 'The followers are the visible community of faith; their discipleship is a visible act which separates them from the world – or it is not discipleship'.[3] While theologians from throughout church history would largely agree with Bonhoeffer's sentiments, they have struggled in locating this 'public' and 'visible' church, making it less, or at least less obviously, visible.[4] The most promising means of such location has been to identify *notae ecclesiae*, or marks of the church. The classical marks of the church arose out of the dispute over which church may claim to be the true church, a question especially salient in the Donatist controversy.

EXCURSUS: THE CASE OF DONATISM

The background for the Donatist schism is the persecutions of Diocletian (303–05), during which North African Christians suffered acutely. In accordance with tradition the church dismissed any clergy who denied Christ or betrayed Christ's scriptures during this time, those known as *traditores*. According to the earliest surviving accounts, however, the seed of the schism was sown apart from the matters of empire: a Carthaginian matron named Lucilla wrongly kissed a relic before communion; she was duly censured by archdeacon Caecilian and bore a grudge against him thereafter. Lucilla then acted on the grudge when the bishop died and Caecilian was chosen as his successor (311). She bankrolled a disgruntled group of priests and enlisted a number of other persons who had previously been censured for theft and thus already had a motive for dismissing Caecilian. Lucilla's party coerced a group of bishops from Numidia (modern Algeria) to denounce the newly instated bishop and instead appoint Majorinus as the new metropolitan bishop of Carthage and primate of all Africa. Caecilian's episcopacy, however, was confirmed by a Lateran council in Rome, and so the schismatics appealed to an even higher authority, Constantine. Constantine convened his own council to investigate (Arles 314), but once again the evidence supported Caecilian, and the Donatists (Majorinus died in 315, succeeded by Donatus, from whom is derived the name of the schismatic party) were instructed to return to the true church. When they refused, the imperial officials treated them as outlaws. The villainous Donatists even enlisted fanatical mercenaries, bandits known as "Circumcellions" who roamed North Africa attacking catholic Christians and generally disrupting the peace, all the while hoping to die in the process as 'martyrs'. The inconsistency of the Donatists was incorrigible: they had appealed to the emperor, but now claimed the emperor had no business in the church; they claimed to be the persecuted church, but they terrorized the countryside and brought the Roman armies down upon themselves; they claimed to be the spotless church (as opposed to the *ecclesiam traditorum*), but their churches were full of thieves and murderers. As a final blow against these heretics, the imperial authorities refocused their efforts and convened a final council (Carthage 411). Therein, both parties were heard, and the evidence once again favoured the Catholic party. The Donatists were defeated.

The above caricature, while accurate in names and dates, is dependent on the accounts of Optatus of Milevis (mid to late fourth century) and Augustine (b.354–d.430).[5] Scholars, who never wholly trusted the depiction of these authors, were nevertheless reliant upon their reporting of the 'facts'. The last few decades of research, however, has witnessed increased sympathy for the so-called Donatist party and increased scepticism about history as written by the winners.[6]

For starters, many deny the validity of the label 'Donatist', since no 'Donatist' claimed this title for him/herself.[7] Moreover, enough evidence is extant to allow for a re-reading of the events: Optatus' and Augustine's works often salvage direct sayings of their opponents; the council proceedings (esp. Carthage 411) allow the so-called Donatists to speak for themselves; and the accounts of Optatus and Augustine include enough inconsistencies to call their version into doubt.[8] Also, the Donatists (we will continue to use this name for the sake of clarity) preserved the ancient tradition of their regional church.[9] Ecclesiologically, the so-called Donatist/Catholic debates about the nature of the church are also being reconsidered.

According to Optatus and Augustine, the heart of the debate involved the boundary of the true church. Both sides agreed there can be only one church, but they disagreed about what invalidates a church: Donatists insisted on the church's ritual purity, or holiness; Catholics insisted on the church's geographical span, or catholicity. In other words, the Donatists believed the Catholic churches had been contaminated by sin; the Catholic churches believed the Donatists had stubbornly cut themselves off from the rest of the church. The Catholics were said to be apostates. The Donatists were said to be schismatics. Augustine was especially able to apply the old rhetorical device of *reductio ad absurdum*: 'If you Donatists think you're the only true church, then the church only exists in the backwaters of North Africa!' (This neatly summarizes the major argument in Augustine's anti-Donatist works).

A more sympathetic reading of Donatist ecclesiology is emerging, however.[10] In this view, Donatists did not in fact require perfect purity for their church members – thus Optatus' and Augustine's charge of hypocritically allowing murderers and thieves to remain in the church is beside the point, if not factually dishonest.[11] Instead, the Donatists insisted on upholding the ancient tradition as they knew it in North Africa – so, if anything, the catholicity of the church is conditioned by apostolicity (e.g. ancient tradition stemming back to scripture itself). Moreover, the holiness of the church is not derived from the purity of its members, but from the purity of Christ. This purity can be forfeited, however, if the church's sacraments are dispensed by a non-Christian (e.g. an apostate). Optatus and Augustine felt the concern over apostate-clerics to be a non-issue because the Donatists' charges against Caecilian were never substantiated. Donatists insisted that they were substantiated at the only synod that mattered – the local gathering of regional bishops in Africa. The Lateran council had no right to overturn the affair. Catholics insisted that appeals were appropriate, the case in point being proved when the Donatists appealed the Lateran council's decision to Constantine himself – no doubt the most strategic mistake made by the Donatist party. The critical mistake on Caecilian's part, conversely, was to concede the point that his ordination was invalid, only stipulating that the Numidian bishops should still recognize his rightful election and ordain him themselves – which they refused to do.[12] Originally and primarily, the jurisdictional question lies at the crux of each argument. The ecclesiological traditions about sacramental validity preceded this event, and the theological applications were then deduced by later advocates of each side. It is these theological renderings of the argument that have survived in the mainstream discourse on ecclesiology, and so it is these – admittedly rhetorically loaded and historically anachronistic – caricatures that we must now pause to analyse before returning to our discussion of the marks of the church.

Augustine offers the most sophisticated response on either side of the Donatist debate, and it is his ecclesiology that will triumph in Western Christendom at least until the Protestant Reformation. Augustine insists that catholicity conditions holiness: while the Donatists may be able to claim a holy church, they certainly cannot claim a catholic church, that is, a church outside of Africa. Therefore, the Donatist holy church is no true church at all because it is not holy and catholic. On the other hand, Augustine must answer the charge that his catholic church is an unholy church. For the sake of argument, Augustine can admit that *traditores* continued to lead in his catholic church. Does this not invalidate it as a true church since it is not holy? No. Because the true church is invisible.

The church catholic is geographically dispersed throughout the Christian world, and it is demographically inclusive of all sorts – including saints and sinners. The literal geographic catholicity is accepted at face value, but the literal demographic unholiness is explained in terms of visibility and invisibility. The church gathers together, including truly elect and those not elect. Only God can accurately 'see' the difference between these two groups. Therefore, we inaccurately 'see' an unholy church, but the (to us) invisible holy church is present notwithstanding. In sum, the visible church contains, but is not equal to the invisible church.

We must note here, that later Protestant and especially ecumenical usage of the visible/invisible distinction employs these terms in virtually the opposite way from Augustine. Whereas the one, catholic church for Augustine is visible, but like a field containing both wheat and tares its holiness is an invisible subset, there is a tendency in ecumenical statements to relegate oneness to the invisible sphere, acknowledging that there are many visible churches (not just one), but that the truly elect members of these churches collectively and invisibly compose the one church. To demonstrate this recent trend, and to address the question of the church's visibility, we can now return to our discussion about the marks of the church and examine the ways in which the church is said to be visible or invisible.

VISIBLE MARKS: THE CONFESSED CHURCH

'We believe in one holy catholic and apostolic church'. These words from the Nicene Creed represent a consensus among early Christians about ecclesiology. Since these marks of the Church are indebted to early Christianity, the following section will largely draw on early Christian examples for their explanation.[13] But as will become evident, they still inform and guide current ecclesiological discussions.

ONE

Why is the church said to be 'one'? The Pauline teaching about the church as the body of Christ inextricably binds one Lord to one body (Eph. 4). If Christ were to have many bodies, he would be a monster. We may think of this in spatial terms: there can be only one church, so wherever on the earth you find 'church' you find *the* church. Add to this spatial dimension, the chronological: the Lord's promise that the church would prevail until the eschaton (Mt. 16.18 and 28.20) denotes that there never will be a new church, a second church, or even a refounded church.[14]

Based on these two premises, Christians have traditionally concluded that no group can claim to be the church separated from the true church (i.e. schism) nor to be the church reestablished after the demise of the original church (i.e. supersessionist groups often called sects or cults). While these two forms of church division may easily be blurred, we believe that the spatial and temporal categories help clarify the discussion: the church is 'one' both spatially and temporally.

Spatially, the separated or schismatic church must claim that they have separated from the false church, which is in fact no church at all, with the separated church therefore claiming itself to be the one true church. It is separated not from another church, but a false church, a church-impersonator. Examples of separated churches include Protestant Lutherans separating from the Roman church and in turn Radical Reform groups separating from the Lutherans.[15] When we examine the church 'catholic' (see below) we will return to this spatial dimension, but for now the church unified needs to be seen as including this spatial dynamic: all Christians *everywhere* (Lat. = *ubique ab omnibus*).

Temporally, the re-established church must likewise claim to be in fact not re-founded but remaining, that is, the remnant of faithful Christians reorganized and re-gathered, examples ranging from certain kinds of Baptists[16] to cult groups such as the Branch Davidians. When we examine the Church 'apostolic' (see below) we will return to this temporal dimension, but for now the Church unified should be understood in a way that is inclusive of the temporal: all Christians *at all times* (Lat. = *semper ab omnibus*).

While the spatial and temporal are important aspects of the church's unity, we must admit that little has been accomplished thus far. Seemingly, any Christian group can claim to be the 'one church'. Are there not more definitive marks of oneness? Beyond these reasons for defining the church as one spatially and temporally, there have been other dimensions noted in the church's oneness or unity, including the doctrinal, practical and the spiritual. The doctrinal dimension has been invoked to suggest that the true church unifies along right teachings (= orthodoxy), especially the core beliefs of Christianity as taught in scripture, the rule of faith and the creeds. Some traditions have expanded orthodoxy to include the councils (e.g. Eastern Orthodox), and later dogma (e.g. Roman Catholicism and some forms of Protestantism [cf. Westminster Confession]). The doctrinal dimension also touches on the church apostolic, which will be discussed below. But at this point, we must raise the question about doctrinal diversity: on which teachings must all Christians be united in order to claim to be one? All of them (including an eschatological framework)? None of them (including the lordship of Christ)? There are no easy answers, and so many have shifted to a more 'practical' definition of unity.

The practical dimension has been invoked to suggest that the true church unifies along right practice (= orthopraxy), especially the essential lifestyle of Christianity as exemplified in Christ and the early church. Some traditions have explained orthopraxy in terms of ritual purity (e.g. Donatists) and others in terms of ethical lifestyle (e.g. Anabaptist groups and some forms of liberation theology). The practical dimension also touches on the church holy, which will be discussed below. But at this point, we must raise the question about Christian practice: In what actions must all Christians be united in order to claim to be *one*? All of them (including forms of worship)? None of them (allowing antinomianism)? Again, there are no easy answers, and so many have shifted to a more 'spiritual' definition of unity.

The spiritual dimension has been invoked to suggest that the true church unifies along right heart condition or right disposition (= orthopathy), especially the orientation of Christian love toward God and others.[17] Some traditions have explained orthopathy in terms of inner piety (e.g. monastic movements) and others in terms of conversion experience (e.g. evangelical movements). The spiritual dimension also touches on the church invisible, which was discussed above. But at this point, we must raise the question about Christian disposition: In what posture must all Christians be united in order to claim to be *one*? In fact, have we not regressed into an individualistic definition of church as invisible, which was problematized in the introductory section? There are no easy answers, and so many have attempted to hold to a blend of two or more of these dimensions in explaining unity.

While Christians differ in their understanding of how the church is 'one', they nevertheless remain firm on this doctrinal tenet. Theologically speaking, this oneness of the church is said to stem from the oneness of God. Despite our lack of understanding and theoretical precision, we can declare that the Father, Son and Holy Spirit, that is the one triune God, unites us, and *not* vice versa. The oneness of the church is ultimately a declaration of faith (*credo*/ 'I believe . . .'), and this faith is faith in God: the Father's work in Christ's body through the Spirit's intervention. The oneness can be affirmed by faith in an invisible unity, or the oneness can be affirmed by faith that some so-called churches are not churches at all. Either statement is a statement made by faith, not by sight. And both statements affirm the oneness of the church. To say the church is *not* one is a heresy that few, if any, have dared to utter. We, therefore, continue through the other 'marks' of the church, recognizing the first and primary mark is a theological confession, and not a visible demarcation.[18]

Holy

'We believe in the . . . holy . . . church'. What is holy about the one church? As discussed in the excursus, this question aims at the heart of the Catholic/Donatist controversy. If the church is holy, can it include unholy, or defiled, people? In the Donatist schism, the matter especially centred on the holiness of the church's clergy. Do the church and her sacraments remain holy when presided over by an unholy cleric? The Donatists, according to their detractors, said no. Augustine argued the opposite: the church is holy, not because of any practical purity of the members or even leaders, but because the church's holiness flows down from its Head, Christ. Augustine concluded that the church is both a house of saints ('holy ones') and a hospital for sinners ('not-so-holy ones'). Luther later compressed these two categories so as to consist of the same people: we are both saints and sinners at the same time (*simul justus et peccator*).[19] Calvin explained the holiness of the church as an eschatological reality toward which the church advances.[20] The church's holiness, in any view, is not easily discerned.

The church is holy while the church's membership is too often questionable. Does this not in fact make the church something separate from the membership? The church is one thing and church members are another. What then is the church in this view? No, one cannot extricate the church from the saintly/sinful members of which it consists: 'We are the Church'; the church is the people of God.[21] After all, in the same letter in which he has to rebuke them for 'sexual immorality among you . . . of a kind that is not found among the pagans', Paul can call the Corinthians 'those who are sanctified in Christ Jesus' (1 Cor. 1.2). We must see the church with the eyes of faith in order to see past, or perhaps deeper than, the faulty, flawed and impure members.[22] The holy forest cannot be lost for the sinful trees. The church, while consisting of Christians who fall short on a regular basis, is more than the sum of its parts, because she has Christ for her head, and because she is filled with the Spirit.

To connect ecclesiology with Christology – as is universally done in claims about the church's holiness – we may recall the doctrine and mystery of the incarnation. John of Damascus (c.676–749) compiled the views of the early church writers to conclude that Christ's divine nature subsisted in his human nature, and there was always a unilateral downward flow from the divine to the human. While the divine

Logos suffered in the flesh (i.e. in the human nature), the finite earthly pain could never overwhelm or conquer the infinite heavenly power (i.e. the divine nature). This explains how ritually impure persons – lepers, women with issues of blood, etc. – could touch Jesus without contaminating him: Christ's power flowed out (Greek = *kenosis*; cf. Phil. 2.6) to heal and sanctify (= 'make holy'), but the direction was never reversed to allow sin, impurity or contagion to overtake and conquer Christ in a final way.[23] Likewise in ecclesiology, all diseased, impure and sinful people who are baptized into Christ, that is, made members of his body, the church, no more contaminate his body than a leper contaminated Christ's earthly flesh. In fact, when Christ took our sin upon himself, his glory shown through more brightly and bleached our sin-stained garments to be whiter than snow. Our baptismal robes, emblematic of this transformation, publicly confess to the world that we have been buried with Christ, and it is now Christ who lives in us, that is in our fallen, diseased bodies. We in turn are united ('The church is one') to Christ's body, and his perfect nature shines through us ('The church is holy').[24]

The conjunction of the 'one' and 'holy' by the council fathers does in fact strike us as impressive, if not inspired. After all, in light of the problems discussed above with 'oneness', namely that any schismatic group can claim oneness, it seems that a dialectic is required between oneness and holiness. While the criterion of holiness by itself could lead to similar ecclesiological narrowness (i.e. 'we are the only true church because we are the only holy church'), it becomes increasingly difficult for a schismatic community to claim to be both holy and one. The only option is perpetual retreatism wherein the group's boundaries are perennially constricted to exclude the unholy, because – as we all know – holiness is graded on a curve. This seems to be symptomatic of some fundamentalist circles wherein the doctrinal or ethical purity is never sufficient and its members must withdraw both from an ever degenerating society and from all other so-called Christians whose *peccator* status (be it moral or theological) is a threat to the schismatic 'church's' self-understanding as holy. In such a downward slide, all claims to 'oneness' smack of special pleading.

Instead, the church must strive for holiness as a calling (Phil. 2.5) while simultaneously recognizing the calling to oneness (Jn 17). Any time we are tempted to risk schism with Christ's body because we have spotted a speck in another member's eye, we remember that the church is one. Conversely, any time we are tempted to tolerate un-Christlikeness and risk lukewarmness, we remember that the church is holy. Any compromise is unthinkable, while any claim to attaining this of our own merit is unbiblical. Are we then trapped in an unsolvable dialectic? Trapped in a theological aporia? Yes. Here we stand. We can do no other. Who then shall rescue us from this body of death? Thanks be to God through our Lord Jesus Christ! The church is utterly dependent upon God's Spirit to lead us into all truth. The holiness of the church must be seen through the eyes of faith in the same way as the church's unity. The church's unity must be seen in light of the church's vocation to holiness. Between any schismatic understanding of these two *notae* God has created the space for the church's existence.

Catholic

While it has become common to explain that the theological term 'catholic' (little C) is quite distinct from the denominational term 'Catholic' (big C), it is worth repeating in order to avoid confusion. When theologians (especially from the first millennium of Christianity) invoke the word 'catholic' (little C), they in no way mean *Roman* Catholic (big C). Instead, the term should be read as synonymous with the word 'universal': we believe in the one, holy, *universal* church.

This translation of the term underscores one of the key meanings for the word 'catholic'. Once again returning to the Donatists, who claimed the moral high ground on the *nota ecclesia* of holiness, they encountered Augustine and his party, who claimed the geographical high ground (or should we say broad ground) with the *nota* of catholicity. How, Augustine asked, can you Donatists claim to be the 'one holy church' when you only inhabit parts of North Africa? We, Augustine claimed, reach to the uttermost parts of the [known] earth! We are catholic, universal, found throughout parts of Africa, as well as Egypt, Syria, Asia, Greece, Italy, Gaul, Spain, and elsewhere. The argument was convincing and would be used again against other regional schisms that developed later in Christian history (e.g. Coptic, Armenian, etc.)

That Christ will be with the church unto the end of the age/earth (Mt. 28.20), and, that there is only *one* church throughout this earth, necessarily implies that a key characteristic, mark or *nota* of the church will be her geographic catholicity, her encompassing the world for Christ. What then is the difference between the spatial dimension of the church's oneness and the church's catholicity? At this level, there seems to be no difference, yet more must be said about what it means for the church to be catholic.

In addition to, or arguably even prior to, the understanding of catholicity as universal, early Christian writers employed the term catholic to mean 'whole' or 'complete'.[25] When a church was completely church it was said to be 'whole' or 'catholic'. Ignatius of Antioch (c.35–107) used the Greek word *katholike* in reference to a local congregation – not a spatially expansive 'universal church'. Similarly, the *Martyrdom of Polycarp*, written soon after his death (156), refers to him as the bishop of the 'catholic church which is in Smyrna' (16.2), and Tertullian likewise speaks of 'catholic churches' in the plural.[26] In what way can a local church be a 'universal' church? Here, the translation as 'whole' proves more helpful.

The local church is a catholic or 'whole' church in that the totality of what it means to be church is found therein. Once again, there has been much debate about what it means to be church and what is required for the wholeness of the church. Perhaps we could start by pointing out that this is a qualitative concern and not a quantitative one. In other words we look to the 'what' of the church and not the 'how many' of the church. Even two or three seem to be sufficient in quantitative terms (see Mt. 18.20a), but these two must be gathered in Christ's name in qualitative terms (see Mt. 18.20b). When we gather in Christ's name, we are the 'whole' church, a complete church, a holistic church, because the fullness of God in Christ is present among us. Christ's body is manifested – not entirely (all Christians every-where from all times), but completely or catholic-ly. The local church is not 'part' of Christ's body, such as a hand or foot (these members referring instead to members of the church in 1 Cor. 12.12–27), but is itself his body. Once again we must look with the eyes of faith to see the catholicity of the church, but theologically there are further expressions of this mark.

One trajectory in early Christianity understood a gathering in Christ's name to be a gathering around Christ himself in the sacrament of the eucharist. Therein, Christ's presence was made recognizable (e.g. Lk. 24.13–35), and to gather in Christ's name was to gather around a common table ('communion') at which all are equal. Around the table, at the partaking of Christ's body, or 'in Christ', all are made one and holy (see Gal. 3.28). Christ's eucharistic presence, his whole presence (not just part of his body in the bread, such as a hand or foot) constituted and manifested the church's wholeness, holistic nature, or catholicity. We have now once again invoked a certain form of communion ecclesiology, eucharistic ecclesiology. But there are still more questions to be addressed about this approach to eucharistic catholicity.

Who then can enact the Lord's Supper and thereby guarantee the church catholic? The answer came in a complementary trajectory: the rise of the monepiscopate (= one city, one bishop). Just as Christ in heaven shepherds the church universally (catholic = universal), so there can be only one shepherd/pastor of the flock on earth locally (catholic = whole). The local shepherd/pastor/overseer stood *in persona Christi*, in the person or role of Christ, and the church thereby understood that it was Christ himself in the elder/priest/ shepherd offering his body to members of his body. Therefore, the local flock needed a shepherd, the local body needed a head, and when Christ acted through the local bishop, the wholeness of Christ (not part of Christ, such as a hand or foot) constituted the eucharistic gathering, the body of Christ, the church catholic.

The necessity and the expanding jurisdiction of the bishop certainly became the dominant ecclesiological trajectory evident in our sources from the second and third centuries of Christianity. Another trajectory, however, must also be addressed, which seems to be in opposition, or at least in tension, with the eucharistic/episcopal emphasis: Irenaeus (c.135–200) insisted that where the Spirit is, there is the church.[27] While Irenaeus most likely meant 'the Spirit of Christ', and while Irenaeus certainly promoted the monepiscopate, his pneumatalogical ecclesiology opens the door to a more organic and less institutional understanding of Christ's presence. There is much debate among scholars about how this tension should be understood in early Christianity, but examples of a less hierarchical and more spiritual or mystical understanding of Christ's presence can be found in groups ranging from the Montanists, to Clement of Alexandria, to Eastern mystics.[28]

While this pneumatological ecclesiology was eclipsed by a more hierarchical/institutional understanding as represented in the monepiscopate, we feel that the debate does beg a question which deserves our attention. Why limit Christ's presence, and thereby the church's catholicity, to sacramental/clerical expressions? Just as gathering around the Lord's table is understood as 'gathering in

Christ's name' visibly/recognizably and thereby enacting the 'whole' church, and just as gathering at the feet of the shepherd/bishop is understood as 'gathering in Christ's name', could we not claim the same for many Christian acts?[29] Why not affirm that the Lord inhabits the praises of his people (Ps. 22.3), and thereby discern the church catholic 'wholly' manifested in hymn singing (which is a more Pentecostal critique)? Why not accept that the Lord is served when we serve society's *anawim* (roughly translated from the Hebrew as 'the least of these'; cf. Ps. 37.11/Mt. 25.31ff.), and thereby the fullness of Christ's body is present both in the serving and in the being served (which is a more liberation theology critique)? Why not insist that wherever the Word of the Lord is revealed in the preaching of the Word, and therein the wholeness of God in Christ creates anew the people of God, we find the church catholic (which is a more Lutheran and Reformed critique)?

Such arguments may seem to stem from 'low church' concerns, but we in fact are following the ecumenical statement of the WCC's Faith and Order commission:

> Visible and tangible signs of the new life of communion are expressed in receiving and sharing the faith of the apostles; breaking and sharing the Eucharistic bread; praying with and for one another and for the needs of the world; serving one another in love; participating in each other's joys and sorrows; giving material aid; proclaiming and witnessing to the good news in mission and working together for justice and peace.[30]

Already, in Vatican II's Constitution on the Liturgy, Roman Catholic dogma had demarcated almost the same means of manifesting Christ's presence:

> Christ is always present in His Church, especially in her liturgical celebrations. He is present in the sacrifice of the Mass, not only in the person of His minister, 'the same now offering, through the ministry of priests, who formerly offered himself on the cross', but especially under the Eucharistic species. By His power He is present in the sacraments, so that when a man baptizes it is really Christ Himself who baptizes. He is present in His word, since it is He Himself who speaks when the holy scriptures are read in the

Church. He is present, lastly, when the Church prays and sings, for He promised: 'Where two or three are gathered together in my name, there am I in the midst of them'. (Mt. 18.20)

Of course Roman Catholic dogma still understands Christ's presence to be manifested 'most especially in the Eucharist',[31] but these other avenues also mediate Christ's presence in his church. Beyond this initial ecumenical consensus on the means of Christ's presence in his visible church, traditional episcopal-governed church theologians still desire more to be said, especially about the role of the clergy in mediating Christ's presence to the church.

Objections to a decentring of the eucharistic gathering under a clergy of apostolic succession usually entail a concern with security: the only way to ensure the truth of the gospel (security from heresy) and the unity of its proclamation (security from schism) is by connecting all congregations and their teachers through a network and/or hierarchy of bishops. This debate between (a) those who understand the church's catholicity or wholeness to be evidenced through innumerable acts of the people of God – this is ecclesiology from below – and (b) those who understand the Church's catholicity or universality to be guaranteed only in episcopally sanctioned acts – this is ecclesiology from above – can be seen as stemming from another question: How did the first century Christians understand church? from above or below? If they understood and practiced church in a free or low church fashion, why not accept this form today? Conversely, if the trajectory of the early Church was towards a monepiscopate, why not insist on this form today? These questions lead us to the notion of apostolicity, but before discussing the next *nota*, we would like to suggest a way forward on the debate about catholicity.

Perhaps the catholicity of the church needs to be seen in dynamic terms, rather than an either/or dichotomy. Instead of constructing a boundary between what is and what is not catholic, we recommend that catholicity be seen on a spectrum. The fullest qualitative and quantitative expression of the church's catholicity (i.e. *ecclesia triumphans*) is found in Rev. 7.9–17. The following expressions of catholicity can be found in this passage: (1) Christ is at the 'centre' and the 'multitude . . . from every nation' of those 'sealed' are gathered around him; (2) the congregation 'worships' God; (3) the Lamb provides food and drink to those who serve him; and (4) injustice and suffering are conquered. The picture is of the eschatological church, the gathering of all the saints from all places and all times, the quantitative catholicity of the church. The picture is also of the triumphant church, the sacramental expression of worship and the celebration of God's enforcement of justice. While this scene will not be entirely realized in the current *saeculum*, the catholicity of this scene can be meaningfully manifested in the church whenever it is gathered in Christ's name – be it for worship, confession, or acts of justice. In any practice performed under the name of Christ the church's catholicity is manifested (i.e. *ecclesia militans*). In this dynamic understanding of catholicity, Christians aim to fully and meaningfully manifest the church's catholicity by becoming the Revelation 7 church. The church can more visibly foreshadow this heavenly celebration when it gathers around Christ's chair and table in worship with the elders and the people, when it is fed and quenched, and when it embodies God's justice for every nation, tribe, people and tongue. In so doing the church, while not visibly encapsulating quantitative catholicity – which can never be fully expressed this side of the *parousia*, is nevertheless visibly manifesting qualitative catholicity (i.e. *ecclesia peregrina*).

By assuming a dynamic understanding of the church's catholicity, space can be created for future dialogue and for constructive understandings of this mark. Those who traditionally have reserved 'full ecclesial status' for certain expressions of church can, on the one hand, see this status as most 'fully' applicable to the Revelation 7 church and, on the other hand, acknowledge that those 'ecclesial communities' not given 'full ecclesial status' retain 'ecclesial status' nonetheless. The dynamic understanding of catholicity also helps to locate 'where' the church is in terms of its manifold manifestations (worship, hierarchy, social acts, etc.). This dynamic application of the term then begs to be juxtaposed to the fourth and final mark of the church, the church's apostolicity.

Apostolic

'. . . the apostolic church'. What could be implied in such a strange adjective? Very few Christian leaders have ever claimed the title 'apostle', and the ones who did belong almost entirely to the first century. To put the matter bluntly, the apostles (i.e. apostles as we have come to think of the twelve, those appointed by Christ) are dead and gone. What have we, today, to do with apostolicity? Clearly, the church apostolic is a *nota* not about its individual clerical titles (modern day apostles), but it may in fact be about its clerical authority.

Who has authority over the church? Or more precisely, who may invoke Christ's authority over the church? teachers? deacons? bishops? everyone? no one? When Christians in the church disagree, who settles the matter? The above mentioned school of thought in early Christianity that promoted monepiscopacy answered that the apostles and (if they are dead) their appointed successors alone have the authority. Thus we have the notion of apostolic succession.

If the apostles invoked Christ's authority (see Gal. 1), and if they appointed successors who would appoint successors (see 1 Tim./Titus), then the church is truly church only when governed by someone within this line of apostolic succession. Irenaeus again is helpful here, for he silenced many by invoking this *nota*. When a so-called church claimed to be church, but taught/practiced/felt something different than the rest of the church, Irenaeus played the credential card. His argument runs as follows:

> From whom did you learn this teaching/practice/disposition, Jesus or another teacher? If another teacher, it is a different Gospel and un-Christian. If from Jesus, then how? He's been dead, risen and ascended for some time now! If from one of Jesus' successors, which one, and how did s/he pass on this information from a century ago to you? We in *the* ['my'?] church can trace our lineage from Jesus to Peter to Linus to Anacletus to Clement, etc., . . . From whom and through whom do you claim to derive this heresy?[32]

Irenaeus' argument was so compelling that even his enemies bought it (thus the Gospel of 'Thomas', Gospel of 'Judas', etc.).[33] From hence forth, the notion of 'apostolic' must be attached to a church for it to be considered truly church, and the church's apostolicity resides in its officer(s). But perhaps this explanation of apostolic is too focused on apostolic 'authority' and apostolic 'office'.

The Reformation, and especially the Radical Reformation, became sceptical of the above outlined understanding of 'apostolic'. After all, Paul himself found churches that he did not found (see Acts and Romans). Were not these true churches, even without apostolic succession? Perhaps, apostolicity is oriented more towards an abstract norm than to an authoritative office.[34] In other words, can we not understand 'apostolic' to be a description of the church, rather than a description of the church's leaders? None of the other *notae ecclesia* refer to the clergy alone. Why apostolicity? Is this a case of *sola clerica*? Perhaps 'apostolic' is better understood as a descriptor of the church's teachings?[35]

This ambiguity is found as early as Irenaeus himself. He seemingly demands both apostolic teaching and apostolic office:

> It is within the power of all, therefore, in every Church, who may wish to see the truth, to contemplate clearly the tradition of the apostles manifested throughout the whole world; and we are in a position to reckon up those who were by the apostles instituted bishops in the Churches, and to demonstrate the succession of these men to our own times; those who neither taught nor knew of anything like what these heretics rave about.[36]

While Irenaeus' statement has traditionally been read as referring to both apostolic teaching ('truth . . . the tradition of the apostles') and apostolic succession ('bishops . . . the succession of these men to our own times'), it has been argued by may Protestant ecclesiologists that even Irenaeus' concern with succession is meant to secure the truth, not the authoritative office, of the apostles ('who neither taught nor knew of anything like what these heretics rave about').

At this point, we want the reader to make no mistake: Irenaeus favoured the authoritative monepiscopate, and he believed that this institution stemmed from Christ himself. The point – or disputed aspect – of the matter is simply this. If Irenaeus and others like him in the second and third centuries championed the succession of apostolic office *in order* to secure the succession of apostolic truth, and if apostolic truth is upheld by a church, then is not that church 'apostolic' with or without a bishop in succession of apostolic office? This point is argued by those who lack apostolic office (bishops) but claim apostolic truth (scripture, creeds, etc.), such as Tertullian, who wrote just after Irenaeus and who apparently could not trace his Carthaginian bishop's lineage back to an apostle.[37] But this point can also be assumed by traditions that do require bishops and do claim apostolic succession, such as the Anglican Church, whose catechism defines 'apostolic' as '[the church's state which] continues in the teaching and fellowship of the apostles and is sent to carry out Christ's mission to all people'.[38] In other words, the church, according to an episcopal denomination, is apostolic *not* because of episcopacy but because of its apostolic teaching and mission.[39]

Lest we sound as though we are denying the need for *episkopoi*, let us clarify the point of our argument by further analyzing Irenaeus' view of apostolicity. Irenaeus certainly insisted on both apostolic office (bishops) and apostolic teachings (Rule of Faith). The succeeding generations of Christians embraced both, including the parallel traditions in the Eastern Orthodox church and the Western Catholic church. What about the Protestants? Did they deny the need for apostolic office? No. All of the magisterial Reformers retained this office, even if preferring alternate titles, such as pastor and teaching elder. They did, however, demand both. To be able to claim apostolic succession but to stray from apostolic teaching is unacceptable. What, then, about the Radical Reformation? Did not they deny the need for apostolic office? Again, the answer is emphatically no. All forms of the Anabaptist tradition embraced the need for this office, even if they did prefer alternative titles and insist that the 'succession' of this office was handed down through faithful churches and bestowed upon called ministers – not handed down by faithful ministers upon called churches.[40] With mainline Protestants and Anabaptists, the emphasis of apostolicity is not upon the office itself – although the office is not denied. With Anabaptists, the notion of apostolicity applies to the clerical office only secondarily – deriving primarily from the church's apostolicity. Irenaeus, no longer available to appear in court and testify on any one party's behalf, can be claimed by all three. What is certain about the church's apostolicity is that it is a mark of the church's connection to the original followers of Jesus. The mark is often invoked to support the episcopate, and yet in all traditions it is primarily a mark about the church itself, not a definitive statement about the church's visible office.[41]

To move forward in this debate, therefore, we suggest that, as with the tension between 'one' and 'holy', we concede a remarkable interplay between the *notae* 'catholic' and 'apostolic'. The mark of catholicity is an expansive one, indicating an eccentric, centrifugal force. The church is universal, and all whole churches are church, wholly church. The emphasis is on the expansiveness and inclusiveness of the church: even when referring to the local church, the church is inclusive and accommodates the 'whole' Christ (who is infinite!) and the 'whole' line of Adam (which includes every nation, tribe and tongue!). The mark of apostolicity on the other hand delimits the church; apostolicity is a concentric, centripetal force. Not everyone who cries 'Lord, Lord' can claim to be church. The church is restricted to include only those who fit the description apostolic. The church should be outward in mission, but the mission and message must be the same as that of the inner core of Jesus' first disciples.

Once again, we suspect true inspiration in the conjoining of these two marks. Any church claiming to be part of the catholic church must also be in accord with the church's apostolicity: no church can teach/practice 'anything it wants' simply because of the expansive freedom implied in the description catholic – the church is apostolic. Likewise, no church can claim to have exhausted the apostolic truth, to claim to have the whole truth – certainly not a monopoly on the Truth – of the church precisely because of her expansive nature. The church is catholic.

The Church is one, holy, catholic and apostolic. Let us attempt to graph the nature of this church, which meets all four of these criteria (see Illustration 1). The church's oneness inflexibly resists any schism. The church's borders are unfenced and open to all – thus, the porous depiction in the illustration. Simultaneously, the church's holiness tirelessly draws her members to Christ-likeness. The church's Centre (Rev. 7.17) is a narrow Way (Mt. 7.14), yet a Light (Jn 1.9) guiding all within ever inward. In the same manner, the church's catholicity exhibits itself wherever (quantitatively/'universally') and however (qualitative/'wholly') the church manifests Christ's name, as shall be finally culminated in the end of days. While at the same time, the church's apostolicity re-orients the ongoing manifestation of Christ to its original manifestation in the first century. This visual illustration of course fails to explain fully the multifaceted and mysterious nature of the church. Yet, we offer it here as an attempt to remove any under-standing of the *notae ecclesiae* as items on a list, independent of each other, and replace such an understanding with a more fluid and dynamic view.

We also offer this explication of the marks in order to pinpoint a lingering dilemma. Where is the church? One concern to which we must return is that of invisibility. In our treatment of these marks, we have underscored the fact that all 'marks' are treated – almost universally – as invisible marks. What exactly is being marked? Do not these marks enable any group claiming the name of Christ to claim to be church? And would not the apparent divisions and differences of all of these so-called churches make the church for all practical purposes indefinable, that is, invisible? Oh church, where art thou?!

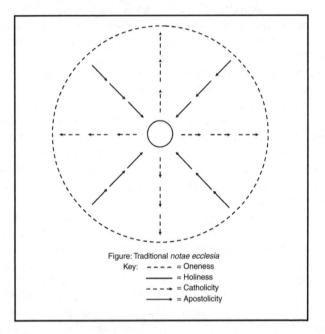

Figure: Traditional *notae ecclesia*
Key: − − − − = Oneness
　　　 ———— = Holiness
　　　 − − − ▸ = Catholicity
　　　 ————▸ = Apostolicity

While this aptly describes the status of current ecclesiological debates, and while we admit up front that we will not be able to solve these ecclesiological counterpoints, we do hope to address possible ways forward (see the conclusion to this chapter). For now, let us confess: to describe the church as 'one, holy, catholic, and apostolic' says less about the church visible than is often assumed; the confession is a theological confession of faith.

Before leaving these marks altogether, we should quell any fears that may arise about being left ecclesiologically speechless (or blind, to keep a consistent metaphor). In keeping with Moltmann's approach, we can understand the church by way of a pneumatological analogy, one that arises naturally enough considering that the *notae ecclesiae* have been attached to the belief in the Holy Spirit in the classical creeds.[42] In pneumatology, we might ask, 'Where is the Spirit?' But such a question would allow no easy answer, even though Christians have always assumed (and rightly) certain signs, seals, gifts, and fruits to be connected to the Spirit's presence. So with the church, its marks are sometimes not sustained, structured, easy-to-demarcate marks. Instead, they 'mark' or 'note' verbally, not substantively, the church in a sometimes sporadic, untraceable manner. 'The wind blows where it chooses, and you hear the sound of it, but you do not know where it comes from or where it goes. So it is with everyone who is born of the Spirit'. (Jn 3.8) So it is, too, Jesus might say, with everyone in the fellowship of the Spirit (i.e. the church).

All evidence from the early church suggests a certain 'spiritual anarchism'.[43] Perhaps we should not fear an element of this pneumatological flux in our ecclesiology today. Moreover, the later Christian centuries understood the church in sacramental (Augustine of Hippo) and iconic (John of Damascus) terms; that is to say, the church points past itself to the ultimate community of persons in the Godhead. The visible marks themselves, therefore, need not be stable, fixed and unmovable. Instead, they iconographically and sacramentally capture our gaze only in order to further it, to reveal a mysterious reality past our earthly horizon.[44] In short, if these marks of the church are matters of 'faith' (*credo*), then they are 'the substance of things . . . *not* seen' (Heb. 11.1).

To reiterate, we still aim to find visible marks of the church; we simply have not found the classical *notae* to be treated as such in any Christian tradition. This does not invalidate these marks; it simply clarifies their role as theological descriptors about the envisageable-yet-invisible aspects of the church, those aspects which require faith. And so, rather than dismissing or discounting these marks, we can embrace them as they are, and simultaneously continue our quest for the visible whereabouts of the church.

Moltmann recognizes the invisibility of the creedal marks, and so he decides to 'move other marks of the true church into the foreground'.[45] While he admits that the four *notae* define the church's 'essential nature', he expresses dissatisfaction with the indefinite nature of the marks: the marks describe the invisible nature of the church. In order to address a visible church Moltmann shifts from a focus on the essential nature to the dynamic process of becoming church.

> Faith, hope and action are the genesis of the form of the church visible to the world in unity, holiness, catholicity and apostolicity. That is why theology cannot withdraw 'to the invisible church', 'the church of the future', or 'the church of pure demands'. The church

lives in one, holy, catholic and apostolic rule of Christ through faith, hope and action.[46]

It is the 'action' or loving practices of the church which manifest the church. The invisible one, holy, catholic and apostolic church becomes the visible church – while of course remaining one, holy, catholic and apostolic – by its activity in the world.

Of course, the Protestant Reformation long ago voiced this very same concern, the concern that any church can claim the *notae ecclesiae* as invisible attributes while displaying unacceptable traits. To retrace these steps may seem undesirable, and all warning signs to ecumenically sensitive travellers read, 'Do not enter! That road leads to schism, and old wounds will be reopened'. Nevertheless, until the Protestant concerns are heard, and the Protestant marks are understood, no way forward will arise that allows for the centuries-old concerns about the church's visible location to be incorporated. So then a survey of how the Reformers attempted to address this issue, and the Roman Catholic responses, may illuminate the possible directions one may take to define further the marks of the church visible, and thereby answer the question, 'Where is the church?'

Before turning to Protestant marks of the church, however, we think it important to locate the Protestant concerns about a church's claim to 'be' the church within the wider ecclesial problem that had plagued Christianity, namely, schism.

EXCURSUS: THE 1054 SCHISM, THE AVIGNON PAPACY AND THE PROTESTANT REFORMATION

Historians typically identify the Protestant Reformation as a debate about soteriology. After all, Luther deemed justification by grace through faith as the doctrine on which the church stands or falls.[47] Ergo, justification lies at the centre of the Protestant/Catholic debate. Without detracting from soteriology's role in the Reformation debates, we suggest another paradigm as equally important for understanding what took place in Western Christianity at this time, a paradigm which is especially apt in our current discussion. Justification is precisely the doctrine on which *the church* stands or falls, and therefore the Reformation must be understood in terms of ecclesiology as well as soteriology. When this paradigm shift is taken into account, Protestantism, with its emphasis on the visible marks of the church, belongs to the older debates about schism, especially the East-West schism (usually dated at 1054) and the so-called Babylonian Captivity of the papacy in Avignon, France, which resulted in three rival claims to Peter's chair.

1054 supposedly represents a moment in history when Eastern Orthodox and Roman Catholic Christians excommunicated each other, resulting in a schism still unresolved to this day. On the other hand the vast consensus of historians and theologians agree the date is somewhat arbitrary, since the two traditions had already parted ways in previous centuries and since the two communions recognized each other's validity for some time thereafter. The difficult task of establishing the objective facts, or at least the facts to which both sides can agree, has been undertaken by a group of scholars from both sides of this divide. The North American Orthodox-Catholic Theological Consultation produced a study which analysed the historical, political, cultural and theological factors of the East-West schism.[48] Their study provides us with a framework for our discussion.

Long before the excommunications of 1054, the Eastern and Western churches underwent diverging trajectories in terms of their language (Greek vs. Latin), their political ties (Byzantine vs. Frankish), and their liturgies. Whenever the two sides of the church clashed, such as when the Franks claimed Bulgaria and expelled the Greek missionaries, the differences became salient, such as when the said expelled missionaries reported to Photios, the ecumenical patriarch of Constantinople, on Western 'abuses' (unleavened bread in the Eucharist, claims to papal supremacy, addition of the *filioque* to the creed, etc.), which prompted Photios' denunciation of Western 'novelties', which in turn prompted Pope Leo III to write his own response defending such practices. A few generations later when Pope Leo IX in 1054 sent Cardinal Humbert to Constantinople, and when Patriarch Keroularios refused to hear Rome's claims, the confrontation resulted in mutual excommunications. The excommunications, however, explicitly addressed the individuals involved, not the entire Eastern and Western churches. Moreover, such scenes of interepiscopal conflict were not new to Christianity, and this event went largely unnoticed at the time. The successive centuries witnessed both instances of business-as-usual-cooperation between both sides and additional scenes of antagonism, the most famous of which was the 1204 razing of Constantinople by Western crusaders. The East/West breach solidified so that a true and lasting schism was established.

Western Christianity then experienced its own internal schism. The Avignon Papacy began when Pope Clement V accepted the French king's invitation to transfer his residence from Italy to the newly built papal palace in Avignon. Dubbed by some 'The Babylonian Captivity' because of the supposed control of the French court over the popes, the move evoked disapproval throughout Western Christendom. When Pope Gregory XI returned the papacy to Rome, the solution was only short lived. Gregory died in 1378, and two popes were elected to replace him: Urban VI, who remained in Rome but alienated many cardinals, and then Clement VII, who represented the faction that denied Urban's rightful papal election and who returned to France.

The details of these papal actions and elections remain shrouded in mystery. The Roman Catholic Church has yet to rule officially as to which pope was valid. One influential study which seeks to understand the relationship between the church and the wider European society is that of Brian Tierney, *Foundations of the Conciliar Theory*.[49] Tierney situates the Western schism in terms of conciliarism, which – to put it in simpler terms than Tierney would allow – is the belief in an ecumenical council's power over a pope, and not vice versa. The conciliarist movement sought to resolve the immediate problems of multiple claimants to the papacy. This viewpoint, however, would not be the official solution for the church.

The Great Schism (as it is often called in the West) or Western Schism, came to a conclusion at the Council of Constance (1414–1418), which needed to resolve what had by then become a tripling of the papacy. In 1409 a council met to denounce the two popes as 'schismatics' and appoint a third pope, Alexander V. The previous two popes remained in power, however, resulting in further chaos. Alexander's successor, John XXIII, summoned the Council of Constance, resigned, and was replaced by Martin V, whose appointment initiated a new, unrivalled line of popes. Although Martin's election officially ended the schism, many continued to call for reform in the ecclesial structures.

The two most famous voices of dissent were John Wycliffe and Jan Hus. Although Wycliffe died before this council, his teachings were condemned there as 'heresies'. Hus appeared at the Council to be condemned for the same, and he was then handed over to the secular officials to be burned at the stake. While many sympathized with these two 'heretics', there were others who simply wished to balance the power of the papacy, the conciliarists.

Conciliarism itself was not debated at Constance; instead, it is probably safer to conclude that the sentiment remained largely unvoiced but widely appreciated. At the Fifth Lateran Council (1512–1517), however, the conciliarist stance was formally rejected, leading to what became known as ultramontanism, which officially invested the pope with unrivalled power in the Western church. So, although the 'Great Schism' had allegedly ended, the conciliarist sentiment which emerged from it lingered into the sixteenth century. It must be admitted, likewise, that the conciliarist movement in fact contributed to (if not created!) the Protestant Reformation, which itself must be seen in terms of schism.

In 1517 an Augustinian monk and professor of biblical theology posted 95 theses on the door to the church in Wittenberg. Martin Luther wished to debate these theses openly, and his argument centred around the selling of indulgences. When copies of Luther's post spread throughout Europe, even arriving at the Vatican, the 'debate' quickly escalated into schism.

Debate has raged for centuries as to how to best understand Martin Luther's actions in the second decade of the sixteenth century, actions which resulted in the Protestant Reformation. One voice in this discussion is David Yeago, who, in his essay 'The Catholic Luther', reframes the young Luther's concerns in terms of the sacramentality of salvation, a very 'catholic' notion.[50] While Yeago explicitly retains soteriology as the primary scope of Luther's contentions, Yeago nevertheless has also encroached upon the ecclesiology of Luther and thereby the entire Reformation. Evidence of this is in Yeago's habit of referring to Luther's 'schism', rather than allowing for Luther's actions to be understood in terms of re-establishing the church. Yeago's primary argument focuses on Luther's 'sacramental and ecclesial concreteness', but additional conclusions result from Yeago's discussion.[51] First, the founding of Protestant churches, or 'the Western schism', was unnecessary, according to Yeago, an accident of history rather than an unavoidable consequence of Luther's teachings. Yeago's evidence is primarily the lack of a fair hearing in any of Luther's trials; had there been such, Luther's soteriology would be in accordance with the 'catholic' tradition. On the other hand, in response to the 'theological obtuseness of the Roman court theologians', Luther himself shares the blame because of his 'impatience and anger' and his rhetoric about the pope as Antichrist which 'made schism inevitable'. Yeago's reading of Luther is helpful to our discussion in that the definition and the definers of schism are seen to contribute to the actual schism more than the doctrinal controversy that preceded it. When Luther questions the validity of the papacy (at the Diet of Augsburg in 1518), and when the papacy responds with entrenched ultramontanism (see *Decet Romanum pontificem, 1521*), excommunicating Luther and any 'schismatics' (ibid., preamble) who advocate conciliarism (see 28th Lutheran teaching condemned by *Exsurge Domine*, 1520), which itself was understood as due to the ongoing influence of Wycliffe and Hus, the perennial Western concerns with ecclesiological authority once again re-emerged.

By positioning Luther as successor to Wycliffe, Hus and the conciliarists, who in turn structurally parallel the Eastern Orthodox, the debate about schism must address two concerns: Rome's relationship to the rest of the church and the definition of schism itself. Although this historical reconstruction may appear as a Protestant apologetic against Rome, we hope to transcend the polemics of the past and better appreciate the reality of the current state of division by questioning the definition of schism itself. Schism in one sense is impossible: the church cannot be divided; the church is 'one'. In another sense, however, we must speak of 'schisms'. But in what sense exactly? When we speak of church schism we inevitably speak of 'those schismatics' who have separated from 'us' and 'our church'. This kind of discourse is especially symptomatic of ecclesiology from above. However, there is hope of a way past this historical and theological impasse.

On 7 December 1965, Pope Paul VI and Athenegoras I, Patriarch of Constantinople, simultaneously lifted the 1054 excommunications.[52] Although hopes were high in the immediate time after this joint declaration, and although many are still optimistic for the future, the Eastern Orthodox and the Roman Catholic churches have yet to return to full communion with each other, as would be manifested in concelebration of the Eucharist: the East and West are no longer *ex*-communicated, but they are not communicated either, due to the question of papal supremacy. Nevertheless, we can trace a veritable inversion of the history of Western schisms from 1965 onward, an inversion of posture and gesture – which offers hope of a completion of this inversion in structure and communion. Pope Paul VI not only lifted the excommunication of the Eastern churches, but he then carried out an aggressive campaign of ecumenism. When Paul VI's mantle fell to John Paul II, the latter continued to reach out to Protestants and Orthodox Christians, the most explicit instance of which is the statement, *Ut unim sint* ('That they may be one', 1995).[53]

Pope John Paul II attempted to reignite ecumenical dialogue by calling for a renewed dialogue over the papacy itself – the office which admittedly has been prohibitive to dialogue in the past: '[The Papacy] constitutes a difficulty for most other Christians, whose memory is marked by certain painful recollections. To the extent that we are responsible for these, I join my Predecessor Paul VI in asking forgiveness'.[54] The pope then defines his office in terms remarkably close to conciliarism:

> All this [i.e. the wielding of authority] however must always be done in communion. When the Catholic Church affirms that the office of the Bishop of Rome corresponds to the will of Christ, she does not separate this office from the mission entrusted to the whole body of Bishops, who are also 'vicars and ambassadors of Christ'. The Bishop of Rome is a member of the 'College', and the Bishops are his brothers in the ministry.
>
> Whatever relates to the unity of all Christian communities clearly forms part of the concerns of the primacy.[55]

This of course is not a conciliarist statement, but it is a commitment to collegialism which could be conceived as including 'all Christian communities'. At this point, Pope John Paul II then offers a remarkable olive branch:

> I am convinced that I have a particular responsibility in this regard, above all in acknowledging the ecumenical aspirations of the majority of the Christian Communities and in heeding the request made of me to find a way of exercising the primacy which, while in no way renouncing what is essential to its mission, is nonetheless open to a new situation.[56]

What this 'new situation' is, and how we are to understand 'open to' is a lingering question from this document. Nevertheless, the pope has re-opened the possibility for ecclesiological re-cognition and communion.

In our excursus on schism, which is admittedly Protestant in its bias, we have not intended to point the finger at Rome, to place the blame of all schism at Rome's feet, nor to label the pope the Antichrist. Instead, our intention is just the opposite: to lay bare the definition of schism by illustrating how schism has always been defined from a top-down vantage point, an approach we find inherently problematic. All parties agree that if the bishop of Rome were to loosen his claims to a universal juridical supremacy (which sounds incredibly close to 'lording one's authority over another' – cf. *Ut unim sint* 88) it is certain that the 1054 schism would be ended. Similarly, would Eastern Orthodox communions desist from defining schism from a top-down approach, the doctrinal differences between the Eastern Orthodox, Oriental Orthodox, Lutheran, Anglican, and other Protestant communions would begin to fade behind the (if not doctrinal, then) ecclesial compatibility shared across these regional and denominational lines – lines which were originally drawn from a top-down vantage point, but which disappear from a bottom-up ecclesial perspective.

Admittedly, new problems would certainly arise in a context where schism (or now, communion) is defined from below – for example, opportunity for mean-spirited divisiveness. So while we do not presume to solve the dilemma, we do insist that schism defined solely from above offers little to no promise for ecclesiological dialogue. Even if the parties agree that schism should be defined from the top-down, there is no agreement (and from all appearances, no *possible* way forward) as to who is at the top: Rome, Constantinople, Canterbury, councils? Alternatively, the question of schism can be addressed, not simply by embracing congregationalism, which of course is the view of our own traditions, but by re-orienting the discussion even within hierarchical traditions.

Our aim in this excursus on schism and our call to redefine 'schism', rather than being a blame-game with Rome, is meant to envision a way to re-engage dialogue with the bishop of Rome with whom all 'schismatics' have ultimately conflicted, but who is himself now open to 'exercising the primacy' of his office 'in a patient and fraternal dialogue on this subject, a dialogue in which, leaving useless controversies behind, we could listen to one another, keeping before us only the will of Christ for his Church and allowing ourselves to be deeply moved by his plea "that they may all be one . . . so that the world may believe that you have sent me" (Jn 17.21)'.[57]

Perhaps, all 'schismatics' could re-engage dialogue with the bishop of Rome and see him in an Irenaean sense as the hub of Christian communication.[58] Perhaps, the bishop of Rome could utilize his office in ways that explicitly 'serve' those other communions over whom he claims to be 'first' (i.e. primacy; cf. Mk 10.42) in a Cyprianic fashion.[59] The bishop's role could even be carried out in an Augustinian approach, as exposited (for the monastery) by Benedict of Nursia:

> Whenever weighty matters are to be transacted in the monastery, let the Abbot call together the whole community, and make known the matter which is to be considered. Having heard the brethren's views, let him weigh the matter with himself and do what he thinketh best. It is for this reason, however, we said that all should be called for counsel, because the Lord often revealeth to the younger what is best. Let the brethren, however, give their advice with humble submission, and let them not presume stubbornly to defend what seemeth right to them, for it must depend rather on the Abbot's will, so that all obey him in what he considereth best. But as it becometh disciples to obey their master, so also it becometh the master to dispose all things with prudence and justice.[60]

If we may correlate the abbot with the pastor (as Gregory the Great did in his *Pastoral Rule*) we can envision the president dialectically holding the position in tension with 'listening' to every member of the flock – because, after all, God can speak through any member of the flock. While Protestants and Eastern Christians will rightly wish for a full explication of what it means to 'obey' before agreeing to these terms, all parties can appreciate the inherent structure of mutual submission in love.

These ancient voices from the early church are simply offered as potential blueprints to guide the conversation into the 'new situation' spoken of by Pope John Paul II, which addresses the schisms of the medieval and modern church. Whether or not his successor(s) will take up this mantle remains to be seen. Whether or not the schism – as defined above – can be healed remains a matter of hope. In sum the notion of schism has perennially entailed conflict with Rome, and so – counterintuitively to most Protestants and many Orthodox – Rome offers the most viable focal point for visible unity. Only now, in our 'new situation', the Bishop of Rome can emerge as the means of communication which can lead us to a visible communion, which will further manifest our faithfulness to Christ's ancient plea 'that they may be one'. To this further 'manifestation' of the church, as expressed in the concerns of the Protestant Reformation, we now turn.

VISIBLE MARKS: THE PRACTICED CHURCH

We began this chapter by asking, not 'what' is the church, but 'where' is the church, a question Martin Luther used to shift from his discussion of councils to a discussion of the church itself in his work, *On the Councils and the Church*. Luther insists that the church is 'a communion of saints, that is a crowd or assembly of people who are Christian and holy'.[61] Luther offers the second phrase as an exposition of the first: the church/*communio* is holy/*sancta*. Here Luther outlines his critique of the Roman Catholic Church on ecclesiological terms in terms of holiness, and lack thereof. Because, according to Luther, the Roman church has ceased to be holy, it has ceased to be church. After contrasting the 'fleshly' religiosity of the traditions of Rome with Moses' two tablets, which serve as 'guides' for holiness, Luther outlines seven practices, each of which entails 'an external sign, by which the church, or Christian people in the world, should be recognized'.[62] These seven signifying practices mark the church, making it visible to the world.

The signifying marks are (1) possession of the holy Word of God; (2) baptism; (3) the altar; (4) the office of the keys exercised publicly; (5) the consecration of ministers, who administer the previous four marks; (6) public worship; and (7) bearing the cross or tribulation. Luther's marks, however, must be read as practices which manifest the church, enabling the church to *become* the church visible, because even these marks, although given as further signs of differentiation between the true church and the false church, nevertheless provide no guarantee of ecclesiality: '[T]hese signs cannot be regarded as being as reliable . . . since some heathen too practice these works'.[63] The church certainly is holy, and this holiness, moreover, manifests itself visibly. And yet, Luther perceives the devil's imitation of God's temple which 'utilized outward things' so as to set up his own chapel, a larger and visible counterfeit. Therefore, while Christ's church is manifested visibly, no guarantee is available for visible ecclesiality, sacramentality, or sanctity; Christ's sacraments 'work spiritually and invisibly and for the future so that his church and bishops can only be smelled, as it were, faintly and from afar, and the Holy Spirit behaves as though he were absent'.[64] The church, which for the late Luther is the elect people of God and only truly known to God, manifests itself fleetingly through its practices which enable the true church to become the visible church. The church's visibility, however, is a 'faint' and fleeting glimmer of its invisible reality, a reality whose full visibility is only available in 'the future'. If we give Luther's reference to the future its full weight, then Luther's ecclesiology defines the church's visibility as an eschatological visibility. This eschatological/ futuristic visibility is not entirely and solely futuristic (*sola futura*), for the kingdom both has come and is coming, and the church is defined as the people destined for the kingdom, a people/church manifested both now – in a sense – and to be manifested in the future – in a sense. Luther's practices, therefore, in no way securely 'mark' the true church from the false church, for wolves remain in sheep's clothing, but they do mark or point us to the future church of Rev. 7. Meanwhile, they manifest fleeting glimpses of the church. This flighty form of visibility left many Protestants dissatisfied, and prompted many to stress discipline, formally deeming it a 'third mark' of the church along with preaching and the sacraments.[65]

Defining the church's visibility via a third mark of church discipline is typically attributed to Anabaptists. Anabaptists, however, are increasingly difficult to define and categorize, and moreover the importance of discipline is shared by a much wider consensus of Protestant Reformers (not to mention Catholics). Nevertheless, one of the key moments in Western theology occurs at the meeting of Swiss Anabaptists in Schleitheim (1527).[66] The resulting confession with its seven articles set forth the Brethren's clarification of orthodoxy, including ecclesiology. The confession aims to draw a clear boundary between true faith (and church) and false faith (and church), and it does so by explicating the so-called radical stances of non-violence and non-oathtaking, and then by delineating the so-called radical enforcement of these practices through the ban and separation.

These articles (baptism, the ban/discipline, breaking of bread/ communion, separation/excommunication, shepherds/oversight, [rejection of] the sword/peace-making, and [rejection of] oaths/ exemplary-honesty) are not 'marks of the church' *per se*. They are items on which the participants agree as to the *practice* of the church. Thereby, of course, these articles function in a Hütterian sense: via these practices the church 'becomes' the church, the church becomes visible. While the ban, excommunication and shunning were practiced to various extents among various Anabaptists groups, the emphasis on church discipline influenced many so-called magisterial Reformers, such as John Calvin.

Calvin, a devoted student of Luther's works and fully schooled in Anabaptist debates, likewise addresses the concern about a church claiming the classical marks of the church while nonetheless representing a 'false church'. In his final book of the *Institutes*, Calvin transitions from the faith requisite for salvation (book 3) to the 'external means' of attaining salvation (book 4). He begins, '. . . we need external helps to beget and increase faith within us' (4.1.1). Therefore, 'it is now our intention to discuss the visible church' (4.1.1).

After stating his goal, however, Calvin must divert his attention to a two-fold problem with the church's visibility. First, the church consisting of the elect is 'visible to the eyes of God alone' (4.1.7). Secondly, within the church on earth, alongside the elect 'are mingled many hypocrites'. In the former Calvin insists on a humble posture for believers: reverence due to the earthly church because only God discerns the heart; in the latter we discern, not the heart as God does, but the practices, namely 'the Word of God purely preached and heard, and the sacraments administered according to Christ's institution' (4.1.9). Attempting to use this criterion, however, reveals a residual ambiguity: who decides if the preacher is preaching 'purely' or if the administrator is administrating 'according to Christ's institution'? Calvin's external means and visible marks are not so external nor so visible. Thus, he must exert his energies in chapters two through eleven in differentiating the true (Reformed) church from the false (Roman) church, the falsity of the latter being largely due to its deviation from scripture and its teaching of false doctrine. Calvin returns to the church's visibility in chapter twelve where he discusses church discipline.

Discipline, it is clear, requires even more spiritual discernment and functions mainly in instances of 'open sins'. Church discipline, therefore, offers a means of excising those who exhibit reprobate lifestyles, but discipline in no way offers certainty or further means of manifesting the church. At the least, church discipline establishes a visible commitment – albeit only one that is manifested negatively via excommunication – to the invisible mark of holiness discussed above by publicly insisting on a righteous lifestyle. Once again, however, righteous lifestyles themselves are no true indicator of ecclesiality, but are only signs thereof. After all, the celibacy of the Roman church is certainly a righteousness of a sort, specifically a false and fleshly righteousness, and Calvin devotes another chapter entirely to this false righteousness (4.13).

In chapter fourteen through seventeen Calvin defines the sacraments rightly administered. These are 'signs' in the Augustinian sense (4.14.3–4) and so the sacraments themselves must exposit the Word rightly. There once again remains, however, the problem of inauthentic claims to ecclesiality, this time found in wrongly administered and understood sacraments, resulting in the polemics of chapters eighteen through nineteen.

In the word preached, in the church disciplined, and in the sacraments administered, Calvin has thrice attempted to mark the 'external means' of salvation, namely the church visible, but in each of these three visible means Calvin never transcends the dialectic between the visible church as an image of the true church and the visible church as a warped (*depravatio*) image which remains masked as much as it continues to manifest. While we laud Calvin's insights on the Divine's 20/20 vision, we are concerned that he leaves humans speechless about the true/invisible church, being forced to speak about a visible church that is not really church at all. The church visible to God is not (yet) manifested on earth.

More positively, Calvin has been able to provide three indicators of ecclesiality: Word/doctrine, discipline/righteousness, and sacraments/sanctification.[67] These indicators, according to Calvin, necessarily occur in true churches because of the Father's sovereignty over Christ's body as enacted by the Holy Spirit. On the other hand, these indicators may also occur in false churches because the devil imitates the Lord's work. Like Luther, Calvin's attempt to define the visible church has only defined what the visible church *should* be.

From Calvin's time through the successive generations of Protestants we can trace the following contours of Protestant 'marks'. While many Lutherans and early Protestants had succinctly defined the church's marks as twofold, many later Reformers added discipline as a mark of visibility. The former is well represented by the Church of England's nineteenth foundational article: 'The visible Church of Christ is a congregation of faithful men, in which the pure Word of God is preached, and the Sacraments be duly ministered according to Christ's ordinance . . .'. The latter represents an acknowledgement of Anabaptist concerns over nominalism, which is represented by the

Wesleys' Holy Clubs.[68] Whether or not these two or three practices should be doctrinally defined as 'marks' of the church is debatable, but there is broad agreement as to the way in which these practices 'mark' the church visibly – or, *almost* visibly.

It is in respect to the Protestant marks of quasi-visibility that Thomas Oden critiques the polarization of ecclesiology into a binary opposition of 'hypervisibility' and 'hyperinvisibility'.[69] Alternatively, 'The dated polemics of Catholics against Protestant teaching on invisibility and of Protestants against the Catholic teaching of visibility, now dysfunctional, must be reconceived'.[70] Oden picks up the history of Western schisms as an attempt fairly to analyse both sides of the visibility debate:

1. The proto-Reformers, such as Wycliffe and Hus, and the earliest Protestants, such as Luther, 'were correct to oppose the reduction of the church to a visible culture-entwined, medieval institution' – i.e. invisibility.
2. Alternatively, the Roman Catholic concern 'was correct to stress the visible corporateness, order, historicity, social palpability, and cross-cultural engagement of the *ekklesia*' – i.e. visibility.
3. Finally, the second generation Protestants' concerns with faith and faithfulness 'was correct to stress the invisible *dimension* of election, grace and faith' – i.e. quasi-visibility.[71]

Oden then further maps Protestant ecclesiology while constantly calling for additional attention to Catholic insights. The Protestant approach carried to an extreme results in 'iconoclasm', 'excessive invisibility', and even 'docetic fantasies'.[72] The Roman Catholic approach, however, remains too top-down in its definition of the church's marks and in defining schism. Oden hopes the two traditions can embrace a *rapprochement*, centred in the revelation of God in Christ: the incarnation reveals *theandric* unity, a unity of 'above' and 'below'.[73] The church, consequently, must exhibit a corporeal visibility united-yet-distinct from its spiritual invisibility; it must 'embrace' both an ecclesiology from above and an ecclesiology from below. Oden's call to embrace both top-down and bottom-up ecclesiology is helpful, and his demand that the in/visibility debate be reconceived is commendable. It is precisely in a redefinition of schism – a definition not defined solely from above – that such reconceptualization may occur.

Thus far, we have traced the Protestant marks/practices of the church as extensions of the classical marks. That is, we have understood the classical marks to be in some sense foundational to Protestant confessions of faith when it comes to ecclesiology; and yet Protestant ecclesiology, emerging as it did from concerns with inauthentic expressions of church, struggles to provide an addendum to the church's visibility, despite this being the stated aim. What then is the future of Protestant ecclesiology? As we see it, Protestants are left with three choices in their ecclesiological prospects:

(a) The various 'confessions' and definitions of church – visible or otherwise – can be further entrenched in doctrinal apologetics, and Protestantism can remain Balkanized along denominational lines. This prospect looks especially bleak in light of the demise of denominationalism projected by virtually all sociological studies.

(b) Protestantism can repent of its schismatic actions, and return to Rome or Constantinople. We neither mock nor deride this option, as it has attracted many of the brightest and most faithful Protestant minds of our time. We do, however, feel the "or Constantinople" clause in this option raises serious problems for this option being a real solution in any sense of the word.

(c) Protestantism can continue to be the *ecclesia reformata, semper reformanda*. While this prospect entails its own set of problems, namely the tendency towards further splintering, it does offer an openness to the future of ecumenical dialogue, a missional commitment to contextualism, and self-critical engagement with tradition.

Of course these three options deserve much more attention than time will allow here, but in terms of Protestant ecclesiology this outline suggests to us that a discussion of 'the emerging church' is worthy of our attention.

THE EMERGING CHURCH

Approximately every five hundred years the church has undergone a radical transformation. The first great emergence (not quite at the five hundred year mark) occurred after Constantine imperialized the church; but the empire itself then collapsed into the 'dark ages', during which time the church became the church of Gregory the Great. The second significant shift occurred in the schism of 1054 in which the Eastern and Western churches recognized their mutually exclusive trajectories. The third transformation occurred in the out-break of Protestantism after 1517. And today, roughly five hundred years after Luther posted something on the Wittenberg door, we are due another revolution. The previous synopsis of church history comes from Phylis Tickle in her book, *The Great Emergence: How Christianity is Changing and Why*.[74] Although Tickle's history is far too cursory and oversimplified (intentionally so for a wide readership, and less so than our sketch of her sketch suggests), her work underscores an important phenomenon in the present state of ecclesiological practice and discourse: the emerging church, which represents cur-rent concerns in ecclesiological discourse and is claimed by some to represent the future of ecclesiological practice. At this point a disclaimer is in order.

For the sake of time and space, we will simply ignore the debate over what this 'movement' or 'conversation' should be labelled; options include emergent, emerging, emergant, remergent, re:mergent, and [re]mergent.[75] The fact remains that no consensus has arisen as to what to call this movement, and so for the sake of discussion we retain the most commonly known term, emerging.

Tickle's discussion of the emerging church is also a helpful starting point because she approaches the phenomenon as an outsider, not a practitioner or propagandist. She is the former religion editor for *Publishers Weekly*, a prolific author, recipient of an honorary doctorate from Yale, and a lay minister in the Episcopal Church. Despite this 'outsider' status, Tickle understands the emerging church to be broadly inclusive of new ecclesial expressions spontaneously arising throughout the world in response to the postmodern condi-tion in which younger churches find themselves. When defined so broadly, the category of 'emerging church' becomes incredibly dif-fuse and virtually unrecognizable, and yet it is only when locating the emerging church within the global and ecumenical scope that this phenomenon may offer something to the question of ecclesiology. It is, therefore, to this global manifestation of the emerging church that wish to turn our attention. But first we must allow emerging church practitioners to speak for themselves and explain to us what is 'emerging' in their ecclesiology. Admittedly, the emerging church, as it is known predominantly from the publications coming out of Grand Rapids, is a small movement of mostly white, mostly (post-?)evangelical, mostly free church, Protestant Christians. And yet this phenomenon merits attention as a current voice in ecclesiological debate.

'Attempting to define emerging church is like trying to nail pudding to the wall'.[76] We confess our inadequacies in defining what the emerging church is, but for the sake of discussion some definition must be ventured nonetheless. In order to capture the competing ideas of what it is and how it should be understood, we offer – as opposed to a Websterian propositionalized definition – a Wittgensteinian 'family resemblance' of characteristics which can be signified by the umbrella-like label 'emerging church'. Before listing these characteristics, let us see an analogy given by one influential thinker in the emerging church, and the founder of Emergent Village.[77]

Brian McLaren, who in his many books has attempted to describe to non-emergents what the emerging church is, has provided several explanations of this 'conversation' he helped to initiate.[78] McLaren prefers, however, to see 'emergent' in an ecological analogy which relates what 'is emerging' to that from which the emerging thing 'emerges from', such as new saplings in a rain forest.[79] Emerging churches, therefore, need not be new churches or churches formally separated from their ecclesial heritage. Indeed, the opposite is the case: emerging churches emerge from and yet cling to the ecclesial soil out of which they arose while also stretching into the new climate of the world. This implies (1) that the emergent church is not confined to post-evangelicals, although a majority of them admittedly are of this stripe, and (2) that the emerging church is oriented toward, and transgresses the boundary of, the world – that is, missions.

In terms of a Wittegensteinian family resemblance of characteristics and concerns, the emerging church entails the following aspects. In appearance it must be conceded that the emerging church is the latest evolution of the contemporary worship movement in evangelicalism, 'worship 2.0' as we once heard Mark Driscoll call it.[80] While most, if not all, emerging worship services fit this description and consist of candles, indie music, and non-traditional locations (such as pubs and warehouses), the worship itself in most instances 'emerges' out of deeper concerns with culture.[81] This deeper concern usually stems from an engagement with postmodern and especially postfoundationalist thought.[82] This philosophical underpinning/accommodation presents the most controversial aspect of the emerging church movement.

There are many detractors of the emergent church who see in this philosophical move a slippery slope to religious relativism.[83] The interest in postmodern thought, however, is most commonly understood in terms of contextualization and mission: as the emerging church attempts to be/come church to the world, it must be contextualized and incarnational to the postmodern condition and culture in which contemporary Christians find both their location and their vocation. In a word, the church is missional.[84] Often, the conversation around the emerging church's 'missional' status, especially when an anti-essentialism and post-foundationalism are prevalent, engenders a prioritization of praxis over doctrine – which once again returns us to the concern over relativism. At this point, however, the cultural (and philosophical) contextualization is dialectically juxtaposed to a return to ancient Christian sources and liturgy, which suggests that most contemporary services are not so 'contemporary'.[85] One instance in which all of these 'family resemblances' come to an acute expression is in the New Monastic Movement.

The New Monastic Movement relates to the current ecclesiological discussion precisely because its leading advocates claim to be embodying ecclesial priorities and practices. New Monasticism's genealogy is as follows. Alistair MacIntyre concluded his influential book, *After Virtue*, by cryptically calling for 'another – doubtless very different – St. Benedict' to usher us through the new dark ages (i.e. postmodernism).[86] Jonathan R. Wilson took up this call as it relates to the church, in turn calling more specifically for a 'new monasticism'.[87] Communities which rallied around this label, many of which existed prior to Wilson or MacIntyre's publications, began to dialogue and further define themselves and their mission.[88] This self-definition by new monastics culminated in the following twelve 'marks' or practices:

1. Relocation to the abandoned places of Empire.
2. Sharing economic resources with fellow community members and the needy among us.
3. Hospitality to the stranger.
4. Lament for racial divisions within the church and our communities combined with the active pursuit of a just reconciliation.
5. Humble submission to Christ's body, the church.
6. Intentional formation in the way of Christ and the rule of the community along the lines of the old novitiate.

7. Nurturing common life among members of intentional community.

8. Support for celibate singles alongside monogamous married couples and their children.

9. Geographical proximity to community members who share a common rule of life.

10. Care for the plot of God's earth given to us along with support of our local economies.

11. Peacemaking in the midst of violence and conflict resolution within communities along the lines of Mt. 18.

12. Commitment to a disciplined contemplative life.[89]

Clearly New Monasticism can claim only the loosest of ties to 'old' monasticism (e.g. no vows of celibacy are required), but it claims to embody the ancient values of the early church. Similarly, the new monastic movement is often considered 'emerging' because of values, 'marks', or practices shared with the wider emerging church phenomenon. A new monastic community should not be confused with a church, according to Jonathan Wilson-Hartgrove, Jonathan R. Wilson's son-in-law and leader of the Rutba House. Instead, such a community serves as a sign to the church of what the church should be/come: 'We are free to imagine what God's kingdom could look like, right here on earth as it is in heaven. I don't pretend that we're getting everything right in new monastic communities – no more than Israel got everything right in the wilderness. But we're in a space where we are free to imagine'.[90] The New Monastics' concern with missions in post-Christendom brings to light the affinity of this element of the emerging church with Newbigin, who states, 'The most important contribution which the Church can make to a new social order is to be itself a new social order'.[91] Moreover, the importance of the 'marks' of New Monasticism in particular and the practices of the emerging church in general have brought us back once again to an explication of the visible church as one of becoming visible in a Hütterian sense, a visibility, however, which is manifested in a local, concrete contextualization.

If the emergent church's primary strength is its ability to retain its 'catholic' roots in an incarnational manifestation of its missional orientation, then perhaps we have come full circle back to the original aims of both the classical marks and the Protestant marks.[92] The externally oriented mark of 'catholicity', when understood as a universal mission, which after all is the ancient concern of the apostles themselves (*apostolos* = sent one), and is thus dialectically also 'apostolic', can be carried out visibly via the concern with 'holiness', especially understood as justice, found in emergent churches. The oneness of the church, it is admitted, has yet to find a visible expression in the emerging church, an admission of less import in light of the above discussion of this mark. Likewise, the Protestant question about the church's authenticity results in additional marks or signs for the true church, marks and signs which perpetually recede from sight yet which offer glimpses of the church visibly. Such glimpses certainly appear in emerging churches, who may not always define doctrine 'rightly' in modernistic propositionalist terms, yet who certainly pursue 'rightly' in pragmatic terms, that is a 'righteousness' emerging churches pray will roll down like an ever-flowing stream.[93] On the other hand, if emerging churches excel in their concrete practices that manifest church, they nevertheless need to deepen their reflection on the universal church.[94] Assumedly, emergents believe in this universal church as an article of faith, and yet in their concern to manifest the church they will also need to find means of manifesting the church's unity. This need not entail a return to hierarchy and tradition in a simplistic and institutional way, but the desire to affirm and disclose the church's unity will likely prompt a 'conversation' (emerging church lingo) that 'reimagines' (new monastic goal) the churches' relationships to one another which is 'open to a new situation' (John Paul II's offer).

Before concluding this section, however, we must return to our initial response to Tickle's book, in her claim that the phenomenon of the emerging church is best understood as part of a global ecclesiological groundswell, even if the 'emerging' language is predominantly championed in the United States. Mindful of this movement's affinity to the missional theology of Newbigin, this is a somewhat natural enough manoeuvre. Contemporary theologians interested in ecclesiology, and indeed all of Christian doctrine, would do well to dialogue with the so-called contextual theologies of 'world Christianity'.[95] The emerging church's vocabulary displays a remarkably high correspondence to the terminology of liberation theology, a correspondence which may reflect direct derivation of thought.[96] Moreover, the North American emerging churches, *mutatis mutandis*, are structurally parallel and phenomenally homologous to Latin American Base Ecclesial Communities, African Independent Churches, and many other 'emerging' expressions of Christianity.[97] The emerging church, now broadly defined, serves the wider church as a sign of a 'new situation', one in which the church must continue to *become* the church visibly through a missional posture to the world. How this 'new situation' and the churches emerging hence will be received by the wider expression of Christianity remains to be seen. (See our final chapter where we return to world Christianity and 'the New Christendom'.) We can, however, recognize the church visibly through its mediation and its mission, two items in which all discourse about the marks of the church find their *telos*, and so it is to the church's mediation and its mission that we now turn.

PENTECOST AND ECCLESIA

It is tempting to resolve the problem of Jesus' absence after the ascension by speaking of his church, that company of people who continue his work on earth. There is something to this. Jesus promised that 'the one who believes in me will also do the works that I do and, in fact, will do greater works than these, because I am going to the Father' (Jn 14.12). But speaking of the church alone cannot resolve the issue. After Jesus' ascension, the disciples were to wait in Jerusalem until Jesus sent the Spirit and they were 'clothed with power from on high' (Lk. 24.49). They waited, and the Spirit came in awesome power at the feast of Pentecost. The disciples' 'greater works' were themselves predicated upon the Spirit's Pentecostal mission.

To understand Pentecost, we have to look further back in the economy of salvation. In a time when all humanity still spoke one language, a group of people spoke with one voice: 'Come, let us build ourselves a city, and a tower with its top in the heavens, and let us make a name for ourselves; otherwise we shall be scattered abroad upon the face of the whole earth' (Gen. 11.4). The Lord, being aware of the power of a unified people ('this is only the beginning of what they will do . . .' – Gen. 11.6), confused their language and scattered them across the earth. The Lord's confusion of the people at Babel stayed their God-denying project of self-exaltation. Like the exile from Eden, the multiplying of languages and scattering of the people protected those at Babel from going from bad to worse.

Later, in the midst of Israel's rather checkered history, Joel prophesies concerning the last days:

Then afterward I will pour out my spirit on all flesh; your sons and your daughters shall prophesy, your old men shall dream dreams, and your young men shall see visions. Even on the male and female slaves, in those days, I will pour out my spirit. (Joel 2.28–29)

At Pentecost, Joel's prophecy is fulfilled and Babel is undone. Jerusalem was packed with Jews who had gathered for the feast (notice the re-gathering of those scattered at Babel), and a group of Jewish followers of Jesus 'were filled with the Holy Spirit and began to speak in other languages, as the Spirit gave them ability' (Acts 2.4). A piercing noise draws the attention of those Jews gathered for the festival 'from every nation under heaven' (Acts 2.5), and they stand amazed and perplexed to hear these Galilean followers of Jesus speaking in the language of every nation represented. In the midst of their confusion, Peter explains that this is what Joel was talking about. The Spirit has filled these followers of Jesus, so that 'in our own languages we hear them speaking about God's deeds of power' (Acts 2.11).

What Pentecost represents – and in this it marks the beginning of the mission of the church – is the unity of the gospel ('one Lord, one faith, one baptism' – Eph. 4.5) communicated in a diversity of languages, all in the power of the Holy Spirit. Note, too, that the unity of proclamation does not require – we might even say, does not *allow for* – a unified language. This signals a Spirit-directed, Spirit-filled flourishing of the many – *as many* – as they are united to the one Lord. Acts 2 finds its further fulfilment, much to his surprise, in Peter's proclamation of the gospel among the Gentiles in Acts 10.

The Spirit is the one who enables the church to confess Jesus as Lord (1 Cor. 12.3). The Spirit unites us to Christ (hence Peter's insistence that baptism, or identification with Christ, accompany reception of the Spirit). The Spirit applies the work of Christ to believers in this union, making us participants in Jesus' death and resurrection (Col. 3.1–4; Eph. 2.5–6). By the power of the Spirit we are made sons and daughters of God in Christ, and we know this by the witness of the Spirit, who enables us to cry, 'Abba! Father!' (Gal. 4.6–7; Rom. 8.15–17). It is the Spirit, we might say, who is the chief means of grace.

As it was in the power of the Spirit that Jesus lived faithfully before the Father, performed great works of healing, exorcised demons, preached the gospel of the kingdom, suffered and died and, on the third day, was raised to new life, so it is in the power of the Spirit that the church lives faithfully as God's people. By the Spirit we are raised to new life with Christ and empowered to put to death the deeds of the flesh (Rom. 8.11–13). It is the Spirit, after all, who 'gives life' (2 Cor. 3.6) and renews us (Tit. 3.5), who gives to the church its diversity of gifts (1 Cor. 12.4–7, 11–13). Jesus gathers the church by his Spirit, and then the church is scattered by the Spirit that more might be gathered into its company. (See, strikingly, Acts 8.1–8.)

How are Christ and the Spirit related in the church? It is by his Spirit that Christ is present here and now. This gives sense to the 'advantage' of the ascension, as Jesus ties his ascent to the Father to the descent of the Spirit.[1] We do best to hold together the departure of Christ in his ascension and glorification at the right hand of the Father with his presence by the Spirit. At Pentecost, we learn that Christ is 'in a manner present and yet in a manner absent'.[2]

Still, we may not simply equate Christ's presence and the Spirit's. While it is true that the Spirit's public office is to witness and bind the church to Christ, his work is no mere repetition or flat reminder of Christ's. He expands the work of Christ – perfect in sufficiency but without purchase in the lives of believers apart from the Spirit, who, in uniting us to Christ, applies Christ's work, locating and contextualizing it in the life of the church. The Spirit universalizes Christ's person and work as the church serves as Christ's witnesses 'in Jerusalem, in all Judea and Samaria, and to the ends of the earth' (Acts 1.8). The Pentecostal gift is nothing less than empowerment for mission in which the Spirit catholicizes the people of God. The Spirit is the one who 'liberate[s] the Son and the economy from the bondage of history. . . . The Spirit is the *beyond* history, and when he acts in history he does so in order to bring into history the last days, the *eschaton*'.[3] The Spirit is also the one who particularizes Christ's person and work, uniting and conforming individuals to Christ. By applying Christ catholically and personally, the Spirit constitutes the church.[4]

Still, we remember even in the time of the Spirit that Christ is in a manner absent. Were we to identify the Spirit's indwelling with the presence of Christ without remainder, we would render unintelligible the church's hope in the final advent of Christ. It is precisely because Christ is *absent*, because we await his coming in glory, that we live by faith in hope. From first to last, in all we do, we are radically dependent upon the grace, gifts and presence of God. And so we pray: 'Come, Holy Spirit'.

CHAPTER 3

MEDIATION

WAITING IN THE MEANS OF GRACE

The question of ecclesial mediation is a particularly vexing one. After all, Paul seems to have dismissed the concept outright in his insistence that, just as there is one God, 'there is also one mediator between God and humankind, Christ Jesus, himself human' (1 Tim. 2.5). Can the church possibly be said to *mediate* God? Does this put God in the possession of the church, which is then free to dispense or withhold his gifts and grace at will? If we make such a claim, are we not simply arrogating a role that properly belongs to Christ alone? And at that point are we mediating between humanity and God, or humanity and the devil?

We must say two things at the outset, and throughout: (1) the triune God binds himself to the church, freely and lovingly determining himself to be for, with and in her life together. Thus we must look first to the church to discern God's activity; we must go to the church to find God. That is where he makes his home with us. (2) The triune God is not thereby limited in his presence and work to the perimeter, parameter, people, possibilities or perfection of the church. He can reveal himself and accomplish much outside, even over against the church. He can work mightily even in the midst of a sinful church. Thus we may not presume upon God, such that we infer an automatic divine sponsorship of the affairs of the church or disparage extra-ecclesial sites in which he may be at work. We will excavate and explore these two commitments in the next few pages.

* * *

First, then, the bondage of the triune God, in which he gives himself in covenantal fidelity to the church, freely and loving determining himself to be for, with and in her life together.

Late in life, John Wesley collected his standard sermons, those sermons meant to set out his evangelical Methodist vision of the Christian life. For one so concerned with *Herzreligion* ['heart religion'] and the centrality of an experience of personal conversion to Christ, it may strike some as odd that Wesley included a sermon on 'The Means of Grace'.[1] After all, it would seem that such a personal religion would eschew the routine, even quotidian character of such means, means which do not change from person to person or even generation to generation. Furthermore, to many 'means of grace' smacks of arid institutionalism, of hollow religious husks drained of spiritual content.[2] Nevertheless, Wesley insisted that 'according to the decision of holy writ all who desire the grace of God are to wait for it in the means which he hath ordained; in using, not in laying them aside' (3.1). These means are the 'usual' or 'ordinary' channels of grace (1.1). God could, of course, use unusual and extraordinary means to give himself to people; that is the implication of the second point above. But he has appointed these means as the ordinary channels of grace, and we would be foolish and ungrateful to look elsewhere.

What are these channels, then? '[F]irst, all who desire the grace of God are to wait for it in the way of prayer. This is the express direction of our Lord himself' (3.1). Wesley speaks of the 'absolute necessity of using this means, if we would receive any gift from God' (3.3). 'Secondly, all who desire the grace of God are to wait for it in searching the Scriptures'. (3.7). Finally, 'all who desire an increase of the grace of God are to wait for it in partaking of the Lord's supper: for this also is a direction himself hath given' (3.11). This final point fuels Wesley's approach to the means of grace. The man who resolved to be a 'man of one book' (*homo unius libri*) looked to that book to discern God's ways with his people and the shape of the Christian life. The means of grace saturate scripture and are God's appointed instruments through which he communicates life to his people in the church.[3] That some have abused, and as a result others have despised, the means of grace does not attenuate their value as 'means ordained by God' and 'the usual channels of his grace' (1.1). Nor does the fact that Christ is the means of grace (as its 'sole price and purchaser') render prayer, the Bible and receiving the Lord's Supper as means of grace (as 'a channel through which the grace of God is conveyed') obsolete (4.3).[4]

What might it mean to 'wait' for God's grace in the means? Waiting combines humble submission, patient faithfulness and expectant receptivity. It refuses to ramble across new territories in a quest for grace but insists on abiding where grace has been promised. This is no mere conservatism, however, and certainly not sloth; rather is it a posture of expectation. Waiting in the means requires trusting in them, that is, trusting that God will meet and bless us there in faithfulness to his promise (4.1).

Waiting further assumes that grace has its source in and ever remains a gift of God. While the means of grace are the site and instrument of God's giving, they must not be confused with the end. They have no intrinsic power, for God alone is 'the giver of every good gift' and 'able to give the same grace, though there were no means on the face of the earth' (2.3). Though the means of grace are where God has ordained he should be sought, they are not what we seek. 'In using all means, seek God alone. . . . Nothing short of God can satisfy your soul. Therefore, eye him in all, through all, and above all' (5.4). 'Remember also, to use all means, *as means*; as ordained, not for their own sake, but in order to the renewal of your soul in righteousness and true holiness. If, therefore, they actually tend to this, well; but if not, they are dung and dross' (5.4). Souls satisfied in God, conformed to Christ and transformed by the Spirit are the end (*telos*) of the means of grace.

What, though, *is* grace? A word used so indiscriminately in casual conversation, and often enough in theological exposition, can threaten to lose all significance. Here is a simple, but comprehensive definition of the theological concept: Grace is the effective presence of the triune God freely given to pardon and to empower.

Let us unpack that a bit. First, grace is *effective presence*. That is, grace is not a 'thing' capable of being abstracted from the personal presence of God. It is less a measurable quality than it is the presence of God to and among his people. And this is an effective presence; it does something. God does not come to his people aimlessly or anemically, but comes to redeem, sanctify and perfect them. Note that 'effective' does not imply 'automatic'. As the personal presence of the triune God among his people, grace does not operate like a machine but within a relational dynamic. That is, it is received in faith.

Second, grace is the effective presence of *the triune God.* A properly theological account of God's grace (as opposed to, though not entirely divorced from, an account of the grace of a ballerina) broadcasts the subject of grace. Nor is this 'god' in general, but the triune God of Christian confession, Father, Son and Holy Spirit. It is this God who is for us, with us and in us in the church. Paul concludes 2 Corinthian with a benediction: 'The grace of the Lord Jesus Christ, the love of God, and the communion of the Holy Spirit be with all of you' (13.13). This is not to restrict grace to a gift of Christ apart from the Father and the Spirit, for grace is the gift of the triune God. We might paraphrase the benediction by putting it thus: The loving Father gave his Son to the world that by his death and resurrection we might be brought into the fellowship of the Spirit between Father and Son. Grace is present when and where the Spirit brings Father and Son to us and us to Father and Son. And that 'when' and 'where' are the church. The church, to return to our earlier discussion, is thus marked above all by the presence of the triune God.

Next, grace is *freely given.* Nothing about this 'when' and 'where' of grace could be predicted on the basis of the 'when' and 'where'. To put it more straightforwardly, the triune God gives his grace to whomever he wants for no reason other than his good pleasure. That he does so preeminently in the church in no way suggests the church's own inherent suitability as a recipient of grace. (That he may also do so outside the church reminds the church of this.) Furthermore, the triune God only ever gives his grace to sinners. Grace is unmerited.[5] The economy of grace knows nothing of *quid pro quo*; grace 'travels outside of karma'.[6]

Finally, grace is the effective presence of the triune God *to pardon and empower*.[7]

Both of these verbs are vital here. The end of pardon is empowerment; the origin of empowerment is pardon. This suggests both the profound brokenness and disorder of sinful humanity as well as God's faithfulness to his creation such that redemption is creation's restoration and vindication. It would do no good to empower sinful humanity; that would only be to abet the further corruption of God's good creation. But if God merely pardoned without providing the empowerment needed to live faithfully before him in the world, the church would be left resourceless. Thus we can say: 'Grace neither destroys, nor merely perfects nature; rather, grace perfects nature through a disruptive event which must be classified as mortification and vivification'.[8]

An objection arises from Alexander Schmemann against the language of 'means of grace'. In his lushly doxological articulations of Christian theology, Schmemann worries that references to the sacraments as 'means of grace' shunt them into 'the peculiar *estrangement* of the sacraments from the Church' in a 'scholastic reduction' whose atomizing impulse leads to the dismemberment of the church.[9] This atomizing, in which the sacraments are reduced to a moment (the consecration or *epiclesis*, in the case of the eucharist[10]) and their meaning is reduced to their validity rather than their fulfilment,[11] isolates the sacraments from the life of the church. Such isolation dissolves 'the indivisible unity of *teaching, liturgical experience,* and *spiritual effort*' – a unity 'that, more than anything else, we need today'.[12] Schmemann worries that talk of 'means' tends to reduce, say, the eucharist, to a delivery mechanism for individuals without reference to source, context and ends of the sacrament. Isolation, then, involves mechanization, in which the sacramental machine is made up of component parts isolated from their Maker. (The analogy itself is deeply foreign to the utterly personal, free and loving – that is, never 'automatic', much less 'automated' – workings of the triune God and his grace.)

Materially, Schmemann is right; but his quibble with the term 'means of grace' is a bit misleading. It is certainly the case that the sacraments are often treated in isolation from the church, and ecumenical discussion has at times tended to over-emphasize issues of validity. On their worst days, the Reformers and the church from which they were cast out were equally, and wrongly, focused on issues of secondary concern like sacramental validity, to the neglect of the mystery celebrated in the sacraments. Here, though, with his integrative and doxological approach, Schmemann makes common cause with Wesley, who never intended in his usage of the phrase 'means of grace' to suggest the reduction of the work of the church to a delivery mechanism for a grace divorced from the triune God. Wesley is clear: 'In using all means, seek God alone. . . . Nothing short of God can satisfy your soul. Therefore, eye him in all, through all, and above all'.[13] Or, as Schmemann puts it, it is 'that "newness of life" in Christ which *is* grace'.[14]

On the other hand, to return to our second guiding principle, God's having bound himself to the church does not imply that he is thereby limited in his presence and work to the perimeter, parameters, people, possibilities or perfection of the church. Barth puts this with apt bluntness: 'God may speak to us through Russian communism, a flute concerto, a blossoming shrub, or a dead dog. We do well to listen to Him if He really does . . .'.[15] The danger of assuming that God only speaks through, say, a blossoming shrub is that we begin to think there is something about the shrub that inclines God to speak there. This is a subtle mistake, but it quickly lands one in the position of ever-narrowing standards as to just where God can speak and act. Suddenly, he becomes a function of our preparation; or, to put it differently, he is allowed to speak and act among the clean, the good and the beautiful. This is hardly good news for sinners, and it is far from the grace which creates, rather than finds goodness.[16] Still, we can speak of a certain providential fittingness in the sacramental symbols, grounded in the unity of God's works in creation and redemption.[17]

In one sense, one simply cannot ask or expect too much of the church. Saints through the ages have rightly treasured the church as the mother who gave them birth, the teacher who reared them in the faith, the hospital where the wounds of sin were healed, the haven protecting them from the evil one, and the heavenly home of their hope. And yet, all of these things are true only and ever derivatively. George Hunsinger offers a helpful distinction at this point, between a saving agent and an acting subject. Christ is the sole saving agent of salvation from first to last. He is also the primary acting subject, but his ministers and people are auxiliary acting subjects.[18] This is an anti-Pelagian caveat.[19] *Solus Christus* is affirmed, such that the action of the church is only ever (at least insofar as it is *holy* activity) a participation [*koinonia*] in Christ's action. What's more, this participation is a participation-in-reception; that is, the church does not add a little something extra to the saving work of Christ. Its action is entirely in the mode of reception through the Spirit's application of it in the church. At the end of his sermon on the means of grace, Wesley cautions his listeners:

> Settle this in your heart, that the *opus operatum*, the mere *work done*, profiteth nothing; that there is no *power* save, but in the Spirit of God, no *merit*, but in the blood of Christ; that, consequently, even what God ordains, conveys no grace to the soul if you trust not in him alone. On the other hand, he that does truly trust in him, cannot fall short of the grace of God, even though he were cut off

from every outward ordinance, though he were shut up in the centre of the earth.[20]

Holding these two guiding principles together, we can affirm that 'while *we* are bound to the sacraments, God is not'.[21] With this in mind, we will look in what follows at four means of grace, beginning with baptism.

BAPTISM

It is quite a distance from Jesus' bracingly immediate call to discipleship, with its absolute expectations invading the lives of those with ears to hear,[22] to babies in pretty white dresses and a few drops of water – or, if you prefer, a teenager dunked in a jacuzzi during a youth group sleepover. If the former represents the heady days of Jesus' life and ministry and the rugged witness of the early church, the latter offers a gilded memorial to an ever-receding bit of antiquity.

Reading Dietrich Bonhoeffer's *Discipleship*, written in the crucible of the Holocaust, one might expect a call to restoration, a desperate attempt to reach back behind an institutional church to its origins in the radical way of Jesus' first disciples. And that is precisely how the book opens. What is surprising, however, is the way in which Bonhoeffer asserts Christ's contemporaneity with the church. Christ *still* calls disciples, and he does so with the same demands for fierce devotion. But how can he do this? As we have already argued, Christ's ascension puts him at a certain remove from us. He is in a manner absent. How, then, can this call reach us? Here is Bonhoeffer:

> What the Synoptics describe as hearing and following the call to discipleship, Paul expresses with the concept of *baptism*. . . . Baptism is essentially a paradoxically passive action; it means being baptized, suffering Christ's call. In baptism we become Christ's possession. . . . Baptism thus implies a *break*. Christ invades the realm of Satan and lays hold of those who belong to him, thereby creating his church-community. Past and present are thus torn asunder. The old has passed away, everything has become new. . . . Long ago, Christ himself had already brought about that break. In baptism this break now also takes effect in my own life.[23]

Few churches consider baptism in this manner. Churches committed to believer's baptism concentrate on a prior moment of decision for Christ as the turning point from death to life, finding in baptism a rite necessary for the mission and edification of the church but one that plays a secondary role at best in the life of the believer. Pae-dobaptists, especially those who subscribe to baptismal regeneration (which excludes the Reformed), are notionally committed to the significance of baptism, but the difficulty of imagining a rite of *transition* for just-born infants quickly domesticates the starkness of which Bonhoeffer speaks.[24]

What, then, happens in baptism? Consider the words of Paul and Timothy to the Colossians:

> In him also you were circumcised with a spiritual circumcision, by putting off the body of the flesh in the circumcision of Christ; when you were buried with him in baptism, you were also raised with him through faith in the power of God, who raised him from the dead. And when you were dead in trespasses and the uncircumcision of your flesh, God made you alive together with him, when he forgave us all our trespasses, erasing the record that stood against us with its legal demands. He set this aside, nailing it to the cross. He disarmed the rulers and authorities and made a public example of them, triumphing over them in it. (Col. 2.11–15)

Most striking in this passage, and yet easily missed, are the prepositional phrases – 'in him', 'with him'. In baptism we are identified with Christ, such that what is true of him becomes true of us. Everything significant that happens to us does so insofar as we are 'in him' and 'with him'. Entirely devoted to his God and Father, Christ walked faithfully to his death and was vindicated as the Father raised him from the dead in the power of the Spirit. In baptism we are included in the history of this one faithful Israelite by the power of this same Spirit; his history becomes ours, such that we can say that we have been circumcised with his circumcision, buried with him, forgiven and made alive together with him. Furthermore, we are no longer under the dominion of other, and false, lords. God disarmed them and triumphed over them in the faithful death of his Son. The humility of the Lord gave the lie to, and thereby defeated, the pride of all other lords.

In all of this, then, the church is included. Our former lives are over, such that Paul and Timothy can say, 'you have died, and your life is hidden with Christ in God' (Col. 3.3). Baptism marks the transition from our lives being found 'in the flesh' set in opposition to God to being found in and with Christ. Transition is a soft way of putting a much starker reality.[25] Due to sin, we are dead. In baptism, we are buried and raised to new life with Christ by the Father as God forgives and erases the record of our sins.[26] The cleansing waters of baptism purify, then, precisely by drowning us, by making an end of our lives lived in the flesh.[27]

This occurs through repentance and faith. Colossians only tacitly treats repentance, though the need for forgiveness is evident throughout (1.13–14, 2.13–14). But repentance lies at the heart of the baptismal movement. John the Baptist preached 'a baptism of repentance for the forgiveness of sins' (Mk 1.4; also see Mt. 3.6). At Pentecost, Peter stands up and announces that:

> 'God has made him both Lord and Messiah, this Jesus whom you crucified'. Now when they heard this, they were cut to the heart and said to Peter and to the other apostles, 'Brothers, what should we do?' Peter said to them, 'Repent, and be baptized every one of you in the name of Jesus Christ so that your sins may be forgiven; and you will receive the gift of the Holy Spirit'. (Acts 2.36–38)

Turning from sin, turning to the one in whose name sin is forgiven, and receiving his Spirit are of a piece.

We are raised to new life 'through faith in the power of God'. In itself, faith is nothing. In fact, one way to ensure missing the point of the gospel is to think faith is something. Faith is a negative concept that opens up space to speak about something else. It has what Webster calls a 'rhetoric of indication', one which is 'self-effacing'.[28] When the Reformers quite rightly spoke of salvation *sola fide*, by faith alone, they did not mean by that to speak of 'this human action, not that', but instead 'God's action, not ours'. So 'faith' serves as shorthand for 'faith in the promises of God fulfilled in Jesus Christ', 'faith in the Word of God' – or, as in Colossians 2, 'faith in the power of God' (v. 12). We cannot say enough about the importance of faith in coming to baptism, but faith is less a condition qualifying a baptismal candidate than it is that candidate's disavowal of all conditions for approaching the water, his confession that he is 'dead in trespasses'. Dead people can do nothing. Even the grammar of baptism suggests this utter helplessness, as one 'undergoes' baptism, 'receives' it or simply 'is baptized'.

We have called this identification with and inclusion in Christ; a more Pauline expression is incorporation. In baptism, we become part of Christ's body, united to him by the Spirit in the church. To be alive with Christ, then, is to be part of his body in the church. It is in this sense that baptism is a rite of initiation. As initiation into the circumcision of Christ, it is entrance into eternal life in the company of God's people, into the covenantal community established by God.[29] Too often the means of grace are treated as isolated applications of grace to individuals, but baptism reminds us of the communal nature of the means. One person baptizes another into the company of God's people in the triune name. Incorporation is into Christ and, therefore, into his church.

In that it is inclusion among God's people, baptism is ordination to mission. The logic of God's blessing follows a similar pattern in scripture. God elects a person or people (Abraham, Israel, David, Jesus, the church) to enjoy the blessing of fellowship with him by joining his mission of reconciling the world to himself. The classic, but not at all unique statement is in God's calling of Abram: 'Go from your country and your kindred and your father's house to the land that I will show you. I will make of you a great nation, and I will bless you, and make your name great, so that you will be a blessing' (Gen. 12.1–2). The pattern is repeated at the Jordan River – where, much to the Baptist's astonishment, Jesus goes to be baptized (Mt. 3.13–17; Mk 1.9–11; Lk. 3.21–22; also see Jn 1.32). Identifying with his sinful people and sinful humanity, Jesus rises from the water to hear the Father speak of his good pleasure in his Son as the Spirit descends on him. From there, 'Jesus, full of the Spirit returned from the Jordan and was led by the Spirit in the wilderness' for a time of testing, in which Jesus' faithfulness was proven (Lk. 4.1). 'Then Jesus, filled with the power of the Spirit, returned to Galilee', commencing his ministry in his hometown by reading from the scroll of Isaiah: 'The Spirit of the Lord is upon me, because he has anointed me to bring good news to the poor' (Lk. 4.14, 18). In baptism, we are included in the life of *this* one. We hear the Father's good pleasure in us as adopted sons and daughters, we are filled by the Spirit and we are ordained to mission in partnership with God. As those ordained to mission, the baptized are ordained to ministry and constitute 'a chosen race, a royal priesthood, a holy nation, God's own people, *in order that* you may proclaim the mighty acts of him who called you out of darkness into his marvellous light' (1 Pet. 2.9).

We will return to the shape of Christian mission in the following chapter, but a brief word regarding the political character of baptism is in order. While the primary meaning of baptism involves our being identified with Christ, the Anabaptist tradition rightly reminds us that such an identification is a confession of allegiance. In baptism, we confess before God and the world in the church that Christ is Lord. We repent of our past allegiance to false gods (repentance at its heart being recognition, remorse and turning from idolatry) and declare our allegiance to the God and Father of our Lord Jesus Christ. In this eschatological declaration of Jesus as Lord, in which the final truth of the world is anticipated (see Phil. 2.10–11), we witness to the disarming and defeat of the rulers and authorities at the cross.[30] *Our* citizenship, we proclaim, is in heaven (Phil. 3.20); our king is not Caesar, but Jesus (see Acts 17.7). If there were any doubt as to the severity of this political claim, and the affront to the world it represents, consider Jesus' ministry, beginning in baptism, empowered by the Spirit and leading to a disgraceful death. As Dietrich, himself painfully aware of the political implications of Christian discipleship, once put it, 'Whenever Christ calls us, his call leads us to death'.[31]

The uniquely receptive, even passive character of baptism suggests that even in a thoroughly political reading of baptism, which recognizes in this declaration of allegiance to Christ a renunciation of all little lords who take the name of 'Caesar' – even in, that is, this bold token of human faithfulness – the form of such politics is utterly receptive. The church is in no sense self-founding but receives its life from its Lord, being built on him as its cornerstone. Consistent with this, the believer's life is given to her as she is identified with another. Her life is taken up in his, and it is this to which she testifies in baptism.

Nor is this an isolated rite with mere 'developmental' or 'religious' significance. As our incorporation into Christ, baptism marks a transition point at which our lives become enfolded in his as we enter the church. The hinge of Colossians comes at the beginning of the third chapter, in which Paul and Timothy detail the implications of our participation in Christ's death and resurrection in baptism: 'So if you have been raised with Christ, seek the things that are above, where Christ is, seated at the right hand of God. Set your minds on things that are above, not on things that are on earth, for you have died, and your life is hidden with Christ in God' (3.1–3). We are to '[p]ut to death, therefore, whatever in [us] is earthly' and 'clothe [ourselves] with love' (3.5, 14). Notice the pattern of death and resurrection, of putting off and putting on.[32] If our lives have been enfolded into the death and resurrection of Christ, we ought to live according to this pattern. As Luther put it, the Christian life is nothing other than a daily return to baptism – first, in a rediscovery of our lives 'hidden with Christ in God' and second in an ever being conformed to the image, or pattern of Christ (Rom. 8.29). This order resists a reduction of the Christian life to moralism divorced from union with Christ, even as the twofold sense of baptismal return resists a reduction to sacramentalism shorn of obedience.

At this point, it might be objected that we are investing baptism with far too much significance, or at least that such an account does not belong in an ecclesiology written by theologians who come from the free church tradition. But to speak of 'baptism' in the New Testament, and indeed throughout the history of the church's reflection on and practice of baptism, is to speak of a diachronic process of initiation into the Christian faith. The biblical witness is varied as to the order of believing, baptism and belonging. Nor should this be surprising, given the quick and relatively decentralized growth of Christianity. At times, the Spirit fell on and filled believers first, in response to which the apostles saw fit to baptism them (Acts 10.44–48). At other times, repentance and belief led immediately to baptism and a later filling with the Spirit (Acts 8.14–17). Less important than the chronology, then, was the concomitance of belief, baptism and filling with the Spirit. In the early church, 'baptism' began with an often lengthy catechumenate in which candidates were instructed in the faith, culminating in the baptismal rite and admission to the Lord's table at Easter.[33] The inversion of that order with the turn to infant baptism suggests the necessity of a post-baptismal process during which the child comes to repent and believe the gospel; it does not suggest faith's dispensability.[34] To argue that the church's faith, or that of the parents and sponsors, suffices in a child's baptism cannot properly imply the non-necessity of the child's faith but only the custodial character of her guardians until the Spirit enables her to believe for, if never by, herself. In any case, what is common is the coordination of repentance, belief, baptism, filling with the Spirit and initiation into the Christian community. They form one unified complex marking the incorporation of believers into Christ in the church and thus belong together, even if separated in time. They are to be synthesized, even if they cannot always be synchronized.

With this in mind, we can approach the diversity of baptismal practice with a bit more flexibility. The very fact that God has clearly been at work as both infants and adults have been baptized in the name of Father, Son and Holy Spirit dissuades us from outlawing paedobaptism or believer's baptism. Even if we find scant biblical evidence, there is ample patristic evidence for infant baptism (certainly by 200 CE).[35] And while the mere presence of an ancient practice does not compel us to accept it today, its near ubiquity for much of Christian history puts a significant burden of proof on those who would dismiss infant baptism out of hand. Understanding the unified, if diachronic, complex of which baptism is a part commends the re-integration of what are often isolated moments. More important than establishing a normative chronology for repentance, belief, baptism, filling with the Spirit and initiation into the Christian community is holding them together theologically (if not always in time). This will suggest certain modifications of practice and theological reflection. At times, free churches can so emphasize decision as the locus of entrée into the Christian life that baptism becomes a distant echo or announcement of an event accomplished 'altogether elsewhere'.[36] On the other hand, churches practicing infant baptism can veer toward treating the baptismal rite as a mechanism by which Christians are automatically made, regardless of its connection to repentance and belief. Infant baptism is incomplete until it is met by the repentance and belief of the child later in life. Either error can foreground particular human actions in such a way that the divine actions of our being identified with Christ and filled with the Spirit are pushed to the wings.

If one had to choose between baptismal regeneration and decisional regeneration, we believe the latter to more faithfully reflect Jesus' call to discipleship and the radical character of Christian conversion. But we resist this dilemma as a false one – and one far too dominant in discussion of the way in which God's salvation comes to be applied to God's people. It is Christ alone who saves, and he does so by grace alone through faith alone; that he does so in baptism (understood as part of a diachronic complex of initiation) need not be seen to mitigate these core soteriological commitments. Nor, of course, are these commitments mitigated in insisting that Christ alone saves in and through bringing people to decision (a necessary caveat, given the subtly Pelagian tendency in many churches to interpret faith as an efficient rather than instrumental cause). *Sola fide* does not equate without remainder to decisional regeneration. Baptism and decision are sites of salvation, therefore, perhaps instrumental causes; but only God is the efficient cause.[37] As Calvin puts it, we ought 'clearly discern in the Father the cause, in the Son the matter, and in the Spirit the effect, of our purgation and our regeneration'.[38] In the synthetic unity of which baptism is a part, we enter the church. In prayer, we learn the church's ways of speaking, loving and living. To prayer we now turn.

PRAYER

Prayer does not come naturally for humanity east of Eden, but prayer is the natural posture of the church. It evinces the graciousness of God and the need of his people and invites their gratitude in response. Wesley draws our attention to the Sermon on the Mount:

> Ask, and it will be given you; search, and you will find; knock, and the door will be opened for you. For everyone who asks receives, and everyone who searches finds, and for everyone who knocks, the door will be opened. Is there anyone among you who, if your child asks for bread, will give a stone? Or if the child asks for a fish, will give a snake? If you then, who are evil, know how to give good gifts to your children, how much more will your Father in heaven give good things to those who ask him! (Mt. 7.7–11)

It is fitting that the one who Jesus invites us to call 'Father' would give his grace to us in response to our asking, just as any father would give his children the things for which they ask.[39] This means of grace teaches us dependence and gratitude, the childlike character of those who receive the kingdom of God (Mk 10.15; Lk. 18.17; see Mt. 18.3).[40] Prayer is, in this sense, the form of the Christian life, the essence of the church. One might call it a – even *the* – basic human action. We ask, God answers. God gives, we receive. There are certainly many questions to be asked about unanswered prayers, but Jesus' teaching and his own undiluted confidence in the constancy and goodness of his God and Father affirm a faithful Father who delights to give good gifts at the request of his children (Jas 1.17). Were he fickle or arbitrary, prayer as a means of grace would be undone, replaced by a mechanism of manipulation – the beggar having become the barterer.[41]

But more needs to be said about the dynamic of prayer in light of God's revelation as Trinity. James Torrance has argued that we are functional unitarians, approaching the triune God in worship and prayer as a counterpart independent from us. In the process of implicitly denying God's being as Father, Son and Holy Spirit we exhaust ourselves in a do-it-yourself spirituality. Here we enter into a contractual relationship with a God 'who needs to be conditioned into being gracious by law being satisfied' rather than living in joyful obedience in response to the covenant of grace.[42] What prayer in a unitarian key neglects is the way in which the triune God works within our praying to draw us into communion with him and one another.

The Father gives good things to those who ask him, but does this smuggle in a requirement that we be particularly discerning in our asking? Surely there are plenty of things he does not want to give, precisely because he is concerned for our flourishing.

> Likewise the Spirit helps us in our weakness; for we do not know how to pray as we ought, but that very Spirit intercedes with sighs too deep for words. And God, who searches the heart, knows what is the mind of the Spirit, because the Spirit intercedes for the saints according to the will of God. (Rom. 8.26–27)

In our fumbling, ignorant praying we are helped as the Spirit prays within us on our behalf in perfect accord with the Father. That his intercession occurs 'with sighs too deep for words' suggests both the gratuity of his help and the mysterious intimacy of one who is 'closer to me than I am to myself' even in my praying.[43]

While the Spirit prays in us, Jesus prays for us. The neglect of Christ's ascension in theology and the church carries with it an amnesia regarding Christ's priestly office, which includes his self-sacrifice in death (Heb. 7.27) but also his role as worship leader (Heb. 8.2) and intercessor at the right hand of God.

> Furthermore, the former priests were many in number, because they were prevented by death from continuing in office; but he holds his priesthood permanently, because he continues forever. Consequently he is able for all time to save those who approach God through him, since he always lives to make intercession for them. (Heb. 7.23–25)

This is good news for those who fail in prayer as in all of life. Where we fail, as Jesus represents us before the Father, he is faithful. 'Jesus takes our prayers – our feeble, selfish, inarticulate prayers – he cleanses them, makes them his prayers, and in a "wonderful exchange" . . . he makes his prayers our prayers and presents us to the Father as his dear children, crying: "*Abba* Father"'.[44] So Paul can trumpet:

> If God is for us, who is against us? He who did not withhold his own Son, but gave him up for all of us, will he not with him also give us everything else? Who will bring any charge against God's elect? It is God who justifies. Who is to condemn? It is Christ Jesus, who died, yes, who was raised, who is at the right hand of God, who indeed intercedes for us. Who will separate us from the love of Christ? (Rom. 8.31–35)

In prayer the church is not left to its own devices or asked to drum up its own resources; instead, it is caught up in a trinitarian dynamic of giving. Prayer does not function as a means of grace insofar as our prayers are perfectly motivated and articulated. Rather, God gives us his grace and with it himself even as we pray.

> Jesus prays for us; he also has prayed before us. He is, in Barth's words, our predecessor in prayer. The distinctive value and importance of the 'Our Father' as the Lord's Prayer consist in the fact that in it Jesus ranges Himself alongside His disciples, or His disciples alongside Himself, taking them up with Him into His own prayer. The 'We' of this prayer is the We to which the Lord attaches Himself with His people. . . .[45]

In light of this understanding of mediation, we can return to the problem raised in the opening of this chapter. Christ is 'the one mediator between God and humankind' (1 Tim. 2.5) in that through his faithful ranging of himself alongside his disciples they are quite literally affiliated into the Son's relation to the Father. Mediation does not mean the maintaining of distance; or, if it does, it is only a distance maintained for the sake of communion. Christ mediates between God and humankind in that he re-establishes their fellowship in his incarnation, death and resurrection and daily witnesses to the sufficiency of that accomplishment before the Father.

Prayer is a form of ecclesial mediation in which we intercede for others in the name of Jesus. Just before proclaiming Christ the one mediator, Paul urges that 'supplications, prayers, intercessions, and thanksgivings be made for everyone' (1 Tim. 2.1).[46] While we cannot do the work of re-establishing communion between God and humanity – nor need we – our small work of mediation in the church involves the prayer that this communion be realized throughout the world. And, as James assures us, 'The prayer of the righteous is powerful and effective' (Jas 5.16). Take Elijah as an example – 'a human being like us' (v. 17) whose prayer stopped the rain for 42 months. We have emphasized the Trinity's place in our praying and the consequent significance of our prayers for the world. But prayer is also 'transfiguring' and 'God's way of transforming our thinking'.[47] In this sense, too, it is a means of grace.

In prayer, we put on the confidence and humility of children of God whose hope is in Christ and whose help is in the Spirit. It remains to make just a few points with reference to the prayer Jesus taught his disciples, in its shorter Lucan version:

Father, hallowed be your name.
Your kingdom come.
Give us each day our daily bread.
And forgive us our sins,
for we ourselves forgive everyone indebted to us.
And do not bring us to the time of trial. (Lk. 11.2–4)

Jesus teaches us to pray by teaching us to pray in the first person plural. We do not pray to 'my Father', asking him to feed and forgive 'me'. Instead, we pray together praising and petitioning 'our Father' (see Mt. 6.9).[48] The Lord's Prayer is the church's prayer before it is the Christian's prayer. Or, and better, it is the Christian's prayer precisely as it is the church's prayer. And it is in the church that we learn how to pray, as it is in the church that we learn all the disciplines of the Christian life.[49]

One might simply summarize the first two clauses as a prayer that all the world might know and celebrate God as Father. Were heaven and earth to hallow his name together (as heaven already does), his kingdom would have come. The Lord's Prayer immediately sets us in the crisis of those children who have come to know the Father but who also see the profaning of his name and the absence of his kingdom all around. Prayer is fundamentally active, then, as we yearn for God's name and kingdom – both signalling his gracious and effective reign – to be universally embraced. The prayer will narrow to more particular concerns, but its broad horizon reminds us of the scope of God's work and the context of our daily needs. From the beginning, the Lord teaches his people to pray with a view toward the Last Day.[50] Indeed, the 'inexhaustible mystery of the few sentences in the Lord's Prayer' could be summarized in the phrase 'eschatology becoming actualized'.[51]

The next three lines seem to follow oddly on one another. What, after all, do physical nourishment and forgiveness have to do with one another? Quite a lot, it turns out. It is key to recognize the 'whence' of our difficulty in forgiving others. The bitterness in which I cross my arms and refuse to forgive you (whoever first called this 'nursing a grudge' had a poet's sense for image and irony) is not for nothing. Rather, it flows out of a feeling of being incomplete. I feel that I need something from you. 'You owe me' an apology – that is, a token of your recognition of being in the wrong, your sorrow and your commitment to doing things differently. At its heart, then, our lack of forgiveness betrays need.

In the previous clause we find the petition for our daily bread – a prayer almost entirely symbolic for those of us in the West. We pray it, but have difficulty entering into the need it expresses. The petition evokes God's provision of manna for Israel in the wilderness. Every morning Israel would awaken and gather the manna – only enough for the day, as its shelf life was just that.[52] 'Bread' is representative here, though, of all that the sovereign Lord provides for his people. It also anticipates God's final provision in the marriage supper of the bride and the Lamb (Rev. 17.7–9). The original Aramaic speaks of 'bread for tomorrow', and Jerome suggests that the sense is, 'Our bread for tomorrow – that is, our future bread – give us today', referring to 'not only the next day but also the great Tomorrow, the final consummation'.[53] When we pray that the Lord would provide us with daily bread – that he would give us everything we need for a life of loving him and others – we remember his past provision, look forward to the heavenly banquet and therefore hope and trust in him to provide today.

And so, by the time we recall the need to 'forgive everyone who is indebted' to us, we can. We no longer have the felt need to collect on our debts, because we have been given absolutely everything we need for today (including, as the middle clause points out, the Lord's forgiveness of our debts). As little as our grudge-clutching hearts might believe this, it is simply the case that the Father of lights, from whom comes every good and perfect gift, the one who gives daily bread because his Son is the bread of life (Jn 6.35), has given us everything we need for life and godliness. So – finally, and thanks be to God – we are released to release others from their debt to us. Wonder of wonders, we can forgive. We can, and we must, as Jesus cautions that those who do not forgive others will not be forgiven by the Father (Mt. 6.15).

The prayer to be kept from the time of trial refers to 'what might buffet us and create a pressure upon our loyalty to God that in our frailty we might not be able to withstand'.[54] Thus the trial in question is one of such severity as to lead to apostasy. What the church asks for here is 'preservation *in* the trial', not 'preservation *from* the trial'.[55] Whether this refers to the final, eschatological trial or to severe trials in this life, in teaching his disciples to conclude their prayer with such bracing realism, Jesus reminds them (and us) of our struggle against sin, death and the devil. In this way, the church's prayer becomes a plea for God's protection and a preparation for war.

As the Lord teaches us his prayer in the church, he includes us in his work. As the Spirit prays in us and unites us in Christ, Jesus prays for us, and we find ourselves praying in the voice of Christ.[56] We turn now to consider the church's book, the Bible, in which the church learns what it means to speak in Christ's voice.

SCRIPTURE

The second of the chief means of grace, according to Wesley, is 'searching the Scriptures' – which 'implies reading, hearing, and meditating thereon'.[57] But for what are we to search? One must have *some* sense about what one is looking for in order to look effectively. Augustine sensed as much in asking, 'But who calls upon you when he does not know you? For an ignorant person might call upon someone else instead of the right one'.[58] Just so, we rightly ask, 'How do we search the scriptures if we do not know what lies hidden in them?'

The church lives in the presence of its risen Lord. All its activity is oriented to this one standing in its midst (Rev. 1.13), this one who comes to judge and pardon and calls the church to faith and obedience. To search the scriptures aright is to orient the reading and hearing of the Bible to *this* one. Put briefly: the Bible is about Jesus Christ.

The *locus classicus* here is the episode on the road to Emmaus, where the risen Lord, 'beginning with Moses and all the prophets . . . interpreted to them the things about himself in all the scriptures' (Lk. 24.27). Here is the scene:

Now on that same day two of them were going to a village called Emmaus, about seven miles from Jerusalem, and talking with each other about all these things that had happened. While they were talking and discussing, Jesus himself came near and went with them, but their eyes were kept from recognizing him. And he said to them, 'What are you discussing with each other while you walk along?' They stood still, looking sad. Then one of them, whose name was Cleopas, answered him, 'Are you the only stranger in Jerusalem who does not know the things that have taken place there in these days?' He asked them, 'What things?' They replied, 'The things about Jesus of Nazareth. . . . But we had hoped that he was the one to redeem Israel . . .' Then he said to them, 'Oh, how foolish you are, and how slow of heart to believe all that the prophets have declared! Was it not necessary that the Messiah should suffer these things and then enter into his glory?' Then beginning with Moses and all the prophets, he interpreted to them the things about himself in all the scriptures. As they came near the village to which they were going, he walked ahead as if he were going on. But they urged him strongly, saying, 'Stay with us, because it is almost evening and the day is now nearly over.' So he went in to stay with them. When he was at the table with them, he took bread, blessed and broke it, and gave it to them. Then their eyes were opened, and they recognized him; and he vanished from their sight. They said to each other, 'Were not our hearts burning within us while he was talking to us on the road, while he was opening the scriptures to us?' That same hour they got up and returned to Jerusalem; and they found the eleven and their companions gathered together. They were saying, 'The Lord has risen indeed, and he has appeared to Simon!' Then they told what had happened on the road, and how he had been made known to them in the breaking of the bread. (Lk. 24.13–35)

Notice a few things. First, these disciples have not connected the dots. They seem to have known the law and the prophets, and Jesus upbraids them for being so 'foolish' and 'slow of heart to believe' what the scriptures (in this context, the Old Testament) indicated about the Messiah. This is not for lack of concern or discussion on their part, nor are they unique among the disciples. *No one* seems to have believed the scriptures. This suggests, on the one hand, that mere familiarity with the Bible is not sufficient to lead one to recognition of or commitment to its subject. On the other hand, it implies that Christology cannot be quickly read off the surface of the text. While all of scripture is about Christ, it has a manifold way of proclaiming him. Moving too quickly to the Christological reference of the text without wrestling with the literal sense can find us missing nuances which enrich our knowledge of and communion with Christ. To take one example: it is right to identify the suffering servant of Isa. 53 who 'was wounded for our transgressions, crushed for our iniquities' (v. 5) with Jesus, but to do so quickly, before considering the servant on his own terms in the context of Isaiah's more immediate horizon, is to miss both the servant and Christ.[59] It is to miss the way in which Israel is called to be God's servant, its failure to do so, and the long wait for the one, true Israelite who is Jesus.[60]

Secondly, we find on the Emmaus Road that Christ is the authoritative interpreter of scripture. Here is affirmed Calvin's principle that 'God alone is a fit witness to himself in his Word'.[61] We might add: 'God alone is a fit interpreter of that which witnesses to himself'. In other words, Christ is not only the ultimate referent of scripture; he is the interpreter of scripture, the pastor and shepherd who feeds his flock on the Word of God. This implies that the only proper interpretation of scripture is within Christ's body wherein Christ – as mediated by the power of the Spirit and through the person functioning *in persona Christi* – gives this interpretation.[62]

Finally, the goal of searching the scriptures is communion with Christ. Notice that, even after Jesus' rebuke and authoritative interpretation of the scriptures, the disciples do not seem to realize who he is. It is only as they enter into table fellowship with the crucified and risen one that 'their eyes were opened, and they recognized him'.[63] We read the Bible in order to know the one of whom it speaks. As we learn about him, we enter into communion with him – communion apart from which we cannot really or rightly know him. Knowledge and communion imply and lead to one another.

It is fitting, then, that the risen Lord's hermeneutic at Emmaus finds dominical grounding in his instruction to 'search the scriptures, for they testify of me'.[64] This is precisely what the Bereans do years later after hearing Paul, and what Paul exhorts Timothy to do.[65] A century later, against Marcion's violent sundering of the testaments, Irenaeus demonstrated Christ from the prophets who came before him, articulating the unity of scripture and the continuity of God's ways with the world.[66]

The place of scripture in the church is to testify to Christ. The centre and *skopos* (or goal) of the Bible is the one in whom God was reconciling the world to himself (2 Cor. 5.21). To call Christ the subject of scripture is not to limit its horizon to the short span of his earthly life, though; or at least, it is not to consider those few years apart from the history stretching from creation to the new Jerusalem. Precisely *as* the *skopos* of scripture, Christ is the one towards whom Israel and the nations strain and from and towards whom the apostolic mission finds its orientation and impetus.[67] Furthermore, this one who stands at the centre of scripture is one who calls God 'Father' and is anointed by his Spirit. As J. I. Packer nicely puts it, scripture is

> God the Father preaching God the Son in the power of God the Holy Ghost. God the Father is the giver of Holy Scripture; God the Son is the theme of Holy Scripture; and God the Spirit, as the Father's appointed agent in witnessing to the Son, is the author, authenticator, and interpreter of Holy Scripture.[68]

Of particular note here is Packer's insistence on the threefold character of the Spirit's work in scripture. Accounts of the Bible's place in the church often place the emphasis squarely on its inspiration at the point of authorship (and, sometimes, editing). But the work of the Spirit is required at every point – from authorship through transmission, collection and canonization, to reading and hearing in the life of Israel and the church.[69] In the midst of arguing strongly for the necessity and sufficiency of scripture in our knowledge of God, Calvin appeals to the Spirit's testimony rather than disputation (or, we might add, proper performance or hermeneutical acumen[70]) as a guarantee of scripture.

> Yet they who strive to build up firm faith in Scripture through disputation are doing things backwards. . . . But I reply: the

testimony of the Spirit is more excellent than all reason. For as God alone is a fit witness of himself in his Word, so also the Word will not find acceptance in men's hearts before it is sealed by the inward testimony of the Spirit. The same Spirit, therefore, who has spoken through the mouths of the prophets must penetrate into our hearts to persuade us that they faithfully proclaimed what had been divinely commanded.[71]

God 'sent down the same Spirit by whose power he had dispensed the Word, to complete his work by the efficacious confirmation of the Word'.[72] Calvin will go on to assert scripture's own self-authentication; but self-authentication is simply another way for asserting the primacy of God's witness to himself in scripture by the Spirit. He will even go on to note a number of arguments for the credibility of scripture, but these are decidedly secondary in his argument and do not in any way render suspect Calvin's sense that God is a sufficient witness to himself by an appeal to the bar of reason.[73] 'We seek no proofs, no marks of genuineness upon which our judgment may lean; but we subject our judgment and wit to it as to a thing far beyond any guesswork!'[74]

In short, to call Christ the subject of scripture is to recognize that the Bible tells the whole story of God and the world. Or, we might put it this way: the triune God's economy of salvation has a Christological centre and goal and grounds the church's reading and hearing of the Bible. This is not an arbitrary or alien hermeneutic, but a fundamentally responsive one in which we wait in the means God has appointed. The church's manner of reading, then, calls for the virtues of humility, patience and deference before the text of scripture.[75] So Calvin rails against 'miserable men' who 'out of curiosity . . . fly off into empty speculations. They do not therefore apprehend God as he offers himself, but imagine him as they have fashioned him in their own presumption'.[76] 'Surely, just as waters boil up from a vast, full spring, so does an immense crowd of gods flow forth from the human mind' – human nature being 'a perpetual factory of idols'.[77] Despite the glorious display of God's majesty in creation, we are blind, overlooking, mis-construing, distorting and manipulating what lies right in front of our eyes. As the Spirit leads us to Christ in the Bible, though, we, like Bartimaeus, and like the disciples on the road to Emmaus, regain our sight and follow Jesus on the way (Mk 10.46–52). The Bible is a pair of glasses, making sense of the world and leading us to God.[78]

It is God the Father who speaks in scripture. It is God the Son, himself the Word of God, who is spoken in scripture. It is in and through God the Spirit that the Word is spoken and heard. A sense of the whole, then, and an obedient reliance on the triune God are abidingly necessary in order properly to search the scriptures. A case in point is Irenaeus' claim that the Gnostics have ransacked scripture, taking the precious jewels, which formed the image of a king, and re-arranging them to form the image of a dog or fox.[79] The mere stringing together of prooftexts is insufficient to render one's thinking 'biblical' without attention to the whole read in light of and reliance upon the triune God.[80]

This is a particularly crucial application of the concept of the hermeneutical circle, whereby one moves between part and whole, asking how each informs the other. In recent debates of homosexuality and the Bible,[81] parties have tended to divide along the lines of commitment to the part that condemns the activity (conservatives) and commitment to the whole that proclaims liberation for all (liberals). A 'liberal' hermeneutic all too easily marginalizes portions of scripture, either by producing a canon-within-a-canon or sidestepping the literal sense through a dismissal of naïve literalism. (On the contrary, to read the Bible literally is not to fall into literalism but to attend to its literary character.[82]) On the other hand, a 'conservative' hermeneutic threatens to isolate the naming of a sin from the economy of salvation which constitutes the whole. Thus, and strangely, discussions of sexual morality become loosed from their proper context in the history of creation, fall, redemption and consummation, which constitutes the story of scripture. We are not consigned to hermeneutical despair, or to forsake scripture as a useless (or all too usable) wax nose. Nor do we need to resign ourselves to an only vague expectation of being led into all truth by the Spirit as we read the Bible together. As Kevin Vanhoozer puts it, 'The clarity of Scripture means that understanding is possible, not that it is easy. . . . The clarity of Scripture is not a matter of its *obviousness* so much as its *efficacy*; the Bible is clear enough to render its communicative action effective'.[83] This need not necessarily mean that its action will be immediate, either; the Holy Spirit's sanctifying work occurs as much in the process of the church's reading and being conformed to the Bible as it does as a result of such reading.

In a series of recent books, William Abraham sharply contests the reduction of the canon of scripture to a criterion of truth, a reduction with tragic results: 'Within the Church of the West, how one knew that one knew the truth about God overshadowed knowing God'.[84] The canonical heritage (which, in Abraham's construal, is wider than scripture) is meant to function soteriologically, not (at least not primarily) epistemologically.[85] Precisely by thinking of the Bible as a criterion, so Abraham, we neglect its primary function as a means of grace.[86] He overstates his case, insofar as a primary recognition of scripture as a means of grace need not preclude a secondary recognition that it at times functions as a means of grace by offering a criterion of truth. His fear that seeing scripture as first and foremost a criterion drastically constricts its sanctifying scope is surely right, however, and offers a much needed corrective to contemporary practices of reading the Bible. His contention that ecclesial renewal does not depend on intellectual proposals (alone, we might add) but a return to the means of grace is salutary.[87] Abraham thus helps us locate our discussion of scripture within the framework of ecclesiology.

Searching the scriptures is a form of waiting in the means of grace in which we submit to the story of scripture, allowing our imaginations, our own construals of the world to be re-inscribed according to the God of the gospel and his ways with the world.[88] This critical insight drives the Reformation slogan: *ecclesia reformata semper reformanda secundum verbum Dei* (the church reformed and always being reformed according to the word of God). In its continual need for reformation, the church confesses its disdain for God's word, its disinclination to attend to the voice of God. When we enter what Karl Barth calls 'the strange new world within the Bible', we suffer the culture shock of finding ourselves in a new home, a home deeply at odds with the old world of sin, the flesh and the devil.[89] Hence our abiding need for reformation.

None of this is to invest scripture with authority divorced from scripture's God. It is insufficient to appeal to biblical authority without invoking the God who speaks in, by and through the Bible. Scripture is the primary organ of the voice of God in the church. Thus, it will stand over-against the church; and the voice of God must not be confused with the voice of the church. Calvin clarifies the matter:

> Thus, while the church receives and gives its seal of approval to the Scriptures, it does not thereby render authentic what is

otherwise doubtful or controversial. But because the church recognizes Scripture to be the truth of its own God, as a pious duty it unhesitatingly venerates Scripture.[90]

Still, what about the church's tradition? Alexander Schmemann rightly insists that tradition is not, as in a two-source model of revelation,[91] '*another* source of the faith, "complementary" to the scriptures. It is the very same source: the living word of God always heard and received by the Church'. Tradition is 'the reading and hearing of scriptures in the Holy Spirit'.[92] Schmemann draws our attention to the Spirit's work of drawing us into all truth as he guides the reading of scripture in the truth. On the one hand, he suggests the inescapably ecclesial reading of scripture. It is impossible (in nearly every case – desert islands notwithstanding) to read the Bible apart from the church. Claims to autonomous interpretation quickly and ironically degenerate into slavish and blind repetitions of long tradi- tions of reading the Bible. Even were it possible to evade the church in one's Bible reading, it would be foolish. If, as Gerhard Ebeling once argues, church history just *is* the history of the exposition of scripture, why would one seek to ignore such a long, detailed, faith-filled conversation?[93] Furthermore, might it not even signal a spurning of the Spirit's gifts if we were to wilfully ignore the ways in which he has led the reading, hearing and receiving of scripture? All this we happily grant.

What, though, are we to make of impoverished or false interpreta- tions of scripture? A more dialectical relation between scripture and tradition is called for, according to which tradition both allows for (by shaping and mediating) a reading of scripture informed by the rule of faith and yet also is at other points checked and corrected by that very reading of scripture. If Alasdair MacIntyre is right that a tradition 'is an argument extended through time', the need for scripture's critical function *vis-à-vis* the tradition is more readily seen. Is this circular?[94] Possibly, in that any reading – even one seeking to be corrected by scripture – is stamped with the impress of context. But it is also an inevitable, and in no sense a regrettable hermeneutical dynamic; it is simply what it means to read and interpret a text. Still, the context for reading the Bible is the church, in whose midst the risen Lord sits as Judge and King over his church. The Spirit leads the church into all truth by leading her to Christ, who comforts her in affliction, confirms her in faithfulness and corrects her in sin and error.

Reflecting on Ps. 119, Luther wrote that the way one becomes a theologian is by listening properly to God's word; and one listens properly by engaging in prayer (*oratio*), meditation (*meditatio* – understood as the public excavation and articulation of the word) and spiritual struggle (*tentatio*). What is of particular note at this point is the place of spiritual struggle. Luther does not assume that the church easily makes its home in the word, but recognizes the martial character of our assimilation to the word. 'For as soon as God's Word takes root and grows in you, the devil will plague you and make a real doctor of you and by his attacks will teach you to seek and love God's Word'.[95] The process by which the Spirit leads the church into all truth is by no means free from peril.

When we search the scriptures, seeking to discern therein the voice of the Lord, we do not thereby betray a sense of his mere absence. The Bible is not a recorded message from God as much as the place and manner of his living and active voice. This does not allow us to move behind or around the text to discern some other God than the God of the Bible beneath the Bible; instead, it emphasizes that to read scripture is to hear and be claimed by the voice of God. Holy scripture is, as John Webster puts it, 'the address of the risen Christ to the saints'.[96] 'The risen one is exalted, "far above" (Eph. 1.21), because he is "before all things" (Col. 1.17). And so infinity is proper to him. His aliveness as the exalted Son is immense; no measure can be taken of it. Divine infinity is both absence of determination and unrestricted access to all created particulars'.[97] The means of grace do not serve, then, as a buffer to keep two parties at a safe distance; they are the avenues of God's gracious presence to us, the ways along which the risen Christ takes advantage of his 'unrestricted access to all created particulars' for the good of the church and the world. And his presence as the king of glory 'is a *communicative* presence' – 'resplendent, outgoing, and therefore eloquent'.[98] Christ speaks to and in his church in scripture. He also gives himself as nourishment to the church in his Supper, to which we now turn.

THE LORD'S SUPPER

Strangely, discussion of the sacraments tends to veer in the direction of articulating just *how* God works in them. *That* he works – and that *he* works – is taken for granted and all too quickly allowed to pass from the scene. To take the Lord's Supper as an example, the astonishing fact that the risen and ascended Christ is present in the power of his Spirit is shunted to the sideline in preoccupation with the *manner* of his presence. Here, though, a basic mistake is made, as we forsake the question of 'Who?' in turning to ask 'How?'[99] The question, in turn, shapes our inquiry. Rather than a personal inquiry into who is present, we ask an impersonal question of mechanics. Better to begin by attending to the triune God who nourishes his people at the table.[100]

Calvin puts it this way:

God has received us, once for all, into his family, to hold us not only as servants but as sons. Thereafter, to fulfil the duties of a most excellent Father concerned for his offspring, he undertakes also to nourish us throughout the course of our life. And not content with this alone, he has willed, by giving his pledge, to assure us of this continuing liberality. To this end, therefore, he has, through the hand of his only-begotten Son, given to his church another sacrament, that is, a spiritual banquet, wherein Christ attests himself to be the life-giving bread, upon which our souls feed unto true and blessed immortality.[101]

Furthermore:

But the sacraments properly fulfil their office only when the Spirit, that inward teacher, comes to them, by whose power alone hearts are penetrated and affections moved and our souls opened for the sacraments to enter in. If the Spirit be lacking, the sacraments can accomplish nothing more in our minds than the splendour of the sun shining upon blind eyes, or a voice sounding in deaf ears. There, I make such a division between Spirit and sacraments that the power to act rests with the former, and the ministry alone is left to the latter – a ministry empty and trifling, apart from the action of the Spirit, but charged with great effect when the Spirit works within and manifests his power.[102]

The Father feeds his adopted sons and daughters in the energy of the Spirit by the hand of his Son, who is both host of the meal and the meal itself. And so the meal has been aptly named a 'eucharist' (from *eucharisteō*, or 'giving thanks').[103]

The eucharist (or Lord's Supper, or communion),[104] then, is a feast, something that is easily forgotten. This feast is the central edifying rite of the church. But it is a strange feast. Consider that it holds together the sweetness of table fellowship and the bitterness of death. Indeed, the centre of fellowship is the Lamb who was slain (Rev. 19.7); and we fellowship with him and one another by feeding on his body and blood. The charge of cannibalism levelled against the first Christians missed the point, but not entirely; it certainly captured the sheer shock that one must know in encountering a God who sustains his people in life by giving them himself.

Of course, there is a certain precedent to this in the life of the people of God. After redeeming them from slavery in Egypt, the Lord fed them in the wilderness through the daily provision of the manna and quail (see esp. Deut. 8.3; Ps. 105.40). Israel knew the Lord as one whose goodness they could 'taste and see' (Ps. 34.8). He is the one who 'prepare[s] a table before me in the presence of my enemies' (Ps. 23.5). Table fellowship was a practice of hospitality, friendship and reconciliation. And God could speak through the prophets of his covenant faithfulness to Israel, his utter commitment to securing her welfare, in surprisingly evocative terms. Jesus 'came eating and drinking' with the unlikeliest of companions, displaying the surprising generosity of God and prompting his critics to exclaim, 'Look, a glutton and a drunkard, a friend of tax collectors and sinners!' (Mt. 11.19; Lk. 7.34) It is fitting, then, that Jesus compares the kingdom of heaven to a royal wedding banquet filled with guests off the streets, 'both good and bad' (Mt. 22.10; also see Lk. 14.16–24).[105] Indeed, all of creation is groaning for the day when the Lamb and his bride sit down to their marriage feast (Rev. 19.7–9), a day when 'the Lord of hosts will make for all peoples a feast of rich food' and his people will proclaim, 'This is the Lord for whom we have waited; let us be glad and rejoice in his salvation' (Isa. 25.6, 9). It is to all of this that the eucharist points.

The eucharist is a tensed action, living equally from the past, present and future. We will examine briefly these three temporal angles in order better to understand what happens at the Lord's table.

We remember his death. As he celebrated his last meal with his disciples at the Passover feast, Jesus enjoined them to continue the breaking of bread and drinking of wine 'in remembrance of me' (Lk. 22.19; 1 Cor. 11.25). This remembrance, or *anamnesis*, occurs as the Spirit brings the suffering and death of Jesus and its benefits into the present. In this, the Spirit of truth glorifies Jesus, by taking what is his and declaring it to us in the church (Jn 16.14). And so it is no mere calling to mind. Or rather, in our being reminded of the sacrifice of Christ we are caught up again liturgically and spiritually in the events surrounding his death. Remembering here involves a kind of dramatic inclusion, grounded in our spiritual union with Christ in the church.[106] At the Passover meal to this day, 'each one is required to regard himself or herself as though he or she had come out of Egypt'.[107] God's deliverance in the exodus happened to *us*, not merely to *them*. Similarly, in remembering his death we rejoice in our exodus from bondage to sin, death and the devil in the death of Jesus. But even as we rejoice, we repent. 'Were you there when they crucified my Lord?' the spiritual asks. At the Lord's Supper, we confess, 'Yes, we were. And it is *us*, it is *I* who crucified him. It was my sin that made the glorious victory of the cross necessary'. At the Lord's table, we know ourselves admitted to fellowship, yes, but always admitted on the basis of a costly grace. Lest we worry that there be no room for such as us at the table, though, the gospels are at pains to underscore Jesus' unconditional gift of fellowship to his betrayer (Judas) and to his deserters (the rest of the disciples) and deniers (Peter).[108] It is these toward whom Jesus takes on the role of slave of all, washing their feet and calling them, in turn, to wash one another's feet.[109]

As a brief aside, consider the heated polemic surrounding the relation of past and present in the eucharist and the question of eucharistic sacrifice. Roman Catholic descriptions of the eucharistic sacrifice suggest to many Protestants a continuation or repetition of Christ's 'single sacrifice for sins' 'once and for all', after which he 'sat down at the right hand of God' (Heb. 10.10–14), where he 'always lives to make intercession' for his people (Heb. 7.25). In fact, the very thing that sets Jesus apart from other high priests is that 'he has no need to offer sacrifices day after day, first for his own sins, and then for those of the people; this he did once for all when he offered himself' (Heb. 7.27). Does the language of eucharistic sacrifice tarnish the death of Jesus? In a careful study of the issues at stake, George Hunsinger suggests the key issue for Rome seems to be whether the sacrifice of Christ is effectively made present in the eucharist. He proposes an ecumenically palatable thesis in response: 'The eucharist brought Christ's sacrifice into the present, while the cross remained its dimension of depth. Although the eucharist added nothing to the perfection of Christ's saving work, the perfection of his work was present and effectual in the eucharist'.[110] If we are to speak of Christ 'continuing' his sacrifice in the eucharist, it is 'only in the sense of supplying it with ever new actualizations and forms'.[111] In the eucharist, we hear God's promise that Christ is Christ *for us* (*pro nobis*).[112] The eucharist is not a repetition nor a *mere* remembrance of Christ's death.[113] Rather, 'the same gift is offered to us again – not in the sense that the gift itself is repeated, which is neither necessary nor possible, but in the sense that it is really extended *to us*'. And so 'this remembrance of him is the means by which he makes us sharers in what he is and has done for us'.[114] This remembrance prompts us to offer our own sacrifice, the sacrifice of praise and thanksgiving. It is not just ours; in setting apart the bread and wine for the purpose of worship, the church incorporates all of creation in its offering of praise to God in Christ. We voice creation's praise and call creation to praise even as we join its praise (see Ps. 98, 148).[115]

Second, *we proclaim his resurrection.* The eucharist is no mere commemoration of a dead founder; it is the proclamation of the crucified *and risen* Lord. We cannot remember his death aright without rejoicing in him as the one death could not hold. This is the heart of the gospel. Paul puts it this way: 'if Christ has not been raised, then our proclamation has been in vain and your faith has been in vain. . . . But in fact Christ has been raised from the dead, the first fruits of those who have died. . . . [A]ll will be made alive in Christ. But each in his own order: Christ the first fruits, then at his coming those who belong to Christ' (1 Cor. 15.14, 20, 22–23). The proclamation of Christ's resurrection looks backwards (signalling his vindication and revelation as the Son of God) and forwards (as the beginning of the eschatological harvest).

The crucified one risen from the dead reigns in our midst as Lord. But what do we mean when we say that Christ is here, that he is *present* in the eucharist? Traditional language speaks of Christ's 'real presence', but does that not already assume too much? And if he is *really* present in the eucharist, is he less so in the rest of the church's life? Why limit his real presence to such a small slice of space and time? The trick is sufficiently to account for both *real* and *local* presence.[116] Eastern Orthodox, Roman Catholic, Anglican, Lutheran and Reformed Christians all proclaim the *real* presence of Christ in the eucharist. Even those traditions (Baptists, to take one example) that deny a technical presence are eager to affirm that 'where two or three are gathered in my name, I am there among them' (Mt. 18.20).

The point affirmed by the former group (with the possible exception of the Reformed) is that Christ is *physically* present, but even here quick qualifiers sprout up. His physical presence takes on sacramental form and is only discernible to the eyes of faith. He is not physically present to us the way we are physically present to one another, in other words. So why insist on a real (physical) presence at all? In part, this is a way to articulate the unique form of Christ's presence in the eucharist. He so saturates the bread and wine to the point that they become identified with him. This is an appropriate liturgical application of the incarnation. Just as the eternal Son took on flesh for our sake, so the risen and ascended Christ gives himself in and through the elements.

Even if he declines to identify the elements as the body and blood of Christ, Calvin makes a similar point, emphasizing the fittingness (or 'aptitude') of the signs and the confirmation they offer of our feeding on the flesh of Christ.[117] But they also all affirm his ascension and glorification at the right hand of the Father, where he 'always lives to make intercession for them' (Heb. 7.25). If we are not to theorize Christ's humanity out of existence (and invite a host of heresies to take its place), we have to describe how this man can remain what he is – fully human, body and soul – while also commune with us *in the flesh* as we gather at his table. Calvin turns to pneumatology. It is not that the elements become the body and blood of Christ, or that his body and blood are hidden in, with and under the elements (the Roman Catholic and Lutheran alternatives); in fact, God's action in the eucharist is not one of descent but ascent. It is not so much that Christ descends to us at the Supper, but that the Spirit lifts us up to him.[118] We are presented to him even more than he to us, and the feast takes place where Christ is, seated at the right hand of God (Col. 3.1). This is not to dismiss the language of condescension, and it is right to pray for Christ to be present among us at his table. But it is to enlist the language of con[as]sumption, attending to the Spirit's work in lifting us up to Christ.[119]

Finally, *we await his coming in glory.* Paul writes that 'as often as you eat this bread and drink the cup, you proclaim the Lord's death until he comes' (1 Cor. 11.26). Because the return of Christ serves as a backdrop to the Lord's Supper and marks its *terminus ad quem*, it is not enough simply to say the feast takes place at the right hand of God. It also takes place on earth. In it we receive a 'taste of the kingdom'. But note: 'To taste is to try the relish; and to say that the eucharist provides a taste of the kingdom therefore allows us to express both the provisionality and yet the genuineness of the kingdom as it flavours the present'.[120] In the mean time, the church prays for the kingdom's coming. She awaits the marriage supper of the Lamb and busies herself as a bride making herself ready for her wedding (Rev. 19.7–8).

Still, for all we rejoice in the promise of his coming, we also know this promise as threat. For God's coming to his people always means judgment. Paul follows his reminder of the Lord's coming with a warning:

> Examine yourselves, and only then eat of the bread and drink of the cup. For all who eat and drink without discerning the body, eat and drink judgment against themselves. For this reason many of you are weak and ill, and some have died. . . . So then, my brothers and sisters, when you come together to eat, wait for one another. If you are hungry, eat at home, so that when you come together, it will not be for your condemnation. (1 Cor. 11.28–30)

Already, the Corinthians had relapsed into a church divided into rich and poor. The poor were excluded in some way from the community meal that was joined to the eucharist. It may be that the working poor arrived too late to partake of the best food, or that they were seated at the worst places. In any case, the rich Corinthians ate better than the poor at their communal meal, making a mockery of the Lord's Supper and failing to 'discern the body'.[121] Could it really be claimed that 'we who are many are one body, for we all partake of one bread' when the rich were the only ones feasting?

Fellowship with Christ in the church around the Lord's table (gathering together the threefold reference to Christ's body in historical, ecclesial and sacramental form) just *is* to live as one and hold all in common. The great exchange in which Christ's riches become ours and our poverty his leads to another exchange in which we bear one another's burdens, rejoicing with those who rejoice and weeping with those who weep. 'The Lord's Supper was originally used as a destratifying tool by Paul. He wanted less hierarchy and pecking order, and more equality amongst the participants'.[122] Or, in the charged prose of William Cavanaugh,

> The Eucharist is the promise and demand that the church enact the true body of Christ now, in time. Worldly kingdoms have

declared the Kingdom of God indefinitely deferred, and the poor are told to suffer their lot quietly and invisibly. In the Eucharist the poor are invited now to come and to feast in the Kingdom. The Eucharist must not be a scandal to the poor. It demands real reconciliation of oppressed and oppressor, tortured and torturer. Barring reconciliation, Eucharist demands judgment.[123]

Judgment does not mean aimless destruction, though, for when the Lord comes to judge he brings justice and rights wrongs. Judgment is cause for rejoicing.[124] The traditional liturgical ordering of the preaching of the gospel, followed by the passing of the peace, followed by the eucharist carves space for the church to hear the gospel of judgment and grace, enact reconciliation in the peace and then come joyfully, and forgiven, to the table to receive nourishment for the journey. It is precisely this fellowship of forgiven and reconciled sinners, fed by Christ on the way to the kingdom, which the Father offers to the world as a sign and foretaste of the kingdom. And it is right to conclude our discussion of the Lord's Supper with this joyful vision, one pointing forward to the last day and a final feast:

On this mountain the Lord of hosts will make for all peoples a feast of rich food, a feast of well-aged wines, of rich food filled with marrow, of well-aged wines strained clear. And he will destroy on this mountain the shroud that is cast over all peoples, the sheet that is spread over all nations; he will swallow up death forever. Then the Lord God will wipe away the tears from all faces, and the disgrace of his people he will take away from all the earth, for the Lord has spoken. It will be said on that day, Lo, this is our God; we have waited for him, so that he might save us. This is the Lord for whom we have waited; let us be glad and rejoice in his salvation. (Isa. 25.6–9)

We often think of the Bible and the core practices of the church as things that come between us and God. Relinquishing the hope of meeting with God personally, we settle for devices that help bring him to mind from time to time. We turn to the means of grace as pious pick-me-ups, being happy to find a bit of bread and water to sustain us in the world. But the means of grace have not been appointed by God as buffers to come between Christ and his church; no, they are avenues along which the Spirit travels, uniting us to

Christ, building us up and sending us out into the world to love and serve the Lord.

There is an ongoing debate over who can administer the means of grace in the church, particularly baptism and the eucharist. In turning to consider the issue of women in ministry, we continue, then, to ask about the nature and, perhaps, the limits of mediation in the church.

EXCURSUS: WOMEN IN MINISTRY

As we finish writing this book, Pope Benedict has just issued an apostolic constitution granting a special dispensation for conservative Anglican groups to re-enter communion with the Roman Catholic Church. The Pope's invitation coincides with the Anglican Communion's attempt to address the divisive question of homosexual ordination. In an editorial written only days after Benedict's announcement, George Weigel traces the Anglican tensions to the debate that preceded homosexual ordination, women's ordination. He explains:

> By the end of the [Catholic-Anglican] exchange, in 1986, a parting of the ways had been reached: the highest authorities of the Catholic Church believed that apostolic tradition, not misogyny, precluded ordination to the priesthood, which Catholics understood in iconographic terms as a sacramental representation of the priesthood of Jesus Christ. Archbishop Runcie and those whom he represented believed that contemporary human insights into gender roles trumped apostolic tradition and necessitated a development of both doctrine and practice. Rome could not accept that as a legitimate development of Christian self-understanding. Catholic authorities also feared that this approach to the authority of tradition would inevitably lead to an Anglican re-conception of the moral law on a host of issues, including the morality of homosexual acts. That, too, happened, fracturing the Anglican Communion in the process.[125]

While Weigel uses the ecumenical event to take a jab at Anglican development (solely faulting Anglicans for ending dialogue because they were the ones who ordained women), we have chosen to begin this excursus by recounting this recent news item because the story neatly encapsulates most of the factors entailed in the question of women's ordination.[126] First, the matter inevitably challenges the church's tradition, going back to apostolic tradition itself. Thus, Weigel suggests that Anglicans 'trumped apostolic tradition' (including scripture) with contemporary gender theory – an accusation which assumes the traditional reading of gender roles was an objective and culturally neutral hermeneutic. Second, the question is most often framed in such a way as to claim an inescapable correlation between the ordination of women and the ordination of homosexuals. Witness Weigel's not-so-subtle claim to Catholicism's prophetic foresight at the time Anglicans approved of women's ordination, which predicted the slippery slope into a 're-conception' of homosexuality's moral value. After the following historical survey of women's ministerial roles, we intend to return to these two questions: what is the relationship between women's ordination and scripture and tradition? And then, what is the relationship between women's ordination and homosexual ordination?

In order to answer these questions better, we will explore the history of women in ministry in general and the matter of women's ordination in particular, especially relying on the work of Ruth Tucker and Walter Liefield in *Daughters of the Church: Women and Ministry from New Testament Times to the Present.*[127] Their study provides both a comprehensive survey and a balanced analysis. As historians who aim to present an 'open centrist perspective', these authors aid the discussion in that they attempt to transcend the conservative/liberal dichotomy.[128] Moreover, while the secondary literature on women and Christianity is now bountiful, Tucker and Liefield's work focuses on women in ministry, which includes but is not limited to women's ordination.[129]

Against the traditional, androcentric interpretation of much of the early Christian witness to women's ministerial roles – which explains them either as subordinate to the three-fold orders of bishops, priests and deacons or as wives of bishops, wives of presbyters and wives of deacons – Karen Jo Torjesen contends for a re-reading of the material with an aim to uncover suppressed clerical roles for women.[130] Torjesen offers a shift in paradigm: because first century Christians met in house churches, and because the *oikos/domus* was considered 'private' space in the Graeco-Roman era, and because women retained the ability to share in the various roles of 'private' spaces in this era, women functioned as house-church leaders; only later does the church manoeuvre into the 'public' space wherein women are barred and therefore can no longer take up leadership roles. Once this is evident, we can see the numerous references to women connected to households as leaders of house churches.[131] While this first century practice disappears in the second and third century, the practice itself could not have disappeared overnight. Thus, Torjesen finds evidence for the survival of this practice in three forms: (1) ancient frescos of women presiding at a liturgical meal/ eucharist; (2) injunctions against the ordination of women by the church fathers, which suggest the practice continued and thus needed to be suppressed and (3) epigraphic statements, mostly on funeral steles, that refer to '*episcopa*' and '*presbytera*'.

Not everyone accepts Torjesen's reconstruction of women's ministries in early Christianity, as seen in Valerie A. Karras' response.[132] Karras finds that each of the three forms of evidence for women's ordination to the sacramental orders to be scanty and unconvincing. The possible exception to this is *presbytides* (fem. 'presbyters'/ priests), but this is found in few sources (Epiphanius' *Panarion*, the *Testamentum Domini*, and the Council of Laodicea can.11). Karras, however, believes these are in essence, if not in name, honoured widows, which may reflect an earlier period in which 'presbyters' – be they male or female – performed jurisdictional oversight but never sacramental celebration.[133] When the presbyterate developed so as to include sacramental functions, the priesthood constricted to a male-only office.

Karras admits that she has not addressed Torjesen's primary hypothesis, the eclipse of the common occurrence of women's leadership in first-century private sphere house churches, but has only analysed the evidence from successive centuries which sporadically allude to 'priestesses' and female 'bishops'.[134] As with so much of historical analysis, the central question is not so much one of facts that 'prove' one position or another – it must be admitted by both sides that the historical data is insufficient. Instead, the historian begins with a set of hermeneutical assumptions and interprets the data accordingly.[135] A reference in the New Testament texts to women associated with house churches could imply either wealthy matrons who support the male clergy or female 'overseers' who performed all of the functions entailed in that role. Similarly, epigrammatic references to *episcopa* and *presbytera* could indicate either the wife of a bishop and presbyter or a female bishop and female presbyter.

The debate centres around the most appropriate hermeneutic for the early Christian context.

When turning to late antiquity and medieval Christian customs, the question of women's ordination usually disappears from scholarly discourse. Women were not ordained, but instead assumed clearly defined roles in the life of the church, as wives or nuns. Because women's roles were so narrowly defined, one could easily dismiss the 'dark ages' as irrelevant to the question of women's ministry. Such an oversimplification, however, would miss the unique ways in which women transcended their gender roles and provided service to church and society.[136] First of all, the medieval church did in fact ordain women, according to Gary Macy.[137] Macy's examples of 'ordination', however, which predominantly refer to nuns, abbotesses and deaconesses, never include the bestowal of sacramental powers, and so the question remains one of which roles women can assume. Yet, even within certain confined roles, women contributed to the ministry and even leadership of the church throughout the middle ages.

One prominent category of women's ministry during the middle ages is monasticism. Ascetic Christianity dates back to the earliest Christian centuries, and scholars have understood this phenomenon in terms of the liberation of women from the cultural gender roles of wife and mother.[138] As monasticism developed and formalized women were both offered avenues of ministry and confined to certain forms of ministry. First, one must acknowledge the diversity of thought and practice in the middle ages: while women may have been treated especially harshly in one expression of the church, other regions and tradition allowed more freedom to women. Christina Harrington cites the example of the Irish church, in which saintly women were so prestigious one pious account went so far as to claim a woman's ordination to the episcopacy.[139] Even in a context where women's docility and subordination was emphasized, women perennially found channels through which to contribute to the life and even the rituals of the church.[140] There are even the stunning instances of women leading the church and the Christian kingdoms, such as Catherine of Sienna and Joan of Arc.[141] While women played numerous and prominent roles in the life of the medieval church, women's ordination and full sacramental participation will be the explicit debate of the modern church.[142]

In 1851 when Antoinette Brown was licensed to preach and ordained by the Congregationalist Church, all the debates involved in the women's rights movement, abolitionism, revivalism and frontierism were certainly at play. But along with the socio-cultural dynamics, many Christians in the new world began challenging the prohibition of women from public ministry and formal ordination. One notable tendency, spanning from the earlier Anabaptist movements through the denominational splinter groups of the holiness movement, is the prominent role of women in those groups with reduced emphasis on hierarchy and authority, such as Quakers, Free Will Baptists and various Wesleyan denominations. Churches emphasizing the call to ministry and the Spirit's leading were generally more accepting of women in preaching and pastoral roles. The mainline denominations, however, with their clearly defined offices and centralized authority, remained resistant to women in public ministry – a stance not altered until the twentieth century.

While exceptions can be found, such as the American Baptists' acceptance of women's ordination in the nineteenth century, the mainline Protestant denominations moved toward a positive stance of women in office in the middle of the last century. As mentioned above, Wesleyans had valued lay-preachers from the beginning of their tradition, which included at times women lay preachers. Yet not until 1956 did the Methodist Church (soon to be known as 'United' Methodist) approve the formal ordination of women. The Presbyterian Church (USA) by this time had already, since 1929, declared women could be ordained ruling elders, and then in 1956 Presbyterian women received equal status in all areas of the church. Lutherans in Europe were approving women's ordination by the 1960s, and a number of major branches of Lutheranism in the United States soon followed suit. Anglicans since 1889 recognized women as deaconesses (though this was an ill-defined office until 1985). The Episcopal Church, USA, approved the ordination of women into the priesthood in 1976.

These formal stances on women's ordination do not, of course, tell the full story of women's ministry. In the modern era women played prominent roles in many of the new expressions of ministry normally deemed 'parachurch'. Women were often at the forefront of charitable societies and socially active organizations. Similarly, women participated in the modern missions movement both through raising support and serving as missionaries. Women were also prominent in Pentecostal and charismatic movements. On the other hand, for every instance where women's ministry and women's ordination gained acceptance there were many other instances of opposition, one of the most prominent being the Vatican's 1977 'Declaration on the Question of the Admission of Women to the Ministerial Priesthood'.

While the issue of women's ordination is divisive to many Christian traditions, and while we do not claim to have solved the question for any other Christian group, let us at least pause to draw some conclusions about women's roles in the church. First, we can quickly affirm – though this is a point that might be overlooked – that Christians from anywhere on the theological spectrum can support women's ministry, even if they have theological objections to women's ordination. Given the overall biblical and historical material that promotes women in ministry, any generalized statement denying the capacity and calling of women to minister in God's church is patently unbiblical and suspect of being shaped more by cultural patriarchy than biblical hermeneutics. On the other hand, the matter of ordaining women is more problematic and requires additional theological analysis.

Women's ordination is clearly not found in scripture. Although this seems like a case-closed kind of statement, it must alternatively be admitted that several arguments could still be given for ordaining women. First, men's ordination is not clearly found in scripture either – although there are cases of 'laying on of hands'. The whole matter of 'ordination' is ill-defined, if not absent, in the New Testament. Historically, it is more plausible to understand the first century Christian 'offices' in terms of their functions and roles, with these 'offices' gradually becoming more solidified in the second and third centuries. If women found the freedom to perform many, if not all, of the ecclesial functions in the first century, why could they not retain – or reclaim – that freedom in the twenty-first century? Another line of argument is to admit that women's ordination is not found in scripture but also to insist that scripture's trajectory is toward egalitarianism. William Webb, for example, argues for a 'redemptive movement' in scripture.[143] While scripture's surface level endorses slavery, its theological momentum pushes the believer to reject slavery ultimately. Likewise, traditional women's roles are endorsed on the surface level of scripture, but women's liberation is promoted by scripture's counter-cultural message about the theological equality of women. Thirdly, and most importantly for our current discussion, the argument can be made that the ordination of women is not so much a biblical question as it is an ecclesiological question.

To admit scripture's ambiguity toward the ordination of women is to shift the debate from a strictly biblical framework to an ecclesial framework. In other words, when scripture is ambiguous, who decides the proper interpretation and application? Does the hermeneutical authority reside at the (a) individual, (b) congregational, (c) denominational or (d) universal level? The question of slavery posed this problem over a century ago, with many claiming that slavery was a biblically defensible practice while others found it to be unbiblical. The debate in effect shifted to an ecclesiological plane – Who decides the church's reading of the Bible? – with denominations forming to support one side or the other. One can validly, therefore, frame the debate about women's ordination in ecclesiological, rather than biblical, terms. Of course in doing so, it must also be admitted that the question of homosexuality can make the same manoeuvre. On the ecclesiological level, if not the biblical hermeneutical level, the question of women's ordination and homosexual ordination are homologous.[144] Thus, every mainline denomination that has previously ordained women is now debating the validity of ordaining homosexuals; the debate, although dependent upon biblical questions, is primarily an ecclesiological matter concerning the locus of hermeneutical authority in answering biblical questions. In turning now to outlining the possibilities for the current debate, we then breach the boundaries of what is strictly the matter of women's ordination: women's ordination in a sense becomes a case study for any ecclesiological dispute.

The possibilities available to the church when facing the question of women's ordination are four-fold:

1. *Top-down enforcement.* This is Constantinianism, with those 'in authority' imposing doctrinal standards on those 'under authority'. In post-Christendom this option is veritably unavailable to the church, and any attempt to enforce conformity through legal or political means must be recognized as a Constantinian stance.

2. *Top-down sectarianism.* This in practice is denominationalism, although it predates the modern denominational movement in scenes such as East-West schism. Even if the first option – enforcement – is dismissed as impractical or undesirable, a theological difference can still be seen as barring communion, and excommunication of other churches/groups can be invoked.

3. *Bottom-up cooperation.* This in its past forms would be known as conciliarism, and it entails a voluntary submission to the wider Christian community without claiming the ability to excommunicate any person (or church) outside of one's own congregation.

4. *Bottom-up non-conformity.* This last option is usually (and derogatorily) deemed provincialism, parochialism. When a church or Christian collective refuses to conform to the wider Christian community, it claims its autonomy and acts unilaterally.

While we do not mean to capitalize unfairly upon the current Anglican dispute over homosexuality, the debate seen across the worldwide Anglican fellowship helpfully illustrates these four options.[145]

Recently, the Episcopal Church, USA, it must be admitted, has taken option four, over and against some of the more conservative Anglican churches, such as the Church of Nigeria, which is currently pressing for option two. The Archbishop of Canterbury hopes to hold both parties together, an appeal to option three.

Likewise, in the wider ecumenical debate about the ordination of women, there are those who claim that the ecumenical and apostolic consensus clearly opposes women's ordination and any churches who contradict this consensus must be excommunicated – option two. In response, it must be admitted: any churches which ordain women are in fact embracing the fourth option.

Thirdly, those who hope to transcend this divide contend that women's ordination is a nonessential which should not bar communication since so many of the essential elements of the faith unite both parties, which is to assume option three. Finally, there would be cases when option one is invoked, such as when a church's property is reclaimed by a denomination, or when members within a congregation sue the church in a secular court over the matter. Thus far, we have defined and illustrated these options. But can we not say more, theologically, about each of the four?

While our above portrayal may lead the reader to think that we are dismissing options one and four as untenable, we wish to qualify our stance. First, it must be admitted that option one is foreign to Christian thinking since it embraces a stance of 'lording authority over' others, and option four smacks of unChristlike stubbornness and unChristian resistance to cooperation. Nevertheless, we believe both options one and four are in fact theologically justifiable. Analogies could be found in just war theory and in theories of civil disobedience.

To borrow from theological discourse on politics and society, there is a long tradition of just war theory which claims that war is always undesirable and yet at times is justifiable. During World War II, Karl Barth opposed theological pacifists because, he insisted, God is free, and therefore free to condone war. Barth then proceeded to clarify that war is to be avoided unless one claims to have spiritual discernment in which God has in fact chosen to go to war, such as in Old Testament times. John Howard Yoder responded to Barth's views first by defending his theological analysis, but second by critiquing his practical application.[146] Yes, God is free to go to war, but how does Barth know that the allies in World War II are in fact carrying out a divine mission? To draw an analogy to our current ecclesiological dilemma, we suggest that Constantinian enforcement of doctrine and practice is justifiable. We most vehemently insist, however, that for one to claim such a stance is to claim a spiritual discernment into an extraordinary event.

As for the justification of non-conformity, we find that this stance can also be theologically valid, if seen as analogous to civil disobedience. Martin Luther King, Jr., most famously championed the theological stance which insists on the righteousness of obeying God over human institutions – another ancient and venerable tradition of Christianity. When asked why the black church cannot wait for the legal system to address racial discrimination, King responded by defending civil disobedience in Christian terms: an unjust law is no law at all.[147] The same can be said about anyone claiming theological validity when dissenting from an ecumenical consensus: an unrighteous tradition is an unauthoritative tradition. As with the theological justification of Constantinianism, we confess the possibility of righteous dissent from an ecumenical consensus or a traditional norm, while we simultaneously caution those who would take this route because it is a claim be a prophetic voice in extraordinary circumstances.

To return to the second and third options, these tend to be – but not necessarily are – polarized along hierarchical and free church lines. The theological defence of either of these options, therefore, becomes a theological defence of either ecclesiology from above or ecclesiology from below, which carries us back to other areas that do not further the current discussion about women's ordination nor provide ways forward in the debate. We do, however, underscore the fact that the two approaches, when meeting in the middle, are virtually indistinguishable. To paint in broad strokes, top-down sectarianism emphasizes the need for churches to submit to the higher authority, while the bottom-up conciliarism emphasizes the need for the submission to be voluntary. Both draw boundaries, and both value cooperation.

To recap, when placed in ecclesiological terms, the question about ordaining women (and *mutatis mutandis* other questions) only allows four possible answers. To take them in the reverse order given above, it must be admitted that any church ordaining women is doing so against the ecumenical and traditional consensus, but it must also be admitted that said church may be a prophetic voice of dissent. Next, churches have the option to submit voluntarily to an ecumenical consensus, and this could involve either egalitarians ceasing to practice women's ordination or complementarians agreeing to tolerate it; both approaches would fall under a conciliarist ideal. Many, however, believe the matter of women's ordination to be of such doctrinal significance that they must break fellowship with the opposing party, and they could either frame the division in terms of heresy ('we are Christian and you are not') or schism ('we are both Christian, but our stances are incompatible'). Finally, it must also be admitted that doctrinal enforcement is possibly a theologically justifiable action. Examples could include the seizure of church property from a congregation that ordains a woman without proper authorization or the installation of a female minister against the wishes of a congregation. Yet, it must also be emphasized that such doctrinal enforcement is an exceptional claim to divine intervention and should be employed with great caution.

While we have not solved this debate in any practical way, we do hope that we have clarified the *status questionis* in ecclesiological terms. We grieve the way in which women's ordination has caused division in the church, and yet we simultaneously grieve the many women (and men) who have been emotionally and spiritually injured in this debate. All sides will surely agree to join in mutual prayer and repentance for wrongs done in the past, while continuing to seek divine wisdom, Christ-like humility and spiritual discernment when addressing this matter in the future.

MEDIATION, AFTER ALL

What, then, of the concept of mediation? We have taken a long, indirect route to this topic, prompting a plausible suspicion on the part of readers that this chapter's title is more useful for its alliteration than its material bearing on our discussion. If we have used a strategy of indirection, though, it is due to our conviction that a concept of mediation arises through attending to God's ways with and in the church. Rather than foist an abstractly generated problematic onto the church, we have begun instead by following the church's own witness to the risen Christ and the sanctifying Spirit in her midst. Even more, we have followed the self-witness of Christ or, to put the same point differently, the Spirit's witness to Christ as he leads and guides us into the one who is the way, truth and life.

Rather than defining mediation and requiring ecclesiology to catch up to our terms, we have been implicitly asking after mediation by listening to and looking at the words and deeds of Christ and his church, to their modes of action, reaction and interaction. What, then, can we conclude about the church's mediation of the presence and work of the triune God?

Let us begin by suggesting what mediation *cannot* mean. First, it cannot mean the church's replacement of Christ. 'For there is one God', Paul told Timothy, 'there is also one mediator between God and humankind, Christ Jesus, himself human' (1 Tim. 2.5). Jesus *is* (not merely *was*) the one mediator, while Paul was 'a herald and an apostle . . . a teacher' (1 Tim. 2.7).

Christ is not only the mediator between God and humankind; he is the mediator between and among humans. 'For he is our peace; in his flesh he has made both groups into one and broken down the dividing wall, that is, the hostility between us' (Eph. 2.14). It is in him that we have peaceful access to one another, even as it is in him that we have peaceful access to God. This extends to the *communio sanctorum* across time as well as space.[148] Robert Jenson acknowledges as much, performing a wise reversal: 'The saints are not our way to Christ; he is our way to them. . . . We may not ask Mary to bring us to Christ; because we are one with Christ we can address Mary'.[149] In other words, mediation does not, need not and cannot imply a distancing of Christ.

At the height of his quarrel with Rome, Luther wrote a letter to Pope Leo X, taking issue with the description of the pope as 'vicar of Christ':

> See how different Christ is from his successors, although they all would wish to be his vicars. I fear that most of them have been too literally his vicars. A man is a vicar only when his superior is absent. If the pope rules, while Christ is absent and does not dwell in his heart, what else is he but a vicar of Christ? What is the church under such a vicar but a mass of people without Christ? Indeed, what is such a vicar but an antichrist and an idol? How much more properly did the apostles call themselves servants of the present Christ and not vicars of an absent Christ?[150]

The church becomes, in Luther's sharp words, the vicar of an absent Christ rather than the servant of a present Christ. Whatever else mediation might suggest, it must be a ministerial rather than magisterial concept – a prioritization John Paul II affirmed in his reclaiming the title 'servant of the servants'. The church's office is to serve the reign of Christ in the world, not to assert herself as ruler over others. All ecclesial mediation is secondary and derivative.[151] To call the church an 'extension' of the incarnation could be a softened form of the error of replacing Christ with the church, one that neglects the doctrine of the ascension and Christ's abiding work as prophet, priest and king.[152] Webster calls for

> an apophatic account of mediation [which] draws attention, not so much to creaturely incapacity as to the utter capacity of God's self-communicative presence in Christ and Spirit, thereby entirely reorienting the task of creaturely witness. Apophatic mediation is at heart *indicative*, the mediating reality – object, activity, person, word – does not replace or embody or even 'represent' that which is mediated, but is as it were an empty space in which that which is mediated is left free to be and act.[153]

None of this suggests that churchly mediation is an inherently incoherent or illegitimate concept. While Christ is the 'one mediator between God and humankind', Paul can speak in the same passage, as we have seen, of other forms of mediation (like intercession) proper to the church (1 Tim. 2.1, 8). Still, we pray and worship – indeed, we *live* – in Christ by the Spirit's power.[154] Every word spoken and deed done in the church is founded on, funded by and enfolded in Christ's mediation as the God-man, the one in whom God and humanity (and warring humans) have been reconciled and restored to fellowship with one another. A proper account of ecclesial mediation must be able to retain the dialectic between (i) the ontological difference between Christ and the church and (ii) the mystical union of Christ with the church. In light of our union with Christ, we can add to Webster's remark a call for a (properly constrained) cataphatic account of mediation.

Luther's robust articulation of the priesthood of all believers emphasized the immediacy of the Christian to God in the face of the thick ecclesial mediation of the medieval church. Mis-appropriations of the priesthood of all believers, coupled with an ascendant individualism in modernity, are complicit in a tendency to marginalize the church in the Christian life. But for Luther, the universal priesthood also involved the Christian's permission and responsibility to come before the Father in the name of Jesus to pray for the church and the world.[155] So individuals do engage in priestly action, but only and ever as part of the church's universal priesthood which itself is oriented to the sole priesthood of Christ.

It may help to compare two texts. One comes from (Pseudo-)Dionysius the Areopagite, who lambasts one who 'could imagine himself capable of disdaining the mediation of the saints and of entering into direct relationship with the divinity'.[156] Indeed, Dionysius can speak of 'the inability of the objects of his providential care to communicate directly with him'.[157] On the other hand, take Heb. 10:

> Therefore, brothers, since we have confidence to enter the holy places by the blood of Jesus, by the new and living way that he opened for us through the curtain, that is, through his flesh, and since we have a great priest over the house of God, let us draw near with a true heart in full assurance of faith, with our hearts sprinkled clean from an evil conscience and our bodies washed with pure water.[158]

Over-attending to ecclesial mediation can lead to the dilution of the mediation of Christ so as to simultaneously de-centre Jesus and distance the triune God to whom we have been invited to draw near. While the mediation of Christ need not be in competition with other, derivative forms of mediation, that they are *derivative* and thus thoroughly *secondary* is of vital importance. As secondary, these forms of mediation must ever be seen as servants of Christ. The abiding danger is that discussion of these secondary mediations will outstrip that of the mediation of Christ, leading to a *de facto* marginalization of Christ's mediation and, in the process, of the abiding significance of his humanity as our great high priest, ascended to the right hand of the Father.[159] In other words, we can be so busy in talking about the church that we forget to do things like invoke the Spirit or pray, 'Maranatha! Come, Lord Jesus!'[160]

Throughout the doctrine of the church, above all in a consideration of ecclesial mediation, it is vital to keep a Christocentric focus and trinitarian shape while also speaking maximally of the reality of the church. If it is an ungrateful error to deflate ecclesiology in the name of Christ, it is a profligate error to inflate ecclesiology in the name of Christ. We will not avoid idolatry by saying less of the church generally (though in certain cases this may be called for), but neither do the incarnation of Christ and descent of the Spirit warrant an ever-expanding ecclesiology. If the former posture is a form of ecclesiological sloth, the latter is a form of ecclesiological pride.

In the concluding chapter, we will find that what is true of ecclesial mediation – its Christocentric focus, Trinitarian shape and attention to the reality of the church – is true of mission. In fact, it may well be that it is the mission of the church, with its orientation to the kingdom of God in the world, that equips the church to speak and think appropriately of itself.

CHAPTER 4

MISSION

A DIRTY WORD

To many in the West, 'mission' is a dirty word. And not without reason. Consider the history of the church, which to a certain extent can be told by recounting the abuses suffered by people in the name of the church's mission. Pick an era: sanctioned coercion of Donatists in the fifth century, the Crusades spanning the eleventh through thirteenth centuries, the wars of religion in the seventeenth century, the colonialism in the later half of the millennium, the anti-Judaism of nearly any era.

Much of contemporary Western distaste for the church can be traced to clumsy, naïve, self-serving and manipulative attempts at missionary engagement in the world. These range from the innocuous and laughable to the insidious and lethal. On the one hand there are the culturally out-of-step attempts at relevance, the funny infection of a pulpit with 15-year-old buzzwords. More seriously, we hear of cultural intimidation and decimation in the name of Jesus, of the gospel being whored out to global interests. There is even news of killing for Christ's sake.

Scarred and embarrassed by such a display, we confess that we still like Jesus, but not the church.[1] We are spiritual, yes, but not religious (by which we mean to eschew any too-close connection to the institutional church). The logic is simple enough: the church's history is everywhere mottled, besmirched by abuses of authority and distortions of truth. If we continue to desire to follow Jesus, we worry that the church can only hinder discipleship. Sure, some are simply bitter, having turned their backs on the church and its Lord. But others who would be faithful to Christ suspect that one cannot adequately follow the crucified one in such inauspicious company.

It is here, then, with the question of the church's mission, that the very being of the church is called into question. Now, let us be clear: To follow Jesus means to join him in calling God 'Father' and those in the church 'brother' and 'sister'. There can be, finally, no question of following Jesus apart from the church. Even if a remnant may at times be called to follow Jesus against the church, it will still do so with the church.

Turning to the church's mission, we reach what may be the most perplexing – and certainly is the most controversial – of topics in ecclesiology. And yet, as Martin Kähler once wrote, 'Mission is the mother of theology'.[2] It is in the midst of her deepening and expansion that the church was forced to sort out the requirements and implications of the gospel entrusted to her, and she did so in transit. From the beginning, then, the church's theology has been driven and demanded by mission; and as such, it has been contextual, a located theology articulated by an *ecclesia peregrina*. Clearly, outlawing mission is nothing other than asking the church to cease. After all, 'there is a centrifugal motive in the Church's existence. It is not something secondary; the Church's mission cannot be added to the reality of the Church as if it belonged to the "well-being" of the Church'.[3]

But we can say more. For mission is not only the mother of theology; mission is the mother of the church. This is, at first glance, an odd claim. We tend to think of mission as a project or program that an already well-established institution takes on. After all, someone or something must be the agent of mission. If we speak of the church's mission (and how else can we speak?) we speak of the church as a prior agent who sets out to accomplish something, who goes on a mission. All of which would seem to render our claim that mission is the mother of the church nonsense.

That is, unless there were another agent of mission prior to the church. And it is here that the rediscovery in the twentieth century of the *missio Dei* ('mission of God') is of such monumental significance.[4]

'WE'RE ON A MISSION FROM GOD'

In the 1980 movie *The Blues Brothers*, Dan Akroyd deadpans: 'We're on a mission from God'. He and his partner are in the process of putting their band back together and are enlisting an old bandmate, and Akroyd's character flatly insists that the divine origin of their project is sufficient warrant for the man to rejoin the band. Missions from God worry us, of course; they remind us of loose cannons and power mongers whose purportedly divine missions always seem to reveal a more diabolical than divine origin. To speak of the *missio Dei*, though, is to make a small, but significant, change in the language. This is not a mission *from* God but the mission *of* God. Where the first emphasizes divine sponsorship of our program and suggests its unassailable character (who, after all, can challenge the credentials of a prophet?), the second emphasizes a divine program in which we graciously have been included.

But that is to get ahead of ourselves. We said earlier that to call mission the mother of the church is to assert an agent of mission other than the church that births the church in and through mission. Trinitarian theology speaks of the sending of the Son and Spirit in terms of the trinitarian missions. Corresponding to the Father's eternal generation of the Son and spiration of the Spirit in God are temporal missions in which the Son and Spirit are sent into the world. So, in the familiar words of John's gospel: 'For God so loved the world that he gave his only Son, so that everyone who believes in him may not perish but may have eternal life. Indeed, God did not send the Son into the world to condemn the world, but in order that the world might be saved through him' (Jn 3.16–17). Or, as John puts it in his first epistle: 'In this is love, not that we loved God but that he loved us and sent his Son to be the atoning sacrifice for our sins . . . . And we have seen and do testify that the Father has sent his Son as the Saviour of the world' (1 Jn 4.10, 14). The Father sends the Son into the world to save it. We will have more to say later about the character of this salvation; certainly it is a salvation from sin, condemnation and death and for eternal life with God and his people in the new creation. Note that here we are speaking of the Trinity's mission, divinely initiated and divinely accomplished, a mission whose end is the salvation of the world. (The Spirit is not absent, Jesus having been conceived by the Spirit, anointed by the Spirit, empowered by the Spirit and raised by the Spirit.)

The church's mission takes its cues from and finds its place in God's mission. Jesus commissioned his disciples to continue his work, and he explicitly connected his mission to theirs: 'As you have sent me into the world, so I have sent them into the world' (Jn 17.18). There is an analogy between the two; even more, the mission of the disciples is included in the mission of the Son. We must say this carefully. Clearly, there is one sense in which the church cannot, does not and must not presume to continue Christ's work. For one, he and he alone is the sacrifice for sins (see the passage from 1 Jn 4 above). He has ascended to the right hand of the Father, where he reigns as King and intercedes as Priest on our behalf. Nevertheless, Jesus expected his disciples to be about his work. 'I tell you, the one who believes in me will also do the works that I do and, in fact, will do greater works than these, because I am going to the Father. I will do whatever you ask in my name, so that the Father may be glorified in the Son' (Jn 14.12–13). These greater works are not autonomously produced, of course; in fact, they are done by Jesus himself in response to our requests in his name. But then again, it is also we who do them. What are we to make of this confusing sense of double agency? It will help to consider a passage later in John, the Pentecostal moment of the gospel. After his resurrection, 'Jesus said to them again, "Peace be with you. As the Father has sent me, so I send you." When he had said this, he breathed on them and said to them, "Receive the Holy Spirit"' (Jn 20.21–22). Again we have the repetition of mission. As the Father sends his Son, so the Son sends his disciples. As a sign and empowerment for this mission, Jesus breathes the Spirit onto them. This is the Spirit who, as Jesus told his disciples just before he died, 'will teach you everything, and will remind you of all that I have said to you'. Furthermore, 'the Father will send [him] in my name' (Jn 14.26). The same Spirit who accompanied and empowered Jesus accompanies and empowers his people. Barth points out that ' "sending" means to be invested with *doxa* [glory], to participate in the dignity, authority and power given to the one commissioned to go to a third party for the discharge of his mission'.[5] The mission of the Son is extended, then, in the mission of the Spirit and the church. As Vatican II put it: 'The pilgrim Church is missionary by her very nature, since it is from the mission of the Son and the mission of the Holy Spirit that she draws her origin, in accordance with the decree of God the Father'.[6]

Not that the mission of the Son and Spirit was an entirely new thing.[7] Jesus is the dénouement of God's mission, not its beginning. He is the 'climax of the covenant' that God established with Abraham, Isaac and Jacob. But he is its *climax*, the point at which God's missional ways with the world and his people are integrated and brought to fulfilment.[8] Whether we consider mission creationally (beginning with

God's establishment of Adam and Eve in Eden and command to serve as a kingdom of priests throughout the earth) or soteriologically (beginning with God's seeking and finding the scantily clad – but clad, because ashamed – Adam and Eve after they had eaten from the tree of the knowledge of good and evil), God's mission of making a home in creation among his people can be traced to the opening chapters of scripture. As G. K. Beale has argued at length, 'God created the cosmos to be his temple, in which he rested after his creative work. His special revelatory presence, nevertheless, did not yet fill the entire earth because his human vice-regent was to achieve this purpose. God had installed this vice-regent in the garden sanctuary to extend the boundaries of God's presence there worldwide'.[9] The rest of the Bible narrates humanity's repeated failures to do just that, and God's various missions – his sending of Noah and Abraham, of Moses and David, of Israel among the nations and, finally, of his only Son (and, in him, many sons and daughters) as a light to the world. God's mission in the world has a long history in only part of which the church is present.

An important implication follows from this rediscovery of the *missio Dei*. God is a missional God. This means that mission is first God's project, not ours. Furthermore, mission antedates the church. In short, an attention to the mission of God suggests a shift from an ecclesiocentric to a theocentric model of mission. Rather than speaking of the mission of the church, we speak of the church's participation in the mission of God.[10] This does not suggest an eclipse of the church but, rather, its placement in the broader horizon of God's ways with the world. The church's existence is not oriented to itself but to God's reign. As such, it is the vanguard of the kingdom.[11] In order better to understand the nature of God's reign in the world, we will turn now to consider the conversion of Constantine and the coming of Christendom.

EXCURSUS: CONSTANTINE AND CHRISTENDOM

In 312, the political turmoil of the Roman Empire came to a head at the Milvian Bridge. Aligned along the Tiber River Maxentius, soon to be known as 'the Tyrant', and his superior number of troops awaited the charge of their opponents. Their opponents, led by Constantine, soon to be known as 'the Great', appeared upon the battlefield brandishing a new symbol: the Chi-Rho (the first two

Greek letters in the word Christ).[12] With this event the religion of Jesus enters the era of Christendom, as Constantine will be victorious and the empire will become Christian. Though we will quickly question some of the implications of this, we will use 'Christendom' to refer broadly to the socio-political consequences of the Christian mission.[13]

As with any cursory summarization, our history here risks skewing the actual events into oversimplified constructs, suggesting a pure church on the margins of empire which then became radically transformed by the institutionalization of Constantine. Such a misrepresentation is common in Christian discourse and is known as the 'Constantinian fall' of the church. By no means do the sources support a sudden shift in Christianity which can be dated by distinct 'before' and 'after' categories of Constantine's conversion (B.C. = Before Constantine/Corruption; A.D. *Anno Diaboli*/Deviation). In fact, Constantine's 'conversion' itself is often questioned: he deferred his baptism until his deathbed in 337 C.E. (or 25 'A.D.' by the count of those who hold to the Constantinian Fall theory), and he continued to function as the 'pontifex maximus' over all religions of the empire, just as previous caesars had before him. Moreover, the Christianization of the empire came about more under Theodosius I (347–395 C.E.) than Constantine – even if the latter invested himself heavily into church affairs, and the acculturation to empire had already begun long before Constantine's reign. What is distinctly novel about the scene at the Milvian Bridge is typified by Constantine's new standard.

While the Chi-Rho appeared on the soldiers' gear, Constantine himself bore his new symbol of both power and religion. His standard, Eusebius of Caesarea reports, was modelled after the sign Constantine and all with him had witnessed in the heavens: a cross. But Constantine's smithies fashioned their replica of this celestial symbol out of a soldier's spear.[14] Of course, the choice of a weapon is fitting, given the message appearing in the sky with the cross, *En toutoi nika*/*In hoc signo vinces*/'In this sign, conquer!'[15] From time immemorial religion had been co-opted for the purpose of power, but never before had Christianity, a religion of loving one's enemies and serving-not-lording, been wedded to political and military power.

The old 'Roman' Empire becomes more 'Byzantine' in the East as Constantine transfers the capital to Constantinople, while the Western political landscape undergoes many upheavals, most memorably in the invasions of the so-called Barbarian hordes. Out of the rubble in the West emerges a new 'Roman' Empire under the reign of Charlemagne. It is new in title because it is now the 'Holy' Roman Empire, but it would be more accurate to see it as new in locale because it is Frankish. The supposed holiness of the empire is the same supposed holiness instituted by Constantine: it is a holy empire because it is a Christian wielding of power. Charlemagne's dynasty would be short-lived, but his novelty would be long-lasting. Many a monarch will vie for the title 'Holy Roman Emperor', and Europe, even with its internal wars, will correspond to Christendom itself, including all the abuses of this 'Christian power'. Christendom will undertake multiple Crusades against the 'Mohammedans', permit frequent pogroms of Jewish communities, institute an inquisition against heretics, and result in wars of religion among its own citizens. When enough is finally enough, modernity will rescue Christendom from Christendom: the Nietzchean critique, for example, of the power invested in the church or the state, and the Kierkegaardian critique, for another example, of wedding the church to the state will eventually end the violence brought on by Christendom – or at least such critiques will bring an end to Christendom itself even if Christendom's violent effects linger. Christendom is dead, says the Enlightenment. But, alas, old ideas die hard.

In 1951, H. Richard Niebuhr published his influential book, *Christ and Culture*, wherein he typologized stances the church can take in relation to the world. On the one hand Niebuhr denounced overly optimistic Christian theologies from church history, such as the Gnostics and German liberals, and on the other hand he critiqued sectarian expressions of Christianity, such as Benedict's monasticism and the Mennonites' non-involvement in politics. Alternatively, Niebuhr believed there is a middle-type, which can navigate a path within culture in order to transform culture.[16] While this seems like a completely benign, if not healthy, approach, Niebuhr's view is not without its problems.

In his book, *Rethinking Christ and Culture*, Craig A. Carter attacks the flawed assumption underlying Niebuhr's five types. After reviewing Niebuhr's overall argument, Carter pulls the pro-verbial rug out from under Niebuhr's outline: 'It is very important to understand [Niebuhr's] book as a product of, and apology for, Christendom'.[17] Niebuhr failed to recognize both the problems and the death of Christendom, and thus his options for Christianity's relationship to culture both misrepresent church history and misguide Christian ethics.

Alternatively, Carter offers a six-point typology which in effect lists three pro-Christendom approaches to culture and three anti-Christendom approaches. While the differences between the six approaches are real and important, the crucial differentiation in one's approach to culture is whether or not one approves of 'Christian coercion' (which Carter finds to be synonymous with Christendom). Coming from a Yoderian perspective, Carter cannot condone any such practice, and so he contends for a complete and utter rejection of Christendom. Carter is not alone in his attack on Christendom. Rarely is a good thing said about it in current conversation. One surprising exception (which at first glance has no bearing upon the present discussion, but we believe furthers the debate) is the work of Philip Jenkins.

Jenkins addresses an emerging phenomenon which cannot be ignored and which could be understood as 'the forces of Crusade, from the Christian Third World'.[18] The growth of Christianity in the southern hemisphere raises questions for how Christianity will change in the coming decades; global Christianity, especially as it is fuelled in large part by Pentecostalism, represents a veritable 'new reformation'.[19] While Jenkins is aware that Christendom is 'an archaic term' which suggests abuses of power and violence in the name of Christ, he nevertheless finds that the new emerging forms of Christianity outside of the borders of old Christendom share so many experiences and values, that a transnational identity, if not entity, is being formed which can be labelled the 'next Christendom'. Jenkins is certainly concerned about, and critical of, the ongoing potential for justified violence.[20] On the other hand, he seems to use 'next Christendom' in a helpful way. By juxtaposing the 'new' with the 'old' Jenkins suggests both a comparison and a contrast: the next Christendom will not be the same as the old Christendom. This new Christendom will continue to have implications for society and the public, but it must avoid the abuses of power that come with coercion. In Derridean terms, it will be a Christendom without Christendom.[21]

Jenkins' work is helpful to the present discussion in two ways. First, in our attempt to analyse ecclesiology we should be concerned with the future of the church – what is 'next'. Secondly, Jenkins points our attention back to the emerging church of world Christianity (see the conclusion to the chapter on 'Marks'). This emerging church, which may offer a Christendom without Christendom, merits further attention in current theological conversation about the nature and mission of the church. While a full-scale interaction with global emergent ecclesiology cannot be provided here, we would like to offer a few examples of conversation partners from the non-Western church.

In 1944, a new church was founded. It was new legally and theologically: new in the former sense because the charter and initial gathering was formed under the joint leadership of Howard Thurman and Alfred G. Fisk; new theologically because it arose out of a desire to address the political and racial turmoil of the mid-twentieth century. The church was named The Church for the Fellowship of All Peoples, and Thurman recounts both the legal establishment as well as the theological underpinnings of this new endeavour in his book *Footprints of a Dream*.[22] To hear the description of the church, one would think it an explication of the emerging church movement:

> From the beginning, an emphasis has been given to the arts in religious life including music, drama, and dance. To this day the importance of cultural pluralism and emphasis on the arts remain important to the church. As we enter the twenty-first century and the church moves into its sixth decade, the importance of building bridges among cultural, racial, and religious communities remains a great need in the increasingly dense and complex world.[23]

Much like current emerging church descriptions, it might be tempting to focus on the visible differences between this church and other churches of this era (e.g. worship and cultural demographic), and yet the true theological novelty rests in its deeper understanding of the church's nature and mission which are merely displayed through visible means.[24]

While the locale of this church (San Francisco, Calif.) does not fit with Jenkins' definition of the 'next Christendom' or with what is normally labelled as 'world Christianity', we offer this church and Thurman's theological vision for it as an example because it is an early and influential voice in black theology which belongs among the so-called contextual theologies and represents an emerging expression of ecclesiology which can be contrasted to the Christian expressions resulting from European Christendom. James Cone, who coined the phrase 'black theology', has argued that churches arising out of the black experience in the United States display a distinct ecclesiology.[25] Cone goes so far as to compare black ecclesiology with the Anabaptist mark of church discipline as a visible sign of the church's prioritization of praxis.[26] While the black church movement in North America is by no means homogeneous, any attempt to set systematic discourse about the church into dialogue with non-European expressions of ecclesiology would benefit from a study of the subject as articulated by past and contemporary black theologians, to name only one example.

Another example is that of the church in Africa. The church in Africa has seen radical shifts in the last century, not only in quantitative growth, but in qualitative changes in ecclesial expression. Studies such as that of Allan H. Anderson, *African Reformation*, have especially focused on the African Independent Churches (AIC), churches which broke from or began independent of mainline missionary churches.[27] The AICs prove especially difficult to categorize because of their diversity, but they generally inculturate themselves to the local society in terms of their leadership, their liturgy, and their local ministry. And yet, even within the so-called mainline denominations, churches in Africa are emerging as something 'authentically African'.[28] Amidst many voices calling for 'indigenization' of the church in Africa, E. Bolaji Idowu, who later became president of the Methodist Church in Nigeria, outlines an ecclesiology for African churches.[29] These churches share many of the same features and values of the emerging church, and they do so out of a similar concern to be authentic, incarnational, and missional.

Another influential movement from the mid- to late-twentieth century is the emergence of liberation theology, which includes an expression of ecclesiology unique to Latin America. Leonardo Boff's *Ecclesiogenesis* charts the emergence of, and a theology for, Base Church Communities (BCC).[30] Whereas North America's black churches largely developed out of a Protestant milieu, and African churches have been most influenced by Pentecostalism, the emerging forms of church in Latin America remain by and large within the Roman Catholic communion. Whereas Africa's emerging ecclesiology proves especially gifted in terms of inculturation, the BCC's may offer guidance in their ability to 'reinvent' the church while still remaining within the ancient tradition of Roman Catholicism.[31]

Although we have barely scratched the surface of possibilities when it comes to new expressions of Christianity in the 'next Christendom', we believe that discourse on the church must be in dialogue with voices from outside of the 'old Christendom', which has too often been the case in systematic treatments and textbooks (we include ourselves in this charge).[32] If Christian churches now worship and minister in post-Christendom, or the 'next Christendom', or Christendom without Christendom, then the churches' theologians will require a constant posture of reflexivity and humility. This excursus began with Niebuhr's more mainline approach to Christendom, and then turned to Carter's more Anabaptist rejection of Christendom altogether. The former remained too uncritical in its acceptance of Christendom, while the latter relied too closely on a 'Constantinian Fall' theory of church history. The church is not the world, and yet the church is located in the world, the whole world. Perhaps, a 'third way' between Niebuhr and Carter can be found in the (broadly and globally defined) emerging churches.[33]

KINGDOM, CHURCH AND WORLD

Central, then, to an account of mission is the proper coordination of kingdom, church and world. Consider the following questions, the answers to which will reflect and direct how we understand the relation of those three terms:

- Where is salvation to be found?
- When is salvation to be found?
- Who can be saved?
- What is salvation anyway?
- For what do we hope?
- What is the pattern and goal of the Christian life?
- How do we think about Jews? About Muslims? About atheists?
- (How) should Christians engage in politics? In culture?
- Should Christians be optimists or pessimists?

Here we have some of the most pressing, pregnant and perplexing questions asked in the church, each of which necessitates a thoughtful understanding of the relation between kingdom, church and world.

Adding to the perplexity is a movement, already seen in the New Testament, from a focus on the kingdom of heaven/God to one on the church of Jesus Christ. Consider Alfred Loisy's comment that 'Jesus foretold the kingdom, and it was the Church that came. . . .'[34]

This suggests two different, maybe even mutually exclusive, entities. Jesus proclaimed, 'The time is fulfilled, and the kingdom of God has come near; repent, and believe in the good news' (Mk 1.15). Paul, on the other hand, resolved to 'know nothing among you except Jesus Christ, and him crucified' (1 Cor. 2.2). Has the church of Jesus Christ replaced the kingdom of God – and if it has, has it parted ways with Jesus himself?

It will be helpful to recall Origen's description of Jesus as *autobasileia*, the 'kingdom-in-person'. Jesus is the one in whom and as whom the kingdom has come. When he announces that 'the kingdom of God has come near', he is not speaking of something other than himself. So when the church focuses its proclamation on Jesus Christ, it does not depart from his message but highlights him as the agent and substance of the kingdom. What, though, is the kingdom?[35] What are Jesus and the church proclaiming? We could do worse than Barth's description:

> And the kingdom of God is the establishment of the exclusive, all-penetrating, all-determinative lordship of God and His Word and Spirit in the whole sphere of His creation. Jesus Himself is this kingdom in all its perfection. In Him this divine lordship is inaugurated. For in Him, this human creature, the Creator and Lord dwells and acts and speaks directly and without restriction in the rest of His creation. In Him the calling of all humanity and indeed of all creation to the service of God, and therefore the unity of all the forms and forces and works of the creature, is already a completed event with a perfection which cannot be transcended.[36]

The kingdom of God is God's universal rule for the good of his creation in which his creation responds in joyful service and praise of its King. God's kingdom is 'not a realm or a people but God's reign. Jesus said that we must "receive the kingdom of God" as little children (Mk 10.15). What is received? The Church? Heaven? What is received is God's rule'.[37] And so to receive Christ is to embrace him as God's anointed King. Oliver O'Donovan argues that 'Yhwh's rule over Israel . . . was founded on his acts of salvation and judgment and on his gift of an inheritance'.[38] In receiving Christ the King and God's reign in him, we entrust ourselves to him as Saviour and Judge and enjoy him as our inheritance.[39] The Spirit of Christ is 'the pledge of our inheritance toward redemption as God's own people' (Eph. 1.14). Sharing in the Spirit, we taste the heavenly gift (Heb. 6.4). Sealed with the Spirit, we enjoy the life of the kingdom even now. Indeed, in Christ, the kingdom has *already* come.

At the same time, it is clear that the kingdom has *not yet* come. Jesus taught his disciples to pray for its coming, and the earliest witnesses to the kingdom knew its implications. They acted 'contrary to the decrees of the emperor, saying that there is another king named Jesus' (Acts 17.7).[40] For this, many of them exchanged their lives. 'In the world you face persecution', Jesus frankly admitted. 'But take courage; I have conquered the world!' (Jn 16.33) As Moltmann has argued, it is precisely the knowledge that the kingdom *will* come even though it has not yet done so that provokes the church to hopeful, prophetic action on behalf of 'the least of these' (Mt. 25.40).[41] The promise of God's reign acts as an eschatological burr in the saddle of a complacent church. So it is that 'the future age now has a social and political presence. A community lives under the authority of him to whom the Ancient of Days has entrusted the Kingdom'.[42]

What is the church in relation to the world, then? It is a sign, foretaste, instrument and agent of God's rule in Christ.[43] It is that company of people who approach the kingdom as a gift and a realm to be received (Dan. 7.18; Mk 10.15; Lk. 18.17), entered (e.g. Mt. 5.20; Lk. 18.24; Jn 3.5), awaited and expected rather than one to be built or extended.[44] The church is not that which it indicates; it is not the kingdom. But it is the site ordained by God to announce the kingdom's coming, and the people among whom it is already here. It is, in short, that company of people proclaiming 'this good news of the kingdom . . . throughout the world, as a testimony to all the nations' (Mt. 24.14).

There is a third factor to consider – the world. A common enough word, 'world' admits two distinct meanings in scripture. On the one hand, it refers to the earth and/or all that is in it, including all people (e.g. Ps. 33.8, 89.11, 98.9; Jer. 51.5). God is creator and king, provider and judge over this world. But the term can also refer to the world (or some portion of it) in antagonism to God. We are not to be conformed to the world (Rom. 12.2) in view of its desertion of God, who has made its wisdom foolishness (1 Cor. 1.20). Does this suggest a disregard, even a disdain for God's good creation? No, but it does

evince the transition that began in Christ from 'the old' to 'the new'.
Paul writes that 'the present form of this world is passing away'
(1 Cor. 7.31; also see 1 Jn 2.17). And so 'the world has been crucified to me, and I to the world' (Gal. 6.14). Neither Christ nor
the church belongs to the world (Jn 15.9, 17.14; Col. 2.20); their
citizenship is in heaven (Phil. 3.20).[45] The church is to keep itself
'unstained by the world', as 'friendship with the world is enmity with
God' (Jas 1.27, 4.4).

It seems the acme of enmity to distinguish the church from the
world. After all, as so many theorists have pointed out in recent years,
these kind of binary oppositions involve and invite power plays. To
call ourselves the church, then call everyone else the world suggests
that 'we' are better than 'they'. It is a subtle form of self-justification;
and so, perhaps, far from an aptly Christian way of speaking, it is a
worldly one, as we seek to secure ourselves by ourselves rather than
rejoice in being justified by God in Christ.

To assert that such an easy, self-justifying distinction between 'us'
and 'them' is illicit is not to leave all such distinctions behind. As
Gerhard Lohfink points out, 'Where distinctions are no longer made,
the old gods return'.[46] It was precisely to stave off idolatry that the
men of Israel were forbidden to marry the women of Canaan and
that the boundaries of the people of God were so clearly defined.

Glee over being part of 'us' rather than 'them' betrays an ignorance,
evasion or rejection of the logic of the gospel with its universal intent.
Similarly, it suggests a misunderstanding of the logic of election,
according to which God calls, chooses and blesses a people that they
might be a blessing to others. Election means vocation to mission,
not an invitation to join an exclusive club. The holiness of the church
over-against the world, its being called out of the world and set apart
as God's people aims towards the ever-widening of the tent and
strains towards the day when enemies will become friends and out-
siders insiders. 'Called out of the world, the community is genuinely
called into it'.[47] 'It is holy in its openness to the street and even the
alley, in its turning to the profanity of all human life – the holiness
which, according to Rom. 12.5, does not scorn to rejoice with them
that do rejoice and to weep with them that weep'.[48] As Vatican II put
it, 'The joys and the hopes, the griefs and the anxieties of the men
of this age, especially those who are poor or in any way afflicted,
these are the joys and hopes, the griefs and anxieties of the followers
of Christ'.[49]

In short, the church exists for the world.[50] Schmemann rightly insists that ecclesiology without the cosmic perspective of being for the world is ecclesiolatry.[51] A church so curved in on itself has lost the gospel and left the mission of its God. It is precisely the world in antagonism to God that God loves. It is *this* world that God was in Christ 'reconciling . . . to himself, not counting their trespasses against them, and entrusting the message of reconciliation to us' (2 Cor. 5.19). Jesus calls his flesh 'the bread that I will give for the life of the world' (Jn 6.51). Still, the world was right to sense in Jesus a threat to its way of life; and so it put him to death in a chaotic rage. Perhaps it sensed better than many in the church that the death-dealing character of sin is of such magnitude that God can only be for us by first being against us. To save the world, God had to bring the world to an end. In Christ 'there is a new creation: *everything old has passed away*; see, everything has become new!' (2 Cor. 5.17) The church will at times be called to live against the world which is passing away, then, though always in the humility and self-criticism of those who know that the world is not merely outside but runs straight through the heart of the church.[52] The world is not only 'them'; it is also (and first) 'us'. Nor can the church's word of antagonism be a final one. The church is finally *for* the world not *against* it, because its King under whose reign it lives is finally for the world.

Baptism, Eucharist and Ministry aptly summarizes the relation of kingdom, church and world: 'The church is called to proclaim and prefigure the Kingdom of God. It accomplishes this by announcing the gospel to the world and by its very existence as the body of Christ'.[53] We turn in what follows to the shape and scope of the church's mission of proclaiming and prefiguring the kingdom of God in Christ.

THE SHAPE OF MISSION

The ministry of reconciliation

We have been speaking rather formally to this point. It remains to specify God's reign among his people, lest it be reduced to the horizon of present need and identified flatly with a particular cause. What happens, one might ask, when God sets up his reign in a world at odds with it? In Christ, we learn that God's response to sinners is to reconcile them to himself and to one another. Paul is clear that 'while we were enemies, we were reconciled to God through the death of his Son' (Rom. 5.10).

> For in him all the fullness of God was pleased to dwell, and through him God was pleased to reconcile to himself all things, whether on earth or in heaven, by making peace through the blood of his cross. And you who were once estranged and hostile in mind, doing evil deeds, he has now reconciled in his fleshly body through death, so as to present you holy and blameless and irreproachable before him – provided that you continue securely established and steadfast in the faith, without shifting from the hope promised by the gospel that you heard, which has been proclaimed to every creature under heaven. (Col. 1.19–23)

Estranged and hostile, we were enemies of God and one another; but it was precisely as such – that is, as sinners, that Christ died for us (Rom. 5.8).

> For he is our peace; in his flesh he has made both groups into one and has broken down the dividing wall, that is, the hostility between us. He has abolished the law with its commandments and ordinances, that he might create in himself one new humanity in place of the two, thus making peace, and might reconcile both groups to God in one body through the cross, thus putting to death that hostility through it. So he came and proclaimed peace to you who were far off and peace to those who were near; for through him both of us have access in one Spirit to the Father. So then you are no longer strangers and aliens, but you are citizens with the saints and also members of the household of God, built upon the foundation of the apostles and prophets, with Christ Jesus himself as the cornerstone. In him the whole structure is joined together and grows into a holy temple in the Lord; in whom you also are built together spiritually into a dwelling place for God. (Eph. 2.14–22)

Note the locus of reconciliation – in the death of Christ, where the world's warring reached its peak, but also where it reached its end. Enmity ended as Christ made one new humanity and made peace. (Even this is only part of the Father's plan to 'gather up all things in him, things in heaven and things on earth' [Eph. 1.10].[54]) In the Spirit

God's former enemies have access through Christ to the Father, and strangers are made citizens and siblings. 'It is finished' (Jn 19.30). Indeed 'everything which was needed for the salvation of all . . . has already taken place'. The consequence is that 'the task of mission can consist only in announcing this to them'.[55]

That God was reconciling the world to himself in Christ does not invite Christian passivity. While it is true that Christ has reconciled both Jews and Gentiles 'in one body to God through the cross' (Eph. 2.16), it is likewise true that followers of Jesus have been entrusted with the message and ministry of reconciliation (2 Cor. 5.18). While Christ's work has accomplished that reconciliation, it remains to be applied to men and women in the power of the Spirit through the preaching and living out of the gospel. 'So we are ambassadors for Christ, since God is making his appeal through us; we entreat you on behalf of Christ, be reconciled to God' (2 Cor. 5.20).

The appeal of which Paul speaks is the church's proclamation of God's reconciliation in Christ and call to the repentance which embraces his reconciliation in gratitude and lives in light of it. It is a plea to walk in the reconciliation of God. But what does reconciliation have to do with God's reign? In reconciling the world to himself in Christ, God has re-asserted his kingship and restored order to his realm. The ministry of reconciliation speaks of this restoration of creation in Christ and calls people to live faithfully before the king. This retrospective aspect fittingly characterizes a ministry whose job it is to serve the already accomplished reconciliation.

> If the origin of this *diakonia* of reconciliation is the divine appointment, its content is primarily *speech*. . . . For apostolic speech is not a making real of the gospel of reconciliation, but a testifying to the fact that in Christ and Spirit it is already realized . . . . The apostolic word *indicates*, and that indication is the first great act of the ethics of reconciliation.[56]

The primacy of speech does not here suggest a logocentric preference for the theoretical and universal over the practical and particular. Instead, it serves to emphasize the prior and complete accomplishment of reconciliation. Nothing can be added to it; the church can only serve as its minister in proclaiming God's love for sinners to the world.[57] This ensures that the church remembers its place as herald of the King. In the proclamation of the gospel, Christ himself offers the fruits of his accomplished reconciliation to the church and the world.[58]

The proclamation of reconciliation extends, too, to the friendship God has established in Christ between former enemies. Christ 'has made both groups into one and has broken down the dividing wall, that is, the hostility between us'. By uniting alienated parties, Christ has rewritten purity and holiness codes. Particular kinds of people are no longer rendered unclean – not even Gentiles or sinners. In his scandalous habit of sharing intimate table fellowship with the least of these (and, we note, not simply the 'deserving' least, but the socially repugnant), Jesus brought the kingdom in which there is 'no longer Jew or Greek, there is no longer slave or free, there is no longer male and female' (Gal. 3.28). He understood his ministry as a Jubilee year, a proclamation of unconditional favour and restoration to the destitute. 'The Spirit of the Lord is upon me, because he has anointed me to bring good news to the poor. He has sent me to proclaim release to the captives and recovery of sight to the blind, to let the oppressed go free, to proclaim the year of the Lord's favour' (Lk. 4.18–19). This is no mere economic do-gooding. It is prophetic speech by the King in which Jesus the Lord 'performs righteous deeds, and judgments for all who are oppressed' (Ps. 103.5). The gospel of the kingdom that we have to proclaim is the good news of *this* King's installation and reign. The ministry of reconciliation tells of God's judgments whereby the poor are restored to favour and alienated parties restored to friendship.

Christ and his kingdom are *proclaimed* in the ministry of reconciliation. They are *prefigured* in a community of reconciliation. The people of God live reconciled, thereby anticipating the kingdom, in two ways. First, they make it a practice to confess their sins to one another and forgive one another. A community of reconciliation is not one in which the need for ongoing reconciliation is eliminated. It is one in which God's reconciliation of the world to himself in Christ makes possible our daily being reconciled to one another. Christ becomes both the source of our forgiveness of others (Isa. 53.5, 12) and the model of our forgiveness (Lk. 23.34; Eph. 4.32). It is farcical to pretend to right relation with God without attending to right relation with one's neighbour. So closely are the two related that Jesus commands that anyone who is offering a gift at the altar and remembers that his brother or sister has something against him must leave his gift there before the altar, go, first be reconciled and only then come and offer his gift (Mt. 5.23–24).

Second, a community of reconciliation is one in which fellowship is shared among people who would have nothing to do with one another apart from the work of the Spirit. Many of us would prefer to go to church with people who are like us, but the catholicity of the church, in its correspondence to the universal reach of God's reconciliation, suggests otherwise. Recall from our earlier discussion that catholicity means both diversity and unity. On the one hand, the church encompasses the communion of saints across time and space. That means that the 120 of us who worshiped at Fountain of Life Covenant Church in North Long Beach yesterday are not the church by ourselves. We are the church with those worshiping yesterday in Auckland and those worshipping last year, a hundred, a thousand years ago throughout the world. We are the church, only and ever with our brothers and sisters in the non-Western world, in the non-modern world. On the other hand, the church's catholicity commands our commitment to her unity. We have 'one Lord, one faith, one baptism' (Eph. 4.5). Confessing the catholicity of the church and refusing to live a life of being reconciled together is what Karl Barth would call an 'impossible possibility' – possible in that it happens, but impossible in that its very happening is utterly foreign to the logic of its own existence. In other words, the blocking of reconciliation in our relationships violates the catholicity we (claim to) confess.

The catholicity of the church was more readily apparent in the medieval parish model. On that model, if you lived in a particular town, you went to its church. There is an inherent catholicity here in that the local church in the parish model reflects the make-up of the community.[59] Even though not everyone from the community shows up, everyone is represented. The poor are there, as are the rich. Men and women, married and single, young and old, black and white are there. In this, the local church mirrors the universal church.

What makes this model attractive is its inherent desegregating orientation. The person sitting in the chair next to me could be *anyone* – young or poor or married. The church thus promises to be one of the few places where people who don't belong together, belong together. It is a place where people who we would not choose for friends become our brothers and sisters. This is fitting, as the church as a whole is a people chosen for no good reason by God through Christ in the Spirit.

And it is for this reason that we are suspicious of catering to our felt needs to be with people just like us in church. There may be a place for groups dedicated to singles, young parents, motorcycle enthusiasts, people with tattoos – but it is only a peripheral, provisional and penultimate place, one that fills a gap and looks to groups of people who are nothing like one another. The heart of the church is difference. Our small groups should be places of difference, where we lived the reconciled life with people to whom we are not necessarily fully reconciled. Clubs are for people who want to be with people like themselves. Churches are not.

Still, as attractive as the parish model is, it does not work as well in the stratified societies of the United Kingdom and North America. We have built entire communities around the idea that sameness is next to godliness. Our churches set up shop, reach a community and, often enough, reflect the homogeneity of that community. But in so doing, they fail to reflect the 'come one, come all' character of the church universal. Structures of sin set society up in such a way that we have to be unnatural (moving to or going to church in a different neighbourhood, say) to be natural (that is, truly *kata holos*, truly catholic). But such catholicity, prefiguring and participating in the kingdom where people from every tongue and tribe and nation worship before the throne of God and of the Lamb (Rev. 7.9) is a vital part of living as a community of reconciliation in and for the world. The church's catholicity is the pudding that proves the words of Paul and witnesses to the work of Christ: 'In Christ there is no Jew or Greek, slave or free, male or female'.

Knowing the unheralded unity the Spirit accomplishes in Christ, the reconciled and reconciling community can imagine possibilities for the world that it cannot see for itself. It will, then, engage at every point in projects of reconciliation, in relation to class, gender, ethnicity, culture or physical ability. Lesslie Newbigin, no alarmist, can, for instance, call 'the ideology of the free market' 'a form of idolatry' which is 'probably [the] most urgent missionary task during the coming century'.[60] Action on behalf of economic and social justice is part of the church's reconciling mission. We are heartened to see intentional communities of relocation, reconciliation and redistribution among the New Monastics.[61] In the work of creation care, the church lives out of God's reconciliation by returning to his mandate to steward the earth well (Gen. 1.26–28) and anticipating the restoration of all things in the new creation. Reconciliation is itself only the beginning, though; it is the process of restoration on the basis of which God enjoys communion with his people and they enjoy communion with him and one another.

THE SCOPE OF MISSION

Ecumenism

We begin our discussion of ecumenism with the brute fact of ecclesial disunity – a fact which, no matter what account we give of its origins, its residual and indirect benefits, possibly even its provisional necessity, we can only finally lament and of which we must repent. Berkouwer describes 'the wailing wall of division' and 'the sin of disunity' with 'its horror, its total disorder in contrast to God's election, calling, and intention'.[62] Such disorder implicates the church in the world's disbelief, as her disunity renders the gospel incredible.[63] 'The call to unity and concord resounds in the Church's present, and the earnestness of this call entirely excludes every eschatological "alibi"'.[64]

Nor has this call gone unheeded. The twentieth century was the century of the church, the century of the modern missionary movement, and the century of ecumenism – and for historical reasons, not to mention theological ones, we must include ecumenism in our discussion of mission (and vice versa). The task of re-uniting a splintered church was rivalled only by a renewed vigour on the part of the various splinters to take the gospel to the ends of the earth. A remarkable, prayerful energy fuelled the project. Not since the sixteenth century have we been so hopeful for and close to ecclesial reunion in the West.[65] Many have hoped, too, for a healing of the East–West schism, such that our confession of 'one, holy, catholic and apostolic church' might again be voiced in confidence. And indeed, ecumenical dialogues have accomplished much by way of theological convergence. Perhaps more significantly, ecclesial practice and piety have paved the way for further partnership. We have lived a 'spiritual ecumenism' – praying together, worshiping together, teaching together, fighting for justice and peace together, even evangelizing together.[66] And yet, we remain a deeply divided church.[67] Robert Jenson has documented a cycle of doctrinal difference, discussion, clarification and convergence that, nevertheless, leads to the location of new divisions, or old divisions that we did not previously acknowledge as obstacles to unity.[68]

There is the further question of just how much convergence really obtains when two communions agree on a statement. Is this merely semantic? After all, concepts and judgments are not the same thing.[69] While she may overstate her case, Daphne Hampson argues trenchantly that the perception of Lutheran and Roman Catholic convergence on justification in the *Joint Declaration*[70] is false.[71] We may say the same things, but these statements are made within different structures of thought. Thus, identical statements reflect very different judgments. In light of this, a modicum of caution seems wise in ecumenical conversation, particularly when easy agreement would belie underlying difference. It also seems charitable, as it requires a full accounting of the beliefs and commitments of all parties to the conversation.

Free churches and ecumenism

How ought free churches to think about ecumenism? We ask this question for two reasons. First, we both come from free church traditions and have witnessed responses to ecumenism ranging from disinterest to hostility among free churches. There is enthusiasm in places, too, though usually in the name of a spiritual ecumenism that neglects issues of central concern to 'high' church traditions. Second, the free churches are an underrepresented voice in ecumenical conversations. Many free church Christians dismiss ecumenism as a watered-down attempt by liberal Christians to pursue love at the cost of truth. This is surely a temptation in any project of reconciliation, though to ignore ecumenism in the name of truth may just as easily be a failure of love, that 'perfect bond of unity' (Col. 3.14). In part, the free churches' (especially evangelicals') commitment to mission may lead them to question the priority of an intramural endeavour. It is telling, then, that the modern ecumenical and missionary movements dawned at the same time, even, one might plausibly suggest, at the same place – in the Edinburgh Missionary Conference of 1910.[72] Indeed, 'evangelicalism is in its very existence an amazing ecumenical fact'.[73] Thus, *that* evangelicals ought think about ecumenism, and not merely to call the ecumenical movement into question, should go without saying.

One approach is to assert that 'the distinctions of the various traditions have the potential to bring richness even in the midst of disagreement, creating a mosaic that, examined up close, may reveal that a few pieces are out of place or misshapen but which nonetheless at a distance becomes an image recognized by all as a beautiful work of art'.[74] What are the implications of the mosaic metaphor? To some extent, it might depend upon the context in which the metaphor is deployed. If it fits snugly into a pluralism suspicious of words like 'doctrine' and 'orthodoxy', then it is likely to do little good beyond underwriting theological and ecclesial sloth. If it is coupled with a breezy account of ecclesial division, then it may do little to provoke the sacrifices of love that Christian unity requires. If it serves to justify ecclesial apathy insofar as every church is partial and expectations need not be too high of, say, evangelism among Anglicans or theological reflection among Pentecostals, then we ought be wary. If, however, it is used to forestall attempts to disqualify other churches or marginalize their contribution to and manifestation of the one, holy, catholic and apostolic church, then it could be a useful and apt metaphor indeed.

We can put the question another way: Can we imagine an 'ecumenically valid ecclesiology' finding a home in the free church traditions?[75] That begs the question of criteria for ecumenical validity. At the very least, an ecumenically valid ecclesiology would seem to require two simultaneous orientations.

First, an ecumenically valid ecclesiology must come from somewhere. This of course initially means our ecumenism must be rooted in and oriented to the Bible and the rule of faith (conceived broadly enough to allow for non-creedal Protestants). While this may seem to follow *pro forma*, the rampant pluralism and biblical laxity of our day suggest it be reinforced early and often. Additionally, we must admit how embarrassment leads many free church Christians to hold their distinctives loosely in ecumenical circles for fear of being theologically jejune. We quickly forswear crucial commitments in an effort to build rapport or, more pathetically, to be validated. This will not do. George Hunsinger suggests that 'ecumenical progress means that no tradition will get everything that it wants, each will get much that it wants, none will be required to capitulate to another, and none will be expected to make unacceptable compromises'.[76]

If Hunsinger is right, ecumenism is not that process in which one communion loses itself in another. We err in thinking that Rome and Constantinople need to trade in their vestments for a Hawaiian shirt and a house on Azusa Street (to take Pentecostalism as an example). True to the principle that evangelical union will involve self-giving love on the part of all churches, then, it is incumbent on Pentecostals to attend to matters of structure and polity and take seriously Roman Catholic appeals to the centrality of ecclesial visibility, refusing to content themselves with 'spiritual unity' and instead seeking the visible unity of the church catholic.[77] Pentecostalism has much to learn from Rome about the living tradition of the Christian faith, about Christian devotion, worship and witness that is faithful to the gospel and contextualized. It has much to learn about the blessing and necessity of the Church our mother who 'brings about the birth of Christ in us'.[78]

But Rome errs, too, if it imagines ecumenism as nothing more than a return home to her. It would certainly be unrealistic, but more, it would be a denial of the ecclesiality of Pentecostal churches (which ecumenical proposals frequently forget about or fail to deal with seriously[79]), if the Roman Catholic Church were to require those churches to align structurally with the bishop of Rome in order to be recognized fully as churches and to enjoy full communion. Such a 'return ecumenism' fatally sidelines the work of the Spirit of Christ in Pentecostalism and the faith, hope and love of Pentecostal churches around the world, insisting on a structural answer to a spiritual question.[80] Indeed, Rome has much to learn from Pentecostalism[81] about the power and presence of the Holy Spirit. In their very eschewal of elaborate or extensive ecclesial form (even if it is some-what naïve) Pentecostals provide witness to God's loving freedom, according to which he can bring new life in the most stripped-down of ecclesial settings. In the process, they caution the church catholic against turning the *bene esse* of the church into its *esse*, thereby seeking to guarantee divine presence through strictly immanent means. It is not that the Spirit is formless (recall, after all, the Spirit's brooding in creation, in which that which was formless and void was shaped and filled, becoming 'very good'); but nor is it that the Spirit needs sharply determined forms in order to unite people to Christ in the church, to renew them, to lead and guide them into the truth which is Christ.

If there is an overly confident assumption on Rome's part that the priority of Christ and the Spirit will be retained in the midst of long discussions of secondary matters, there is an overly anxious assumption on Azusa Street's part that speaking of secondary matters cannot but lead to an eclipse of Son and Spirit. We are attending to habits of speech here in large part because the problem is not only one of material commitments; it is also one of emphasis, one reflected in liturgical and theological style and accent even if not always outright disagreement.

Secondly, an ecumenically valid ecclesiology must be going somewhere – namely, to the unity for which Jesus prayed, 'Holy Father,
keep them in your name, which you have given me, that they may be
one, even as we are one' (Jn 17.11). Jesus asks the Father to protect
the church in unity with the Father and Son by the power of their
Spirit, and this unity is ordered to the watching world. The union of
believers with one another and their union with the Father and Son
are 'so that the world may believe that you have sent me' (Jn 17.21).
The union that we seek is *evangelical* union – union around the gospel of Jesus Christ and marked by a self-giving love conforming to
this gospel (see Phil. 2.5–11).[82] An ecumenically valid ecclesiology,
then, will employ a hermeneutic of charity in the name of a generous
orthodoxy in engagement with ecclesial others and subordinate its
decisions to the rule of love.[83] This final note about the rule of love is
hardly insipid and requires far more self-sacrifice and commitment
to the truths of the gospel than many would suppose.[84] Nor, again,
does it suggest a disregard for truth.

'Visible unity' is the watchword of the ecumenical movement,
and it is grounded in Jn 17.[85] To speak of the end (*telos*) of ecumenism without mention of visible unity is immediately to lose
most communions. If it is the boon of the ecumenical movement
to insist consistently on visible unity, it is its bane to fail to imagine
the diversity of forms such visibility could take. Eucharistic fellowship is a *sine qua non* for visible unity, but it is not the only one;
surely shared worship, service and mission are similarly essential
for the church's unity with the triune God, and these ecclesial practices are manifested visibly so that the world might know that
the Father sent the Son and loved the church even as he loved the
Son (Jn 17.23).

For any of this to occur, we must be converted. Ecumenical theology
'will succeed only by a deeper conversion of all traditions to Christ'.[86]
Indeed, 'the way to unity of the Church can only be the way of her
renewal. But renewal means repentance. And repentance means
turning about: not the turning of those others, but one's *own*
turning'.[87] Repentance is hopeful, though, trusting in the Spirit
of resurrection to bring life to the dead and rejoicing in the unity
of the church achieved at the cross and abiding even in the face of
its division. The gift of unity (and it is a gift before it is a task), like
all of God's gifts, is irrevocable.[88]

The limits of ecumenism

Finally, and carefully, we must ask whether and when division might be legitimate.[89] Both division and union can succumb to the 'temptation of distance', in which safety is sought in irony rather than having to suffer the pain of intimacy.[90] Consider Schleiermacher's comment:

> [That] there are frequently also efforts at union which do not origi-
> nate in the Spirit of the Church, and the success of which cannot
> therefore be regarded as a gain, reminds us that there may also be
> divisions which are not due to the worldly elements in the Church,
> but must ultimately be reckoned among the effects of the Holy
> Spirit. . . . But just as those unions may only be apparent, and the
> united elements may certainly tend to separate from the whole body
> in some other fashion, so too that which is in fact only seeking closer
> union within the great fellowship in a way that will do it no injury,
> or again that which is really a return to a formerly abandoned
> fellowship with earlier forms of the Church, may seem to be a
> division, and yet not be such. Hence it is universally true that the
> Spirit unites, and that it is the fleshly mind that disunites. But the
> application of this may be difficult; and when several communions
> separated from each other exist side by side in Christendom, it must
> be left to criticism to decide on which side the disuniting principle is
> entrenched, and which therefore is responsible for division. This is a
> question which it will often be as difficult to solve as the question
> which of two sides in a war has been the aggressor'.[91]

Questions of division suffer from a dilemma which is all too often put in terms of truth *versus* unity. That these could stand on opposite sides of the field reveals how far they have moved in our rhetoric from their Christian home. Jesus Christ is truth. And to be united in the church means nothing less than to be united with Christ the truth. Truth and unity are mutually presupposing and edifying.

That being said, is it ever appropriate for a denomination to divide or a church to leave its denomination over an issue? Certainly, it is incumbent upon Christians to pray and think carefully before separating from one another. All should count the cost and consider it a last resort, a horrible, radical amputation when all other treat-ments have been tried. Simply put, splits (whether denominational or in individual churches) rend the house of God and grieve the Holy Spirit (Eph. 4.30). And sadly, some have seemed all too eager in this regard. Ecclesial division can only be wept over. Schleiermacher once again:

> A complete suspension of fellowship in this sense is unchristian as long as the communion that has been cut off retains its historical connexion with the preaching of the gospel by which it was founded, and does not, itself breaking the connexion, trace the origin of its present form to a different revelation.[92]

In Schleiermacher's judgment, separation is only an option in the face of idolatry. When 'a different revelation' founds a communion, that communion is *de facto* no longer Christian. And at this point, the church only acknowledges what the severed communion has already confessed – that whatever it is, it is not Christian. Anything short of the proclamation of a different gospel is an illegitimate cause for division (see Gal. 1.6–9); the church of Christ knows no irreconcilable differences.

The difficulty is that few, if any, communions will come out and say, 'We are now idolatrous'. To determine when and if a communion has broken the connection, then, can be challenging. The further difficulty is knowing that our own hearts are petri dishes of idols.[93] Not that this excuses the church from the hard responsibility to, on (very) rare occasions, cut ties. Rather does this recognition of our own wayward hearts bring humility and sobriety to judgment. We know that we stand under judgment. And so the judgments we make in turn demand patience, caution, humility and provisionality.[94]

Of course, they also demand courage, the courage to say 'No!' as well as the courage to repent. In fact, in an ecclesial setting where (if you will pardon the expression) 'you're damned if you do and damned if you don't', it may be that we have to be ready to repent of actions that, nevertheless, seem morally and theologically necessary. That is, there may come a time in a particular church or larger communion where ties have to be cut in the name of Jesus and for the sake of the truth which he is and the unity which he establishes. But it may be that the best we can say on Judgment Day when accounting for the severance is, 'I repent. Lord, have mercy'. After all, separation is foreign to the church, a counter-witness to the reconciliation of enemies in one body through the cross.

But how far ought ecumenism extend? To all the 'people of God' (which suggests Israel)? To all the 'children of God' (which suggests other religions)? We turn now to the difficult questions of the church's relation to and engagement with Israel and other religions.

Israel

How is the church to relate to Israel? What does faithful participation in the *missio Dei* entail in this relationship? We do well to begin with Paul's dilemma as set out in Romans. Always a zealous Israelite, Paul encountered the risen Christ on the road to Damascus and was called to be an apostle to the Gentiles. But he continues to wrestle with the implications of this expansion of the people of God for 'my kindred according to the flesh' (Rom. 9.3). How is he to think of them?

> They are Israelites, and to them belong the adoption, the glory, the covenants, the giving of the law, the worship, and the prom-ises; to them belong the patriarchs, and from them, according to the flesh, comes the Messiah, who is over all, God blessed forever. Amen. (Rom. 9.4–5)

The church's first task, then, is one of remembrance and gratitude. This is vital for a church with a long history of anti-Jewish polemic, a tendency to race past the witness of Israel on the way to the witness of Christ and a world still living in the wake of the Holocaust. 'The evidence of Israel-forgetfulness in Christian theology is so ubiquit-ous as almost to escape notice, like skin at a nudist colony'.[95] If Paul can call the church of Jews and Gentiles 'the Israel of God' (Gal. 6.16), this is no mere dismissal of Israel according to the flesh. It is a deeper revelation of the nature of Israel and, as much, an identification of the church with Israel. It is an insertion of the church in Israel's identity rather than an exhaustion of Israel in the church. Indeed, 'the church is an event within Israel'.[96] For the gifts God has given Israel and which have now come to be shared by the church, we can only be grateful. Israel is the root, some of whose branches were broken off due to unbelief in order that the wild branches of the nations might be grafted in. Paul holds out a warning against arrogant presumption on the part of the latecomers and also hope for the re-grafting of his kindred according to the flesh onto the root (Rom. 11.16–24). Indeed, 'all Israel will be saved' (Rom. 11.26), though how one is to understand 'all' (every individual, or a representative remnant?) and 'Israel' (only spiritual Israel, excluding the unevangelized Jews-according-to-the-flesh of the diaspora?) at this point is ambiguous. Paul's conclusion that the judgments of God are unsearchable underscores the eschatological reserve appropriate at this point.

We can ask, though, what it might mean for Israel to be saved. For one, it would not mean Israel according to the flesh becoming something other than what it is. While it would require repentance and belief, it would not involve it changing its identity but coming to understand in a deeper way its identity as the people of God. O'Donovan puts it nicely:

> What Israel has yet to accomplish, however, is a shift of understanding about the centre of its own identity. If at an earlier stage it came to see the possession of the land as transcended and fulfilled in the possession of the law, so now it must come to see the possession of the law fulfilled in Christ, the 'end of the law'. . . . Israel must learn to see itself in terms of him; and when it does so, the struggle for Israel will have borne fruit.[97]

The apostles did not invent a new religion. They proclaimed the lordship of the one true God who had identified himself in, as and with Jesus.[98] Kendall Soulen rightly comments that 'the church *has no God of its own,* and must not have one on pain of ceasing to exist as the church of God. The God revealed in the gospel is the God of Israel'.[99]

At the same time, the God of Israel *has* revealed himself in the gospel. The God of Abraham, Isaac and Jacob has acted definitively in Christ and, just as one cannot speak well of the God of Jesus without reference to the Jews, so, now, one cannot speak well of the God of Abraham, Isaac and Jacob without reference to the one in and as whom he has made himself known, Jesus. We recognize how difficult this position is in a post-Auschwitz era. We must admit that within this Pauline differentiation between 'true Israel' and 'Israel according to the flesh' remains a structural supersessionism[100] in which the church says to Israel, '(a) You aren't who you think you are. [and] (b) We are who you think you are'.[101] To frame this point so bluntly is an admission to a certain lack of parity in any dialogue. Still, it should be pointed out that when we claim to worship Israel's God and follow Israel's Messiah, Israel has traditionally made the same declaration to Christians: '(a) You are not who you think you are.

(b) We are who you think you are'. Thus, this is more balanced than it first appears.

How are we to determine what it means to be the people of God in light of all this? Here we discover that to ask about the identity of Israel is also to ask about the identity of the church. One cannot think one without thinking the other. David Bosch offers a sustained, subtle treatment of this question, arguing that we have to hold together two equally basic claims:

1. Salvation and incorporation into the people of God comes about through trusting in Jesus.
2. God keeps his promises and will not abandon Israel forever.[102]

Now, Paul does refer to the church in Galatians 6 as 'the Israel of God', so maybe we can think of (2) that way. One way in which God is faithful to Israel is to draw Gentiles who worship the God of Israel through Christ into his people. The New Testament does not, after all, envision the church as the 'new' Israel, but as an extension or expansion of Israel and, insofar as it meets YHWH in Christ, the 'true' Israel. Bosch notes the significance of this, and Paul's preoccupying wonder at God's inclusion of the Gentiles. Israel, then, is revealed to be that people chosen by God, rooted in Abraham and God's covenant to bless the nations in him, whose life is gathered around worship of Abraham's God as he is found in Christ. This renders dubious any simple identification of the people of God without remainder with the modern nation-state of Israel, as if the mere occupation of territory plus lineage sufficed to identify God's people, whose *true* identity is constituted by the saving and sustaining action of God and a response of gratitude and worship from a faithful people.

It would seem a strange faithfulness, though, were the God of Israel to be content with casting off Israel according to the flesh entirely. If God simply and fully transferred the meaning of 'Israel' away from Israel according to the flesh to a fully spiritualized Israel, then is this not equivocation? At what point is this still *Israel*? What are we to do with Israel according to the flesh? Really, this is a poor way to put it. The church's history of doing things *with* Israel according to the flesh has usually involved a doing things *to* Israel according to the flesh, and those things have too often been an ugly history indeed. Better to ask what *God* will do with Israel according to the flesh.

Here Paul's passionate fumbling in Rom. 9–11 comes in, with the affirmation that 'God is able to graft them in again' such that 'all Israel will be saved . . .' (11.23, 26) We ought not think this final salvation will occur apart from faith in Jesus (see Bosch's first claim), but neither ought we neglect the hope to which Romans 11 invites us. Indeed, Israel has always looked to the spiritual nature of circumcision and sacrifice (Deut. 30.6; Ps. 51.16–17) and Israel continues to look to the day when God will gather her people back to Jerusalem, along with the nations (Isa. 11.12; Jer. 29.13–14; Ezek. 20.39–44). We see an initial and representative ingathering in Jesus' election of the twelve disciples (recalling the twelve tribes) and their authoritative ministry under him.[103]

All of which is to say, the church which 'longs for his appearing' (2 Tim. 4.8) longs for more than that. As we wait for Jesus, we do well to find our place among the waiting saints of Israel (holy ones like Simeon and Anna) who seek the consolation of Israel. Jesus is that consolation, but many in Israel remain, as yet, unconsoled. And so we do well to befriend them – first, in the humble gratitude of those who were strangers to the promises of God and who remain wild branches only lately grafted onto the root of Jesse; and second, in the hopeful prayer of those who have known the consolation of Israel's God in Christ, await the final consolation on the day of his return and desire that all of Israel according to the flesh might be grafted back in, to enjoy the fulfilment of their long hopes in the Messiah and King, Jesus Christ.

Barth is right: 'Mission is not the witness which [the church] owes to Israel'.[104] Mission implies an alien proclamation, whereas the proclamation of the church is rooted in YHWH's ways with his people. So while the church does owe its witness to Israel, it is not an alien witness. It is, instead, a witness of those whom Israel will be surprised to find included within its midst. The sight of an unexpected people – those who were *not* God's people and *not* his beloved (Rom. 9.25; cf. Hos. 1.10) – enjoying the blessings of God's promises *as* his people is meant to create a longing in Israel to return to these promises. 'But through their stumbling salvation has come to the Gentiles, so as to make Israel jealous' (Rom. 11.11). Thus is the problem of Israel a family affair.[105]

To return to the promises of God, though, means a venturing forth. Israel cannot return home until it sets out on pilgrimage. For God's promises are confirmed, even crystallized – that is, they find their most succinct summary and also are further focused – in Jesus, so that affiliation with him is now the way in which we come into those promises. Around Christ all of the Father's promises coalesce, so that even those promises fulfilled prior to Christ's coming in the incarnation look forward to Christ as the fulfilment of God's ways with his people.[106] To appreciate a promise's fulfilment we must enter into the long years during which it remained unfulfilled. But while all of the promises of God are confirmed in Christ, and many of them are fulfilled in Christ, and while Christ will ever be at the heart of God's promise-making and promise-keeping as the one in whom God is with and for us *(Emmanuel!)*, Paul strains toward a day in which Israel will return to her Lord.[107]

Israel has much to offer the church. After all, to her belongs 'the adoption, the glory, the covenants, the giving of the law, the worship, and the promises . . . the patriarchs, and from them, according to the flesh, comes the Messiah, who is over all, God blessed forever'. What the church has to offer Israel is gratitude, the humility of a younger sibling, and a joyful witness to the faithful God of Israel who has saved the world and vindicated his people in Christ.[108]

But what does the church have to offer the world? Is that even an acceptable question in our contemporary climate? We turn now to consider the church's mission among the world religions.

Other religions

An old tale has it that a series of blind men approached an elephant. John Godfrey Saxe tells a version of it in which the six could feel something of the elephant – tusk or trunk or tail – though none knew the whole of it. In fact, their extrapolations from limited experience led them to very different conclusions (tusk = like a spear, trunk = like a snake, tail = like a rope), though each was convinced of the truth and sufficiency of his description. The moral of Saxe's story?

> So oft in theologic wars,
>   The disputants, I ween,
> Rail on in utter ignorance
>   Of what each other mean,
> *And prate about an Elephant*
>   *Not one of them has seen!*[109]

None of us comprehends the whole of reality, so we had better pool our experience and insight to better grasp the whole. Many deploy a Kantian distinction at this point. We can only describe *phenomena* when it comes to talk of God; we cannot get at the *noumenal* realm, at God *in se*. God is beyond our knowing, and we, like the men in the story, are all blind. After all, who can say he has seen God? This projects a confidence ill-fitting to a God who transcends our small minds and experience. More, and worse, would not the claim to have seen God be the height of presumption and the root of religious violence?

There is surely something to all this. The church could do with some chastening at many points, perhaps above all in its manner towards non-Christians. The move from confident joy in the proclamation of the gospel to arrogant patronization and imperviousness to criticism has been made at many points in the history of the church. Furthermore, to rejoice in having come to know God in Christ is not at all to claim infallibility – on matters religious or otherwise. The church should be ready to admit sin and error. It should, too, be eager to listen and learn from those outside its walls.

And yet, even given all this, the church must continue to hear the words of testimony from another blind man: 'One thing I do know, that though I was blind, now I see' (Jn 9.25). At the heart of its confession, the church rejoices in having seen God. This is not an accomplishment, but an unanticipated gift given in the incarnation of God's Son. Thus, in the oft-cited and oft-abused words of Jesus, 'I am the way, and the truth, and the life. No one comes to the Father except through me. If you know me, you will know my Father also. From now on you do know him and have seen him' (Jn 14.6–7). Jesus is not a downgraded partial vision of deity. He is the one in and as whom the invisible God is known. The beloved disciple can affirm that 'no one has ever seen God'. But he goes on: 'It is God the only Son, who is close to the Father's heart, who has made him known' (Jn 1.18; cf. Col. 1.15). In Christ the invisible is rendered visible, the unknowable knowable – not unambiguous, we hasten to add, nor knowable apart from faith – a point relevant for the church, in both its nature and mission. For the unknown God (Acts 17.23) is now known at a particular site, in the incarnation of the Son, and in a particular posture, in the faithful obedience of disciples. None of this ought be enlisted to re-install the church in a position of unassailability or finality. It is simply meant as an undeconstructible centrepiece. Whatever else Christians affirm, they confess that God is known first and last in Jesus Christ. The church itself is thus a means of grace to the world, precisely because it knows something. That its way of life has yet to catch up to its knowledge accounts for a significant portion of the failure of its witness in the world.

With this in place, we will ask two significant questions about the church's relation to other religions. First, how is the church to engage in mission in its encounter with other religions? We have described mission under the rubric of the ministry of reconciliation. Such a ministry invites people into God's reconciliation in Christ, a reconciliation known and witnessed to in the church. A hospitable church, one which would welcome others into this reconciliation, treats its interlocutors as sinners loved by God. A church can do this because Christians know *themselves* as (i) sinners and (ii) loved by God. One might reverse the order of those clauses for good reason, but both are nevertheless true. And good hospitality involves taking both these aspects seriously.

We begin with the recognition of this other, this stranger, as one loved by God. She is the one created by the Father, the one for whom the Son died, the one whom the Spirit would bring to new life. It is in the triune God that she lives and moves and has her being (Acts 17.28), and it is from him that every gift of her life proceeds (Jas 1.17). That there is much about her life which we ought to receive with gratitude, then, ought not surprise us. She is not merely 'one of them'; she is 'one of us'. This is all put finely, and carefully, in *Nostra Aetate*, Vatican II's 'Declaration on the Relation of the Church to Non-Christian Religions':

> The Catholic Church rejects nothing that is true and holy in these religions. She regards with sincere reverence those ways of conduct and of life, those precepts and teachings which, though differing in many aspects from the ones she holds and sets forth, nonetheless often reflect a ray of that Truth which enlightens all men. Indeed, she proclaims, and ever must proclaim Christ 'the way, the truth, and the life' (Jn 14.6), in whom men may find the fullness of religious life, in whom God has reconciled all things to Himself.
>
> The Church, therefore, exhorts her sons, that through dialogue and collaboration with the followers of other religions, carried out with prudence and love and in witness to the Christian faith

and life, they recognize, preserve and promote the good things, spiritual and moral, as well as the socio-cultural values found among these men.[110]

There is a common good hinted at here towards which the church is called to work in partnership with those of other religions (including, to put it pithily and with some provocation, atheists). The recognition, preservation and promotion called for here, and the real, sustained engagement through dialogue and collaboration are not to be under-estimated or assumed. This is a vital posture and activity of the church in the world, and we may well find ourselves in rather surprising partnerships in the years to come.

In meeting this religious stranger, we recognize her as not only 'one of them' but as 'one of us'. It is also true, and this further qualifies the church's relation to other religions, that *we* are not merely 'one of us', either; we are always, this side of Christ's return, also 'one of them'. We are strangers to ourselves; we are antagonists to the kingdom. In *The Lausanne Covenant*, a document by evangelicals united in the common task of 'the whole church taking the whole gospel to the whole world', the authors acknowledge that 'a church which preaches the cross must itself be marked by the cross. It becomes a stumbling block to evangelism when it betrays the gospel or lacks a living faith in God, a genuine love for people, or scrupulous honesty in all things including promotion and finance'.[111] This is too often the case. We are, in Luther's unrelenting words, '*simul iustus et peccator*'. It is not that the church has achieved an unassailable position over against the world. For even as it speaks the gospel, the church is undone and driven to pray, 'God, be merciful to me, a sinner!' (Lk. 18.13).[112] 'This is at once the miracle and the tribulation of the Church, for the Church is condemned by that which establishes it, and is broken in pieces upon its foundations'.[113] The church is able to welcome sinners into its midst because the people of God know that to be a sinner *is* to be 'one of us'. We, too, are sinners; and we, too, are loved by God.

And yet, it is hardly humility or hospitality to shield sinners loved by God from their being (i) sinners and (ii) loved by God – and loved by him in Christ. To collapse our encounter with religious strangers to dialogue without remainder, to banish proclamation and persuasion as passé, even unacceptable tools of cultural conquest is to surrender the gospel itself and to do a singular disservice to another. While we may make significant common cause with others, the church's first and final cause is Christ the King. Even the most unnoticeable of churchly activities arises from, and is oriented to, the reign of God in Christ, and the church's great hope is in the day when people from every tongue, tribe and nation will join her in worship of the Lamb who was slain that they might be reconciled to God (Rev. 7.9).

So we do invite others to become 'one of us' in the church – not in an arrogation of moral superiority but in a proclamation of the wideness of God's mercy. In keeping with the church's indicative character, we do not invite a person to look to us, but to call on the name of the Lord.

> For, 'Everyone who calls on the name of the Lord shall be saved'. But how are they to call on one in whom they have not believed? And how are they to believe in one of whom they have never heard? And how are they to hear without someone to proclaim him? And how are they to proclaim him unless they are sent? As it is written, 'How beautiful are the feet of those who bring good news!' (Rom. 10.13–15)

This is the normative pattern of evangelism, the way in which the gospel is proclaimed and people come to believe in Christ. Faith comes by hearing (Rom. 10.17). If it is normative, though, it nevertheless fails to account for many people in the history of the world.[114] What about those before Christ (an issue we will put to the side) or those to whom the gospel was never proclaimed?[115]

This leads us to our second question: (How) are we to evaluate the soteriological status of people outside the church who have not heard the good news of the King and his reign? Whether we should do so is a legitimate question. It is not at all clear that the scriptures are interested in evaluating the soteriological status of those who have never heard the gospel. Clearly the universal horizon of scripture inclines God's people to mission and to hope for the salvation of the world, but beyond the necessity and ubiquity of the gospel's proclamation, the New Testament takes little interest in speculation as to the fate of those outside God's people who never hear the good news. Its emphasis 'is always on surprise'.[116] The church is simply commanded to proclaim the kingship of Christ and call all to receive his reign in humble obedience and worship.

On the question of the salvation of non-Christians, George Lindbeck cautions humility and notes that the New Testament's talk of judgment is exclusively with reference to the in-group of believers such that, while we affirm Cyprian's *extra ecclesia nulla salus*, that must be balanced with the statement that there is also 'no damnation outside the church'.[117] Here we have a rigorously non-speculative answer; it is complemented by Hans Urs von Balthasar's argument in *Dare We Hope "That All Men Be Saved"?*[118] His answer: We may hope and pray that this is so, even if we may not assume it. Two parallel themes run throughout the New Testament whose tension will not be resolved this side of the *eschaton*: the very real threat of hell and damnation and the universal love of God and his desire that all would come to salvation.[119] Hell's threat, so Balthasar, invites self-scrutiny and decision, not speculation about others (see, e.g. Mt. 8.11–12; Heb. 10.26–27). The virtue of both these accounts is their reminder that judgment begins with the household of God (1 Pet. 4.17), coupled with a restraint in insisting that we cannot conduct an ecclesial census and thereby know the population of the new Jerusalem.[120] But, the threat of hell remains in scripture, and in close juxtaposition to the hope of salvation (see Rev. 21.7–8). If we may hope for the salvation of those outside the church, we must also fear for their damnation. Furthermore, and most importantly, the church's primary task with reference to those outside the church is not to assume their salvation or their damnation; it is to go to them to proclaim the good news of the kingdom.

There is much, then, that we cannot say. But what can we say? Consider again the Cyprianic dictum: *extra ecclesiam nulla salus*.[121] What are we to make of Cyprian's gnomic remark?[122] A distinction between the visible and invisible church is relevant at this point, though it cannot be recruited to dissolve the issue. The church faces two temptations – 'to imagine there can be a total coincidence of identity and form' and 'to dissociate the identity and the outer form'.[123] In a soft sense, Cyprian is right: to be saved by God is to be saved in and into his church. But, because there can be no total coincidence of identity and form this side of the *eschaton*, one can meaningfully ask about a person's affiliation with the eschatological church *even as he is currently outside the church's form*. Yet this does not invite us to abstract questions of salvation from the church's outer form, as if it had nothing to do with, or were even antagonistic to, the new life of God's kingdom.

Jesus describes the life of the kingdom as knowing 'you, the only true God, and Jesus Christ whom you have sent' (Jn 17.3). This is the knowledge of communion, of fellowship, and to be saved is to enter the living fellowship of the triune God with his people in his kingdom. The church is that company of people who have come to know *this* God and to live in his kingdom by virtue of his having come to reconcile and dwell among them in Christ and opened their eyes and hearts to him in the Spirit. The church is where we learn this. It is a school of the kingdom in which we learn the grammar of salvation, where we learn to discern God's action and respond in faith and obedience.[124] Even if there may be salvation *then* apart from affiliation with the church now, there is no salvation *now* apart from the church.

A common argument needs mentioning here, which runs as follows: With those who have heard, God saves through faith rather than works. With those who have not heard, though, God considers their charity, their having done their best, possibly their good intentions. The problem here is that the economy of grace has been traded away in a well-intentioned, even deeply moral attempt not to lose the best and brightest outside the church. However God considers those who have never heard, we can say that the God in whom is no shadow of turning (Jas 1.17) only ever saves people by grace through faith in Christ. Attempts to smuggle pious pagans into the kingdom by virtue of their virtue fail in that they posit a different economy in God's relations with these others, thereby deserting the economy of grace and suggesting that God may be other than the one we meet in Christ. If and when God saves people who never entered the company of God's people, it will only be as the Spirit brings them by grace to faith in Christ.

Just as mission needs to be seen in light of the *missio Dei*, the question of the salvation of the unevangelized needs to be seen in light of the Trinity. A recent proposal re-describes Cyprian's dictum in trinitarian terms: 'Outside the Trinity, there is no church; inside the Triune God's church, there is salvation'.[125] Or, a bit more exclusively: 'Outside the Trinity, there is no salvation, no redemption, not even for the church. Outside the church of the Triune God, there is no salvation'.[126] The key point in these different formulations is the migration of soteriological exclusivism from ecclesiology to the doctrine of the Trinity, or, at least, and more precisely, the subordination of the ecclesiological weight of Cyprian's claim (*extra ecclesiam nulla salus*) to the doctrine of the Trinity. This staves off ecclesial trium-phalism in its location of the church against the broader horizon of the triune God. But, and here we should be clear, this is not an invitation to stray from the church as the centre of God's saving work. Just as God has appointed ordinary means of grace in the church, he has appointed the church as the means of grace – the ordinary means of salvation – in the world.

In a sense, this is what we have argued for throughout the book – for a foregrounding of the triune God and the economy of salvation along with a robust doctrine of the church whose tent is big enough to include all those the Spirit has led to the Father in the Son but whose end is not in itself but in the kingdom of God.

PAROUSIA AND ECCLESIA

Finally, then, and to round out our rehearsal of the church in the economy of salvation, ascension and Pentecost need to be seen against the horizon of the final return of Christ – when Christ will be finally, utterly present. If Christ's ascension marks his absence from the church, and if Pentecost marks him both present in the Spirit and absent in the body, parousia is the time of pure, unambiguous presence. 'See, the home of God is among mortals. He will dwell with them; they will be his peoples; and God himself will be with them' (Rev. 21.3).

At his return, Christ will come in judgment, revelation and victory. As judgment, it is the day on which he will separate the righteous from the wicked, vindicate the righteous and consign the wicked to the wrath of God. This is a day on which the *corpus mixtum* will become the pure church. She will be 'the new Jerusalem, coming down out of heaven from God, prepared as a bride adorned for her husband' (Rev. 21.2). As revelation, it is the day on which 'the earth and everything that is done on it will be disclosed' (1 Pet. 3.10). No longer the incognito incarnate one, at the Last Day, Christ will be manifest for all to see (Rev. 1.7). His enemies, too, will be revealed; and it is Christ's own revelation and 'the breath of his mouth' that destroys them (2 Thess. 2.8). So his return means victory.

Short of his return, the church and the world are difficult to disentangle. Short of his return, the hopes and fears of all are ambiguous. Short of his return, the church is *simul iustus et peccator*. Holy in Christ, its words and deeds carry a corresponding holiness at times, a shocking profanity at others. Short of his return, we must continue to distinguish the church as it is and the church as it will be, the church in its earthly and heavenly modes, the church militant and triumphant. At the Last Day, such ambiguities and distinctions will cease. God's holy people will be vindicated. The church will be purified and 'gathered together to him' (2 Thess. 2.1). Jesus will rescue those who have eagerly waited for him from the coming wrath (1 Thess. 1.10; Heb. 9.28). He will reward them, too. 'From now on there is reserved for me the crown of righteousness, which the Lord, the righteous judge, will give me on that day, and not only to me but also to all who have longed for his appearing' (1 Tim. 4.8).

If the church longs for his appearing – and it does – it nevertheless remains vigilant. Vigilance involves faithful waiting, the watching and praying Jesus called his disciples to in a time of temptation. We should be wary, in our *in via* state, of easy and careless identification of ourselves with the vindicated. Jesus warns of an eschatological surprise at his return, as eternal life and punishment are allotted, respectively, to those who did and did not care for 'the least of these' (Mt. 25.31–46; also see Rev. 22.12).

Why, we might ask, has the Lord not returned? Why does he, to use an older word, tarry?

> The Lord is not slow about his promise, as some think of slowness, but is patient with you, not wanting any to perish, but all to come to repentance. But the day of the Lord will come like a thief, and then the heavens will pass away with a loud noise, and the elements will be dissolved with fire, and the earth and everything that is done on it will be disclosed. (1 Pet. 3.9–10)

The Lord is patient. He would have all come to repentance. There is an utter finality to the last day; as the day of judgment, it is the end of repentance. The Lord wants none to perish, and so he waits. The time of the church occurs in this interim, and the church's mission of inviting 'all to come to repentance' reflects the compassionate patience of its God. Thus, the church's waiting is a peculiarly *active* waiting in mission rather than a marking time. And its missional expectation looks forward to the worship of God's people in the kingdom:

> After this I looked, and there was a great multitude that no one could count, from every nation, from all tribes and peoples and languages, standing before the throne and before the Lamb, robed in white, with palm branches in their hands. They cried out

in a loud voice, saying, 'Salvation belongs to our God who is seated on the throne, and to the Lamb!' (Rev. 7.9–10)

If *now* is the time for mission, *then* is the time for worship. And so:

> Missions is not the ultimate goal of the church. Worship is. Missions exists because worship doesn't. Worship is ultimate, not missions, because God is ultimate, not man. When this age is over, and the countless millions of the redeemed fall on their faces before the throne of God, missions will be no more. It is a temporary necessity. But worship abides forever.
> Worship, therefore, is the fuel and goal of missions.[1]

It is thus in light of the end that the church busies itself between the two advents of Christ in the power of the Spirit. This vision of heavenly worship reminds us that, important though the church's mission in correspondence to the divine patience is, its hope and orientation are to the day of Christ's return, a day when 'All shall be well, and / All manner of thing shall be well'.[2] Every word and action of the church strains toward the day of his coming, such that the church's life is captured, disclosed and fulfilled in the prayer of '*Maranatha*'.

> The Spirit and the bride say, 'Come'. And let everyone who hears say, 'Come'. And let everyone who is thirsty come. Let anyone who wishes take the water of life as a gift. . . . The one who testifies to these things says, 'Surely I am coming soon'. Amen. Come, Lord Jesus!' (Rev. 22.17–20)

NOTES

INTRODUCTION

1. See Nicholas Healy's critique of 'blueprint ecclesiologies' in his *Church, World and Christian Life: Practical-Prophetic Ecclesiology* (Cambridge: Cambridge University Press, 2000).
2. See *The Catechism of the Catholic Church*, p. 442.
3. It should be noted that even extreme views, such as the notion that Jesus never existed and that Christ is a recycled myth from ancient mystery cults, which was earlier championed by Bruno Bauer (1809–1882) and James George Frazier, *The Golden Bough* (1890), can be still be found in scholars such as Earl Doherty, *The Jesus Puzzle: Did Christianity Begin with a Mythical Christ?* (Ottawa, Canada: Canadian Humanist Publications, 1999); and Timothy Freke and Peter Gandy, *The Jesus Mysteries: Was the 'Original Jesus' a Pagan God?* (New York: Three Rivers, 2001). Similarly, in what could better be classified as a conspiracy theory, Hugh J. Schonfeld, *The Passover Plot* (New York: Bantam Books, 1965), Jesus is said to have intended to fake his death. These types of theories have found few adherents. G. A. Wells, for example, first held to this view, but later conceded that Jesus must have existed, but most accounts of him are legendary (see Wells, *Did Jesus Exist?* [Amherst, N.Y.: Prometheus Books, 1987] and Wells, *The Jesus Myth* [Open Court Publishing Company, 1998]). A more representative view of the whole scope of scholarship would be E. P. Sanders (*Jesus and Judaism* [Minneapolis, Minn.: Fortress Press, 1987]) delineating categories of certain, highly probable, probable and so forth.
4. These examples are listed because they are each the most popular within their own approach. There are many scholars who would be between Ehrman and Wright, and between Wright and Strobel (just as there are scholars who would more to the left of Ehrman and more to the right of Strobel). These three, however, are some of the most accessible.
5. Although the following discussion does not agree point-for-point with the specific conclusions of David Catchpole, *Jesus People: The Historical Jesus and the Beginnings of Community* (Grand Rapids, Mich.: Baker Academic, 2006), much of our method follows Catchpole's approach in that an application of the historical critical method, even when applied with a strong 'hermeneutic of suspicion', still results in a Jesus of history founding a 'church'.

6. Again, the present summary grossly oversimplifies the scholarly discourse. However, we have roughly followed the kinds of 'criteria of authenticity' found in scholars like John P. Meier, *A Marginal Jew: Rethinking the Historical Jesus* (New York: Doubleday, 1991), 1:167ff.; and Gerd Lüdemann, *The Great Deception: And What Jesus Really Said and Did* (Amherst, N.Y.: Prometheus Books, 1999) and Lüdemann, *Jesus After 2000 Years: What He Really Said and Did* (Amherst, N.Y.: Prometheus Books, 2001).

7. Schweitzer, *The Quest of the Historical Jesus: A Critical Study of Its Progress from Reimarus to Wrede*, trans. W. Montgomery (London: Adam and Charles, 1910 [Germ. orig. 1906]).

8. G. Tyrrell, *Christianity and the Crossroads* (London: Longman's Green, 1963 [1909]), p. 49.

9. A more recent example of such a Schweitzerian reconstruction can be found in Paula Fredriksen, *From Jesus to Christ: The Origins of the New Testament Images of Jesus* (New Haven, Conn.: Yale University Press, 2000). It should be noted, however, that the members of the Jesus Seminar have come to the opposite conclusion: it was John the Baptist and Paul who were apocalyptic and whose apocalyptic teachings were later confused with Jesus. See Robert Funk, *Honest to Jesus: Jesus for a New Millennium* (San Francisco: HarperCollins, 1997).

10. Attempts to make this last, rather radical and evidentially weak, claim usually revert to Paul as the 'founder' of Christianity; for example, Hyam Macoby, *The Mythmaker: Paul and the Invention of Christianity* (San Francisco: HarperCollins, 1987); Gerd Lüdemann, *Paul* (Amherst, N.Y.: Prometheus, 2002).

11. For a recent example, see Richard Bauckham, *Jesus and the Eyewitnesses: The Gospels as Eyewitness Testimony* (Grand Rapids, Mich.: Eerdmans, 2008).

12. James D. G. Dunn and Scot McKnight, *The Historical Jesus in Recent Research* (Winona Lake, Ind.: Eisenbrauns, 2005), p. xi.

13. Dunn, *A New Perspective on Jesus: What the Quest for the Historical Jesus Missed* (Grand Rapids, Mich.: Baker Academic, 2005). Similarly, see Luke Timothy Johnson, *The Real Jesus: The Misguided Quest for the Historical Jesus and the Truth of the Traditional Gospels* (San Francisco: HarperCollins, 1997).

14. The work of Sanders has been especially influential on the scholarly debate in that Sanders insists on Jesus being in keeping with Second Temple Judaism, not a radical break from it (see Sanders, 'Jesus in Historical Context', *Theology Today* 50:3 [1993], 429–48). Sanders' view shares much in common with the earlier work by Geza Vermes, *Jesus the Jew* (London: SCM, 1973). Sanders' and Vermes' work influence much of scholarship in that it is now rarely asserted that Jesus would have intended to make a radical break from the Judaism of his day. Supersessionism (especially in an anti-Semitic form) would have been a later Christian development.

15. For example, Robert Eisenman, *James the Brother of Jesus* (London: Penguin, 1998).

16. For example, compare the views of Gerd Theissen, *The Historical Jesus: A Comprehensive Guide* (Minneapolis, Minn.: Fortress Press, 1998), who sees Jesus as intending to re-establish the 12 tribes in the 12 apostles, and Robert Stein, *Jesus the Messiah: A Survey of the Life of Christ* (Downers Grove, Ill.: InterVarsity Press, 1996), who argues for the traditional understanding of Jesus as foreknowing his death and resurrection and intending to establish the church. The noteworthy aspect of these two views is that Jesus did intend to establish 'the people of God' in some form.

17. A few detractors of this position can be found of course: for example, Burton Mack, *The Lost Gospel: The Book of Q and Christian Origins* (San Francisco: Harper SanFrancisco, 1994), p. 222, who nevertheless concedes that the last supper is a historically verifiable occurrence, only that Jesus was celebrating a traditional Passover meal.

18. See John Dominic Crossan, *The Birth of Christianity* (San Francisco: HarperSanFrancisco, 1999).

19. Note how the broad range of sources that agree on Jesus' words over the bread and wine at the last supper (Mk 14.22–25; 1 Cor. 11.23–26; cf. Jn 6.51–58) pass the historical criterion of 'multiple attestation' both quantitatively and qualitatively.

20. Even Schweitzer, in seeing Jesus as an apocalyptic prophet, concedes that Jesus taught a temporary ethical code for his followers until the world's imminent end arrived. More recently, see this view in Ehrman, *Jesus: Apocalyptic Prophet of the New Millennium* (Oxford: Oxford University Press, 1999). On the other end of the spectrum from Schweitzer, Stephen Patterson, *The Gospel of Thomas and Jesus* (Sonoma, Calif.: Polebridge Press, 1992), sees Jesus as a sage who never intended to sacrifice himself and yet who insisted that his followers adhere to a radically new form of living.

21. Horsley, *Jesus and the Spiral of Violence: Popular Jewish Resistance in Roman Palestine* (Minneapolis, Minn.: Fortress Press, 1992), p. 240.

22. Borg, *Meeting Jesus Again for the First Time* (San Francisco: HarperSanFrancisco, 1995), p. 119.

23. Paul Ricoeur, *The Symbolism of Evil*, trans. Emerson Buchanan (Boston: Beacon Press, 1967).

ASCENSION AND ECCLESIA

1. The title of Douglas Farrow's justly lauded *Ascension and Ecclesia: On the Significance of the Doctrine of the Ascension for Ecclesiology and Christian Cosmology* (Grand Rapids, Mich.: Eerdmans, 1999).

2. See Deut. 18.15–18, 34.10–12.

3. The incarnation is perhaps the truest, most profound illustration of Marshall McLuhan's quip that 'the medium is the message'.

4. In his commentary on Mt. 12.14; cited in Joseph Ratzinger, *Eschatology: Death and Eternal Life*, 2nd edn (Washington, D.C.: Catholic University of America Press, 2007), p. 34.

CHAPTER 1 – MODELS

1. All available in translation on the Vatican's website (http://www. vatican.va/archive/hist_councils/ii_vatican_council/).
2. 'Begins' in an ecclesial sense, not a chronological one. Vatican II arose out of debate and was characterized by debate. We do not treat here issues pertaining more internally to the Roman Catholic Church, such as Neo-Thomism and Ultramontanism. For full treatment of these matters, see the sources in the footnotes below.
3. *What Happened at Vatican II* (Cambridge, Mass.: Harvard University Press, 2008).
4. Matthew Lamb and Matthew Levering (eds), *Vatican II: Renewal within Tradition*, (Oxford: Oxford University Press, 2008). Even the history of the history of Vatican II is much disputed. Compare the reviews of O'Malley by contributors to *The Washington Post* and in *First Things* (October 2008). The former finds O'Malley's work helpful and well researched, the latter finds it to be left-leaning propaganda that ignores the evidence. (It should be noted that similarly polarized reviews can be found for Lamb and Levering.) The most complete, yet accessible, history of this council is in Giuseppe Alberigo and Joseph Komonchak (eds), *The History of Vatican II*, 5 vols (Maryknoll, N.Y.: Orbis; Leuven: Peeters, 1995–2006), but this work has also been criticized for its liberal agenda. We also recommend Melissa J. Wilde, *Vatican II: A Sociological Analysis of Religious Change* (Princeton, N.J.: Princeton University Press, 2007).
5. The most famous example would be Archbishop Marcel Lefebvre, who founded the Society of St. Pius X in opposition to Vatican II and which refused to recognize the post-Vatican II popes in Rome as the rightful heirs to Peter. As a side note, Pope Benedict XVI recently (2009) lifted John Paul II's 1988 excommunication of this group's leaders.
6. One example where this can be seen is in the role of Mary. Whereas the Council of Ephesus (431) defined Christology by declaring Mary 'Mother of God' (*theotokos*), at Vatican II Pope Paul VI defined ecclesiology by describing Mary as 'Mother of the Church' (*Mater Ecclesiae*).
7. This shift is especially seen in *Gaudium et Spes* and *Lumen Gentium*, wherein the church is defined as the communion of believers, not as a hierarchy of bishops. Also, the controversial teachings of salvation found outside of the Church's 'visible confines' and non-Catholic Christians deemed 'brothers by baptism' arguably imply a shift in ecclesiological thinking from Cyprian's earlier dictum, *Extra ecclesiam nulla salus* ('Outside the Church there is no salvation').
8. Tillard, *Church of Churches: The Ecclesiology of Communion*, trans. R. C. De Peaux (Collegeville, Minn.: Liturgical Press, 1992).
9. See Ernest Skublics, 'The Rebirth of Communion Ecclesiology within Orthodoxy: From Nineteenth Century Russians to Twenty-first Century Greeks', *Logos* 46:1–2 (2005): 95–124.

10. For a prominent mainline example, see Robert Jenson, *Systematic Theology*, vol. 2, *The Works of God* (Oxford: Oxford University Press, 1999). For a prominent free church example, see Miroslav Volf, *After Our Likeness: The Church as the Image of the Trinity* (Grand Rapids, Mich.: Eerdmans, 1998).

11. Thomas P. Rausch, *Towards a Truly Catholic Church: An Ecclesiology for the Third Millennium* (Collegeville, Minn.: Liturgical Press, 2005), p. 84: 'As we have seen, the term *koinonia* or communion is a rich theological concept that lies at the heart of the nature of the Church'.

12. See discussion in Dennis M. Doyle, *Communion Ecclesiology: Visions and Versions* (Maryknoll, N.Y.: Orbis Books, 2000).

13. Paul S. Minear, *Images of the Church in the New Testament* (Philadelphia: Westminster Press, 1977 [1960]).

14. Minear, *Images of the Church*, p. 66.

15. For example, Hans Küng, *The Church*, trans. Ray and Rosaleen Ockenden (New York: Sheed and Ward, 1967); and WCC Faith and Order, *The Nature and Purpose of the Church* (Faith and Order Paper #181; 1998), available online at http://www.oikoumene.org/en/resources/documents/ wcc-commissions/faith-and-order-commission/i-unity-the-church-and-its-mission/previous-stage-the-nature-and-purpose-of-the-church-a-stage-on-the-way-to-a-common-statement.html, and WCC Faith and Order, *The Nature and Mission of the Church* (Faith and Order Paper #198; 2005), available online at http://www.oikoumene.org/en/resources/ documents/wcc-commissions/faith-and-order-commission/i-unity-the-church-and-its-mission/the-nature-and-mission-of-the-church-a-stage-on-the-way-to-a-common-statement.html.

16. See both Ernst Käsemann, 'Unity and Diversity in New Testament Ecclesiology', *Novum Testamentum* 6 (1963): 290–97; and Raymond E. Brown, 'Unity and Diversity in New Testament Ecclesiology', *Novum Testamentum* 6 (1963): 298–308. Both articles were originally speeches before the WCC, and so their positions have influenced later biblical scholars as well as theologians.

17. Minear, *Images*, pp. 173–74.

18. Dulles, *Models of the Church*, expanded ed. (New York: Doubleday, 2002 [1974]).

19. Dulles, *Models of the Church*, p. 4.

20. Dulles, *Models of the Church*, pp. 26–27.

21. Ferdinand Tönnies, *Community and Society* (New York: Harper Torchbooks, 1963 [orig. *Gemeinschaft und Gesellschaft* 1887];) and see also Ernest Troeltsch, *The Social Teachings of the Christian Churches*, 2 vols (New York: Macmillan, 1956), who distinguishes between 'church' and 'sect'.

22. See Alistair E. McGrath, *Christian Theology: An Introduction*, 4th edn (Oxford: Blackwell, 2007), pp. 397–402; although it should be noted that McGrath explains how Calvin defined the church primarily as herald. Luther and Calvin are seen as most consistent in the following terms: the institutional aspects of the church remain necessary, but are in themselves insufficient (one must also rightly preach the Word).

23. See the WCC Faith and Order, *The Nature and Mission of the Church* (Faith and Order Paper #198; 2005), §5.
24. Dulles, *Models of the Church*, p. 32, and see p. 36 where 'honest scholarship' cannot find these in the ancient sources.
25. Dulles, *Models of the Church*, p. 27.
26. Alasdair MacIntyre, *After Virtue: A Study in Moral Theory*, 2nd edn (Notre Dame, Ind.: University of Notre Dame Press, 1984).
27. Michel Foucault, *The Archaeology of Knowledge*, trans. A. M. Sheridan Smith (New York: Pantheon Books, 1976 [French orig. 1969]).
28. Nicholas Healy, 'Communion Ecclesiology: A Cautionary Note', *Pro Ecclesia* 4 (1995), p. 450, cited in Dennis M. Doyle, *Communion Ecclesiology* (Maryknoll, N.Y.: Orbis, 2000), pp. 5–6.
29. Dulles, *Models of the Church*, p. 40.
30. *Ecclesiogenesis* (Maryknoll, NY: Orbis, 1997 [1977]), p. 1; ref. Yves M.-J. Congar, 'Os grupos informais na Igreja', in *Communidades eclesiais de base: utopia ou realidade?*, ed. Alfonso Gregory (Petrópolis, Brazil: Vozes, 1993), pp. 144–45.
31. Boff, *Ecclesiogenesis*, p. 5.
32. Boff, *Ecclesiogenesis*, p. 7.
33. Boff, *Ecclesiogenesis*, p. 10.
34. Boff, *Ecclesiogenesis*, p. 26.
35. Boff, *Ecclesiogenesis*, p. 37. Boff furthers this idea in his conclusion to *Church: Charism and Power*, trans. John W. Diercksmeier (New York: Crossroad, 1985 [1981]).
36. Boff, *Ecclesiogenesis*, p. 8.
37. Dulles, *Models of the Church*, p. 29, suggests as much.
38. Walter Bauer, *Orthodoxy and Heresy in Earliest Christianity*, eds Robert A. Kraft and Gerhard Kroedel (Philadelphia: Fortress Press, 1979 [1934]).
39. James D. G. Dunn, *Unity and Diversity in the New Testament: An Inquiry into the Character of Earliest Christianity* (Philadelphia: Westminster, 1977).
40. The debate between traditional Roman Catholics, Rudolph Sohm, and then in response Adolf von Harnack and Hans von Campenhausen would require an entire chapter.
41. For bibliography and a helpful discussion of the Philippians 1:1 passage, which has 'exercised the minds of exegetes', see Markus Bockmuehl, *Epistle to the Philippians* (Edinburgh: Continuum, 2006 [1996]). On Paul more generally, see Robert Banks, *Paul's Idea of Community*, rev. ed. (Peabody, Mass.: Hendrickson Publishers, 1996).
42. While this explanation is still common among scholars, R. Alistair Campbell, *The Elders: Seniority within Earliest Christianity* (Edinburgh: T&T Clark, 1994), has championed a 'new consensus' that we find more convincing. The Pauline churches were never entirely charismatic and without structure, and the synagogue-model is ill-attested in the evidence.
43. In what follows, we treat extra-canonical sources in chronological order, but we do not engage in the dating and influence of Acts and the Pastoral Epistles. For such a discussion, we recommend Patrick Burke,

'The Monarchical Episcopate at the End of the First Century', *Journal of Ecumenical Studies* 7 (1970): 499–518; and I. Howard Marshall, *The Pastoral Epistles* (International Critical Commentary; Edinburgh: T&T Clark, 1999), pp. 52–57.

44. A key passage is Acts 20.17–38, where the 'elders' from Ephesus come to Paul, and Paul calls them 'overseers' and commands them to 'pastor' the flock. See also the where the terms 'bishop' and 'presbyter' seem to be interchangeable in 1 Tim. 3 and Tit. 1. This is assumed by Burke, 'Monarchical Episcopate at the End of the First Century'; and Everett Ferguson, 'The Ministry of the Word in the First Two Centuries', *Restoration Quarterly* 1:1 (1957): 21–31. See Everett Ferguson, 'Church Order in the Sub-Apostolic Period: A Survey of Interpretations', *Restoration Quarterly* 11:4 (1968): 225–48, for a survey of other theories.

45. See Campbell, *The Elders*. However, Benjamin L. Merkle, *The Elders and the Overseer: One Office in the Early Church* (SBL 57; New York: Lang, 2003), disputes Campbell's notion that 'elder' intonated a place of honour, regardless of office. Instead, 'elder' and 'bishop' should be seen as synonymous. We still find Campbell's position more convincing. See his response to Merkle in Campbell, 'The Elder and Everseer: One Office in the Early Church', *Evangelical Quarterly* 77:3 (July 2005): 281–83.

46. The discovery of the *Didache*, however, has all but ruled out this option for modern scholars.

47. For the first view, see Eric G. Jay, 'From Presbyter-Bishops to Bishops and Presbyters, Christian Ministry in the Second Century: A Survey', *Second Century* 1:3 (Fall 1981): 125–62. For the second view, see Allen Brent, *Hippolytus and the Roman Church in the Third Century* (Leiden: Brill, 1995); Brent, 'St Hippolytus, Biblical Exegete, Roman Bishop, and Martyr', *St Vladimir's Theological Quarterly* 48:2–3 (2004): 207–31; and Alister Stewart-Sykes, *Hippolytus: On the Apostolic Tradition: An English Version with Introduction and Commentary* (Crestwood, N.Y.: St. Vladimir's Seminary, 2001).

48. Ware, 'Patterns of Episcopacy in the Early Church and Today: An Orthodox View', in Peter Moore (ed.), *Bishops, But What Kind? Reflections on Episcopacy*, (London: SPCK, 1982), pp. 1–24.

49. Ware, 'Patterns of Episcopacy', p. 2.

50. Ware, 'Patterns of Episcopacy', p. 4.

51. Ware, 'Patterns of Episcopacy', p. 5.

52. Ware, 'Patterns of Episcopacy', p. 3.

53. Ware, 'Patterns of Episcopacy', p. 6; ref. Ignatius, *Polycarp*, 7.2.

54. Ware, 'Patterns of Episcopacy', p. 5. It should be noted that Ware's assumption that second century churches gathered in one eucharistic assembly per *polis* is without evidence. Ignatius himself mentions other 'gatherings' apart from his congregation in Antioch, but these are of course deemed heretical, and the Christian practice of meeting 'house to house' cannot have disappeared entirely. Ware is helpful, however, in his faithfulness to Ignatius' own framework: all questions of historical

occurrences aside, Ignatius' *argument* assumes the church to be one eucharistic fellowship gathered around its bishop.

55. Ware, 'Patterns of Episcopacy', p. 8.
56. Ware, 'Patterns of Episcopacy', p. 12.
57. For further discussion of Irenaeus' understanding of the episcopate, see R. J. R. Paice, 'Irenaeus on the Authority of Scripture, the "Rule of Truth" and Episcopacy (Part 1)', *The Churchman* 117:1 (2003) 57–70; and Paice, 'Irenaeus on the Authority of Scripture, the "Rule of Truth" and Episcopacy (Part 2)', *The Churchman* 117:2 (2003): 133–52.
58. Ware, 'Patterns of Episcopacy', p. 12.
59. Ware, 'Patterns of Episcopacy', p. 14.
60. Ware, 'Patterns of Episcopacy', p. 16.
61. Cyprian, *De unitate* 5; discussed in Ware, 'Patterns of Episcopacy', p. 17.
62. Ware, 'Patterns of Episcopacy', pp. 17–18.
63. Ware, 'Patterns of Episcopacy', p. 18.
64. Ware, 'Patterns of Episcopacy', p. 18.
65. See Ignatius, *Rom* 9: 'In your prayer remember the church in Syria, which has God as its shepherd in my place', trans. Bart D. Ehrman, *The Apostolic Fathers*, vol. 1 (Loeb Classical Library; London: Harvard University Press, 2003), p. 281. In other words, even Ignatius admits that a bishop-less church is still a church, only now Christ himself is its bishop until another representative can be appointed.
66. As he did for all seven of the ecumenical councils.
67. 'An Outline of the Faith, Commonly Called the Catechism', in *Book of Common Prayer* (New York: Seabury Press), p. 857. Note this wording is almost verbatim to the Council of Trent.
68. One of us, coming from the Baptist tradition in North America, is especially sensitive to those who prefer the term 'ordinance'. We recommend Gordon T. Smith (ed.), *The Lord's Supper: Five Views* (Downers Grove, Ill.: IVP Academic, 2008). The contributors firmly stand by their respective traditions, and yet they are still able to agree on the importance and general 'outward sign, inward grace' motif – even Roger Olson, who demonstrates how 'sacramentalism' is anything but antithetical to the Baptist tradition.
69. See further Gary Badcock, 'The Church as "Sacrament"', in *The Community of the Word: Toward an Evangelical Ecclesiology*, eds Mark Husbands and Daniel J. Treier (Downers Grove, Ill.: InterVarsity Press, 2005), pp. 188–200; Günther Gassmann, 'The church as sacrament, sign and instrument: the reception of this ecclesiological understanding and ecumenical debate', in *Church, Kingdom, World: The Church as Mystery and Prophetic Sign*, ed. Gennadios Limouris (Geneva: World Council of Churches, 1986), pp. 1–17; Timothy George, 'The Sacramentality of the Church: An Evangelical Baptist Perspective', *Pro Ecclesia* 12:3 (September 2003): 309–23; Robert W. Jenson, *Unbaptized God: The Basic Flaw in Ecumenical Theology* (Minneapolis, Minn.: Fortress Press, 1992), pp. 90–103; John M. McDermott, 'Vatican II and the Theologians on the Church as Sacrament', *Irish Theological Quarterly* 71 (2006): 143–78; Eberhard Jüngel, 'The Church as Sacrament?',

in *Theological Essays I* (Edinburgh: T&T Clark, 1999), pp. 189–213. For a critical response to Jüngel, see Geoffrey Wainwright, 'Church and Sacrament(s)', in *The Possibilities of Theology: Studies in the Theology of Eberhard Jüngel in his Sixtieth Year,* ed. John Webster (London: T&T Clark, 1994), pp. 90–105.

70. *Lumen Gentium* 48; and *Sacrosanctum Concilium* 26, ref. Cyprian, *De unitate* 7.

71. Rome: 28 May 1992; available online at http://www.vatican.va/roman_curia/congregations/cfaith/documents/rc_con_cfaith_doc_28051992_communionis-notio_en.html.

72. Ratzinger, *Letter to the Bishops*, p. 1.

73. Ratzinger, *Letter to the Bishops*, pp. 1, 3.

74. Ratzinger, *Letter to the Bishops*, p. 3.

75. Ratzinger, *Letter to the Bishops*, p. 4. Elsewhere, Ratzinger had already affirmed this: *Principles of Catholic Theology: Building Stones for a Fundamental Theology*, trans. Mary Frances McCarthy (San Francisco: Ignatius Press, 1987 [1982]), pp. 47–48.

76. Ratzinger, *Letter to the Bishops*, 8.

77. Ratzinger, *Letter to the Bishops*, p. 10, and see p. 12.

78. Ratzinger, *Letter to the Bishops*, p. 11.

79. The Orthodox response is no less 'institutional'. It merely diffuses the required visible/outward element from Rome to each bishopric. See the response of Metropolitan Maximos of Pittsburgh, 'Will the Ecclesiology of Cardinal Ratzinger Influence the Pontificate of Pope Benedict the XVI?' in *The Pontificate of Benedict XVI: Its Premises and Promises* (Grand Rapids, Mich.: Eerdmans, 2009), pp. 79–96.

80. Ratzinger, *Letter to the Bishops*, p. 13.

81. Ratzinger, *Letter to the Bishops*, p. 17.

82. *Sacrosanctum Concilium* 41. The same is the case for the famous statement in *Lumen Gentium* 8, where 'the one Church of Christ . . . subsists in the Catholic Church'.

83. Cf. his later statement: Benedict XVI, *Deus Caritas Est*, 14, 'this sacramental "mysticism" is social in character'.

84. Cf. his section entitled, 'The Church as the Sacrament of Salvation' in *Principles*, pp. 45–55.

85. The famous 'Ratzinger Proposal' asserts: '. . . Rome must not demand from the East more recognition of the doctrine of primacy than was known and practiced in the first millennium' (Ratzinger, *Principles of Catholic Theology* [Fort Collins, Colo.: Ignatius Press, 1987], p. 199).

86. Dulles, *Models of the Church*, p. 67.

87. It should be noted: the Faith and Order commission could not come to any consensus on the sacramental model of the church precisely because there is wide-spread resistance to declaring that the church is sacrament; see *The Nature and Mission of the Church* (Faith and Order Paper #198; 2005), discussion box after §48.

88. Ratzinger, 'The Transmission of Divine Revelation', in *Commentary on the Documents of Vatican II*, vol. 3, eds Herbert Vorgrimler et al. (New York: Herder and Herder, 1969 [1967]), p. 194, uses this distinction

to explain the relationship between scripture and tradition, which are interdependent and inseparable but not indistinguishable: the church has defined what scripture 'is', while only defining what tradition 'does'.

89. So far, our three-fold explication of church (as institutional, communal and sacramental-as-outward-manifestation) has much in common with the ecclesiological framework of Hendrikus Berkhof, *Christian Faith: An Introduction to the Study of Christian Faith* (Grand Rapids, Mich.: Eerdmans, 1979). Berkhof, however, evaluates these three dimensions differently.

90. Dulles, *Models of the Church*, p. 69.

91. See Alistair McGrath, *Iustitia Dei: A History of the Christian Doctrine of Justification*, vol. 2 (Cambridge: Cambridge University Press, 1984).

92. Both of course derive from the respective interpretations of Mt. 16:18. If the 'rock' on which Jesus will build the church is Peter (Greek, *Petros* = English, rock), then the church is built on the papacy. If, however, the *petra* (i.e. with the feminine ending in Greek, as opposed to the masculine name *Petros*) on which the church is said to be built signifies Peter's confession, 'You are the Christ', then the church is founded on the proclamation of the gospel.

93. Webster, *Confessing God: Essays on Christian Dogmatics II* (Edinburgh: T&T Clark, 2005), p. 153.

94. Webster, *Confessing God*, p. 153.

95. Webster, *Confessing God*, p. 156. Oliver O'Donovan shares this worry in his description of 'the complex suburbs of ecclesiology, a branch of theology threatened more than any other by uncontrolled suburban sprawl' (O'Donovan, *The Desire of the Nations: Rediscovering the Roots of Political Theology* [Cambridge: Cambridge University Press, 1999], p. 159).

96. Webster, *Confessing God*, p. 163.

97. Webster, *Confessing God*, pp. 172–74; cf. Ratzinger's/Pope Benedict's ecclesiology of *totus Christus*; and see further exposition and critique in Volf, *After Our Likeness*, pp. 46–47.

98. Webster, *Confessing God*, p. 170.

99. Webster, *Confessing God*, p. 166.

100. Webster, *Confessing God*, p. 175.

101. Webster, *Confessing God*, p. 183.

102. Volf, *After Our Likeness*, pp. 133–34.

103. *Communion Ecclesiology*, p. 166. Edward Schillebeeckx, *Church: The Human Story of God* (New York: Crossroad, 1990), is even more sympathetic to this kind of argument.

104. Dietrich Bonhoeffer, *Letters and Papers from Prison* (New York: Macmillan, 1967).

105. For example, compare how Daniel L. Migliore, *Faith Seeking Understanding: An Introduction to Christian Theology*, 2nd edn (Grand Rapids, Mich.: Eerdmans, 2004), pp. 259–61, who follows Dulles' outline, devotes more time to this model than any of the other four.

106. See the discussion of the controverted question of why and whether Bonhoeffer might be recognized as a martyr in Craig J. Slane, *Bonhoeffer*

as Martyr: Social Responsibility and Modern Christian Commitment (Grand Rapids, Mich.: Brazos Press, 2004).

107. Even famous targets of over-optimistic ecclesiologies, such as Walter Raushenbusch, upon closer read do not simply define the church as 'servant' (see Scott Bryant, 'The Optimistic Ecclesiology of Walter Rauschenbusch', *American Baptist Quarterly* 27:2 [2008]: 117–35). While oversimplification is a symptom of analytical models in general, it is a serious problem for this model in particular.

108. Michael W. Goheen, '*As the Father Has Sent Me, I am Sending You':* J. E. *Lesslie Newbigin's Missionary Ecclesiology* (Zoetermeer: Uitgeverij Boekencentrum, 2000), p. 6.

109. Newbigin, Lesslie, *A Word in Season: Perspectives on Christian World Missions* (Grand Rapids, Mich.: Eerdmans, 1994).

110. Newbigin, *A Word in Season*, p. 52.

111. Newbigin, *A Word in Season*, p. 52.

112. Newbigin, *A Word in Season*, p. 53; emph. orig.

113. Newbigin, *A Word in Season*, p. 53.

114. See discussion in Joon-Sik Park, 'Ecclesiologies in Creative Tension: The Church as Ethical and Missional Reality in H. Richard Niebuhr and John H. Yoder', *International Review of Mission* 92:366 (July 2003): 332–44.

115. Cf. Newbigin, *The Open Secret: An Introduction to the Theology of Mission*, rev. ed. (Grand Rapids, Mich.: Eerdmans, 1995), p. 32, 'Those who are chosen to be bearers of a blessing are chosen for the sake of all'.

116. Newbigin, *A Word in Season*, p. 54.

117. Newbigin, *A Word in Season*, p. 57.

118. Newbigin, *The Open Secret*, p. 33, 'The elect must suffer. The church must lose its life'. For discussion of Newbigin's criticism of ecclesial 'introversion', see Park, 'Ecclesiologies in Creative Tension', pp. 332–44.

119. Newbigin, *A Word in Season*, p. 57.

120. Newbigin, *A Word in Season*, p. 62.

121. Newbigin, *A Word in Season*, p. 60.

122. Newbigin, *A Word in Season*, p. 61.

123. Newbigin, *A Word in Season*, p. 61.

124. Newbigin has been consistent in his treatment of the church's essential and functional definitions: 'It is precisely because she is not *merely* instrumental that she can be instrumental' (*The Household of God: Lectures on the Nature of the Church* [New York: Friendship Press, 1954], p. 169, orig. emphasis).

125. Newbigin, *One Body, One Gospel, One World: The Christian Mission Today* (London: The International Missionary Council, 1958), p. 42.

126. Newbigin, *A Word in Season*, p. 62.

127. Newbigin, *Truth to Tell: The Gospel as Public Truth* (Grand Rapids, Mich.: Eerdmans, 1991), p. 85.

128. Newbigin, *A Word in Season*, p. 62.

129. Newbigin, *A Word in Season*, p. 61.

130. Newbigin, *A Word in Season*, p. 61.

131. *Suffering Divine Things: Theology as Church Practice*, trans. Doug Stott (Grand Rapids, Mich.: Eerdmans, 2000).

132. A point Hütter credits to Barth.
133. On this point see de Lubac, who champions a sacramental model of the church and emphasizes the 'becoming' nature of the church. His discussion of the three meanings of the 'body of Christ' in Thomas Aquinas and modern theology is especially relevant: *Corpus Mysticum: The Eucharist and the Church in the Middle Ages* (London: SCM Press, 2006); cf. David Grumett, *De Lubac: A Guide for the Perplexed* (Edinburgh: T&T Clark, 2007), pp. 56–63.
134. Also akin to Hütter is how the church must be understood in 'dynamic' terms, not 'static' ones (see Newbigin, *The Household of God*, p. 50; and Newbigin, *One Body, One Gospel, One World*, p. 42). The dynamic aspect for Newbigin, however, lies in the church's movement from being called of God to being sent by God.
135. Hütter, *Bound to Be Free: Evangelical Catholic Engagements in Ecclesiology, Ethics and Ecumenism* (Grand Rapids, Mich.: Eerdmans, 2004), pp. 36–37.
136. On the importance of attending to the sinfulness of the church as one considers its concreteness and the Spirit's role in convicting the church in its sinful failure to practice well as well as empowering the church in its practices, see Healy, *Church, World and Christian Life*; Healy, 'Practices and the New Ecclesiology: Misplaced Concreteness?', *International Journal of Systematic Theology* 5 [2003]: 298–99. Also see Healy's caveat in the latter article that, while practices are indeed formative, they are so 'only as they are performed with appropriate intentions and construals' (p. 295). Apart from these, they can devolve into counter-practices that form us in pagan ways.
137. Hütter, *Suffering Divine Things*, pp. 5–15; *Bound to be Free*, pp. 28–30.
138. See, for example, Jeff B. Pool, 'Seizure by Divine Raptor: The Pathic Theology of Reinhard Hütter', *Perspectives in Religious Studies* 30:1 (Spring 2003): 55–69, who finds Hütter especially unconvincing at the point of the contextual and local – points we attempt to address in the following paragraph.
139. See Newbigin, *Truth to Tell*; *The Open Secret*; and throughout his writings.
140. Hütter, *Bound to be Free*, p. 36.
141. Hütter, *Suffering Divine Things*, passim; see *Bound to be Free*, p. 36, for a summative list.
142. Hütter, *Bound to be Free*, p. 35.
143. Hütter, *Bound to be Free*, p. 35.

CHAPTER 2 – MARKS

1. *De Catechizandis Rudibus* 25.48.
2. David S. Yeago, 'The Church as Polity? The Lutheran Context of Robert W. Jenson's Ecclesiology', in *Trinity, Time and Church: A Response to the Theology of Robert W. Jenson*, ed. Colin E. Gunton (Grand Rapids, Mich.: Eerdmans, 2000), p. 203.

3. Dietrich Bonhoeffer, *Discipleship*, trans. John D. Godsey (Minneapolis, Minn.: Fortress Press, 2003), p. 113.

4. Another question, which we can only acknowledge here, is about the question of the church's *being visible* versus its *clarity*. Might it on occasion help to speak of the all-too-visible church whose own mixed allegiances and ambitions obscure, or at least fog, its source and goal in Christ?

5. Optatus wrote *Against the Donatists* in 367, and then added a seventh book in 385. For his historical reconstruction of the events, see esp. 1.13–28. For discussion, see W. H. C. Frend, *The Donatist Church: A Movement of Protest in North Africa* (Oxford: Clarendon, 1952). Augustine contested the Donatists from the time he was ordained (391) until the Council of Carthage (411). His anti-Donatist works can easily be accessed by English readers in the *Nicene and Post-Nicene Fathers*, series 1, vol. 4. For discussion see Peter Brown, *Augustine of Hippo*, new ed. (Berkeley: University of California Press, 2000).

6. See R. A. Markus, 'Christianity and Dissent in Roman North Africa: Changing Perspectives in Recent Work', in *Schism, Heresy and Religious Protest*, ed. D. Baker (Cambridge: Cambridge University Press, 1972), pp. 21–36.

7. Brent Shaw, 'African Christianity: Disputes, Definitions, and "Donatists"', in Shaw, *Rulers, Nomads and Christians in Roman North Africa* (London: Variorum, 1995), essay XI.

8. The most egregious example is where Optatus (*Adu. Don.* 1.22–24) claims to have copies of correspondence between the Donatists and Constantine that was written prior to the Council of Arles (314). Therein, Donatus the bishop is named and denounced; Donatus, however, is not appointed bishop until 315. The most complete treatment to date is Paul Monceaux, *Histoire littéraire de l'Afrique chrétienne depuis les origins jusqu'a l'invasion arabe* vols. 4–7 (Paris: E. Leroux, 1901–1923). But for an explicitly revisionist – and widely influential – account, see W. H. C. Frend, *The Donatist Church: A Movement of Protest in Roman North Africa* (Oxford: Clarendon Press, 1952). A more accessible introduction is the essay by James Alexander, 'Donatism', in *The Early Christian World*, vol. 2, ed. Philip F. Esler (London: Routledge, 2000), pp. 952–74.

9. J. Kevin Coyle, 'The Self-Identity of North African Christians', in *Augustinus Afer: Actes du colloque international Alger-Annaba, 1–7 avril 2001*, eds Pierre-Ives Fux, Jean-Michel Roessli and Otto Wermelinger (Fribourg: Éditions Universitaires Fribourg Suisse, 2003), pp. 70–72.

10. See especially the works of Maureen Tilley, 'From Separatist Sect to Majority Church: The Ecclesiologies of Parmenian and Tyconius', *Studia patristica* 33 (1996): 260–65; and Tilley, *The Bible in Christian North Africa: The Donatist World* (Minneapolis, Minn.: Augsburg Fortress, 1997) and James J. O'Donnell, *Augustine, Sinner & Saint: A New Biography* (London: HarperCollins, 2005), pp. 209–43.

11. On ritual purity in earlier North African Christianity and its accommodation by the Donatists, see J. Patout Burns, *Cyprian the Bishop* (London: Routledge, 2002), pp. 166–76.

12. Optatus, *Adu. Don.* 1.29.

13. For an introduction to the terms and primary sources for these marks, see Thomas Oden, *Systematic Theology*, vol. 3: *Life in the Spirit* (New York: HarperSanFrancisco, 1992), pp. 297–365.

14. While we do not intend to attack Mormonism, it is worth comparing this early Christian concept with the teachings of The Church of Jesus Christ of Latter-day Saints. The early Christians could not accept that *the* church could cease, i.e. all Christians become apostate, and then be re-founded by Christ in 'latter' times. This same concern was raised during the Reformation against the 'Protestant Church' (see discussion below).

15. Of course, the events of the Protestant Reformation are much more complex than we let on here. For instance, Luther did not leave but was excommunicated. Moreover, it should also be noted that both the Roman Catholic Church and the Eastern Orthodox churches have made this claim in regard to their schism. See the excurses below in this chapter.

16. This view in Baptist thinking is known as Landmarkism (an idea borrowed from the Stone-Campbell Movement): the unbroken line of 'true churches' that have perpetually been re-established in opposition to the false church (examples usually include Montanists, Donatists, Waldensians, etc.) Landmarkism is rarely (if ever) taught by Baptist schools, but it was promoted in the early twentieth century and still holds the imagination of many practitioners.

17. This aspect could be seen as uniting the previous two in dialectical tension; cf. the conclusion to the previous chapter which interacts with Hütter's 'pathic' framework.

18. All traditions agree on this principle, although some attempt to add visible elements to the theological principle. For example, in the *Catechism of the Catholic Church* §815, the 'bonds of unity' are additions to the theological unity of §813–14.

19. It should be noted that Luther's *simul justus et peccator* primarily concerns individualized soteriology, and is therefore better translated 'simultaneously just and sinner'. Augustine, too, recognized that each of us is both holy and sinful. But where he saw the Christian life as a journey from sin to holiness, the other spoke of the Christian as *at once* entirely righteous in Christ and entirely sinful in ourselves. See James F. McCue, '*Simul iustus et peccator* in Augustine, Aquinas, and Luther: Toward Putting the Debate in Context', *Journal of the American Academy of Religion* 48 (1947): 81–96.

20. Calvin, *Institutes of the Christian Religion*, vol. 2, ed. John T. McNeill, trans. Ford Lewis Battles (Louisville, Ky.: Westminster John Knox Press, 1959), 4.1.17.

21. Volf, *After Our Likeness*, pp. 9–10. Cf. Mt. 18.20; 1 Cor. 3.16; and 1 Pet. 2.5–10. Cf. Vatican II's *Lumen gentium*.

22. The ecumenical consensus on this mark is again that it is an invisible 'matter of faith' (*Lumen gentium* 39, as translated by the *Catechism* §823).
23. We are aware of the current debate about the hypostatic union and kenosis. We recommend Sarah Coakley, 'Does kenosis rest on a mistake? Three kenotic models in patristic exegesis', in *Exploring Kenotic Christology*, ed. C. S. Evans (Oxford: Oxford University Press, 2006), pp. 246–64.
24. John of Damascus, *De fide orthodoxa* 3.
25. The *Catholic Catechism* (§830–31) prioritizes the meanings in this same order.
26. Tertullian, *Praescript Against the Heretics* 26.4.
27. Irenaeus, *Adversus Haereses* 3.24.1.
28. See Hans von Campenhausen, *Ecclesiastical Authority and Spiritual Power in the Church of the First Three Centuries* [Kirchliches amt und Geistliche Vollmacht], trans. J. A. Baker (Peabody, Mass.: Hendrickson, 1997 [1969]).
29. We are here furthering the discussion from the previous chapter in which that which constitutes the church is debated, especially in light of what manifests the church.
30. *The Nature and Mission of the Church* (Faith and Order Paper #198; 2005), paragraph 32.
31. *Catechism of the Catholic Church*, no. 1373 (p. 383).
32. A very free translation of *Adversus Haereses* (especially Sections 3. pref.–3.3).
33. As will soon be admitted, this whole line of argument is a caricature and too simplistic. Even this claim about Gnostic claims is less than helpful: see the arguments of Elaine Pagels, *Beyond Belief: The Secret Gospel of Thomas* (New York: Random House, 2003).
34. For bibliography of this view as an 'ecumenical consensus', see Veli-Matti Kärkkäinen, 'The Apostolicity of Free Churches', *Pro Ecclesia* 10:4 (Fall 2001): 475–86. This is not to deny the historical stance of some traditions which defend apostolic succession (for discussion see Charles J. Conniry, 'Identifying Apostolic Christianity: A Synthesis of Viewpoints', *Journal of the Evangelical Theological Society* 37:2 [June 1994]: 247–61). Instead, we merely point out that the exposition of the creedal affirmation of an 'apostolic church' is normally and most commonly framed in terms of the church's nature, not in terms of the church's officers.
35. Thus, the WCC Faith and Order, *The Nature and Mission of the Church* (Faith and Order Paper #198; 2005), §56, in defining 'the essential apostolicity of the church', exclusively discusses apostolic truth with no reference to apostolic office.
36. A more strict translation of *Adversus Haereses* 3.1 (from *Ante-Nicene Fathers* 1, ed./trans. Alexander Roberts and James Donaldson [Edinburgh: T&T Clark, 1873; reprint, Grand Rapids, Mich.: Eerdmans, 1979]).
37. It should be noted that Tertullian insisted the church be defined as a fellowship of the Spirit, and not by the bishop. This, however, should not be understood as a 'Montanist' view, since Tertullian is no longer

understood to have converted to Montanism (see David Rankin, *Tertullian and the Church* [Cambridge: Cambridge University Press, 1995]). Whatever view Tertullian held about 'new prophecies', he did so within and as part of mainstream Carthaginian Christianity (see Wilhite, *Tertullian the African* [Berlin: De Gruyter, 2007]).

38. *Book of Common Prayer*, p. 854.
39. So the Anglican Webster can write of the way in which an episcopal polity can and must serve the gospel. See John Webster, 'The "Self-Organizing" Power of the Gospel: Episcopacy and Community Formation', in *Community Formation in the Early Church and in the Church Today*, ed. Richard N. Longenecker (Peabody, Mass.: Hendrickson, 2002), pp. 179–93.
40. Which still aligns with the late patristic tradition as Jerome knew it (see *Ep*. 146.1).
41. That some dogmatic statements on apostolicity will also address the episcopate is no surprise, and simply demonstrates a desire to comprehensively address a certain tradition's explication and application of this mark. For example, Constas H. Demetry, *The Orthodox Catechism: With the Most Essential Differences of Other Principal Churches Scripturally Criticized* (Chicago: s.n., 1929), p. 46, states, '[The church is] apostolic because it traces its beginning back to the Apostles, holds the teachings of the Apostles entire and unadulterated, and is governed by the canonical successors of the Apostles whose successors have received Holy Orders from them in uninterrupted succession'. We note, however, that these 'canonical officers' are listed last, almost in a derivative order. Moreover, the 'uninterrupted succession' need not be an uninterrupted succession of officers, but an uninterrupted succession of churches. While the former is the more natural reading, the latter is required by the exceptions that must arise when a church's officers are martyred and the laity appoint new clergy. The same phenomenon (almost to an exact parallel) occurs in the *Catholic Catechism* (§857), while the Anglican catechism (*Book of Common Prayer*, p. 854) drops the last stipulation about officers and only defines apostolic teaching and apostolic mission, and most other Protestant statements follow the Apostles' Creed wherein 'apostolic' is not used (e.g. Luther's catechism and Calvin's *Institutes*). Cf. Bp. Tikhon, *The Catechism of the Orthodox, Catholic, Eastern Church* (San Francisco: Murdock Press, 1901), pp. 51–52, who answers the question 'What does the Creed teach us, when it calls the Church Apostolic?' by stating, 'It teaches us to hold fast the *Apostolic doctrine and tradition*, and eschew such doctrine and such teachers, as are not warranted by the doctrine of the Apostles'. The next question, derivative and yet secondary, is then 'What Ecclesiastical Institution is there through which the succession of the Apostolic ministry is preserved?' Also cf. Bp. Fan Styli an Nolin, *Eastern Orthodox Catechism* (Boston: The Albanian Orthodox Church in America, 1954), p. 47, 'The Church is apostolic, because it has been transmitted to us by the Apostles and their duly consecrated successors without any interruption, deviation, or alteration'.

42. Jürgen Moltmann, *The Church in the Power of the Spirit: A Contribution to Messianic Ecclesiology* (Minneapolis, Minn.: Fortress Press, 1993 [1975]).

43. Adolf von Harnack, F. L. Pogson, trans. and H. D. A. Major (ed.), *The Constitution & Law of the Church in the First Two Centuries* (London: Williams & Norgate, 1910), p. 198.

44. We are influenced here by Jean-Luc Marion, *God without Being: Hors-Text*, trans. Thomas A. Carlson (Chicago: University of Chicago Press, 1991); orig. *Die sans letter: Hors-text* (1982); see especially chapter one, 'The Idol and the Icon' (pp. 7–24).

45. Moltmann, *The Church*, p. 340.

46. Moltmann, *The Church*, p. 340.

47. For discussion, see Carl Braatan, *Justification: The Article by Which the Church Stands or Falls* (Minneapolis: Fortress, 1990).

48. NAOCTC, 'The *Filioque*: A Church-Dividing Issue?', *St. Vladimir's Theological Quarterly* 48:1 (2004): 93–123.

49. *Foundations of the Conciliar Theory*, new ed. (Studies in the History of Christian Thought #81; Leiden, Brill: 1998). See also Renate Blumenfeld-Kosinski, *Poets, Saints, and Visionaries of the Great Schism, 1378–1417* (University Parks, Pa.: Penn State Press, 2006); and the earlier study of Thomas E. Morrissey, 'After Six Hundred Years: The Great Western Schism, Conciliarism, and Constance', *Theological Studies* 40:3 (September 1979): 495–509.

50. Yeago, 'The Catholic Luther', in *The Catholicity of the Reformation*, eds Carl E. Braaten and Robert W. Jenson (Grand Rapids, Mich.: Eerdmans, 1996). For a complementary argument, see Phillip Cary, 'Why Luther is Not Quite Protestant: The Logic of Faith in a Sacramental Promise', *Pro Ecclesia* 14:4 (Fall 2005): 447–86.

51. Quote from Yeago, 'The Catholic Luther', 33, but the additional conclusions which follow are from 33–34.

52. Available online at the Vatican's website: http://www.vatican.va/holy_father/paul_vi/speeches/1965/documents/hf_p-vi_spe_19651207_common-declaration_en.html.

53. Available online at the Vatican's website: http://www.vatican.va/holy_father/john_paul_ii/encyclicals/documents/hf_jp-ii_enc_25051995_ut-unum-sint_en.html.

54. *Ut unim sint*, p. 88.

55. *Ut unim sint*, p. 95.

56. *Ut unim sint*, p. 95.

57. *Ut unim sint*, p. 96.

58. Irenaeus, *Adversus Haereses* 3.3.2–4.

59. For discussion, see G. S. M. Walker, *The Churchmanship of St. Cyprian* (Ecumenical Studies in History 9; Richmond, Va.: John Knox Press, 1969).

60. *Rule of St. Benedict*, trans. Rev. Boniface Verheyen, OSB (1949), available online at http://www.ccel.org/ccel/benedict/rule2/files/rule2.html.

61. in *Luther's Works* 41, ed. Eric W. Gritsch (Philadelphia: Fortress Press, 1966; orig. *Von den Konziliis und Kirchen* 1539), p. 143.

62. Luther, *Luther's Works* 41, p. 149.

63. Luther, *Luther's Works* 41, p. 167.
64. Luther, *Luther's Works* 41, p. 170.
65. For a review of Protestants, stemming from Luther to Calvin, who added discipline as a mark of the church, see Robert M. Kingdon, 'Calvin and Church Discipline', in *John Calvin Rediscovered: The Impact of His Social and Economic Thought*, eds Edward Dommen and James D. Bratt (Louisville, Ky.: Westminster John Knox Press, 2007), pp. 25–31.
66. This confession has been translated by John Howard Yoder, *The Legacy of Michael Sattler* (Scottsdale, Pa.: Herald Press, 1973), and is available on the Mennonite Church U.S.A.'s website (http://www.mcusa-archives.org/library/resolutions/schleithiem/index.html).
67. We avoid labelling discipline as a 'mark', following Calvin: see James C. Spalding, 'Discipline as a Mark of the True Church in its Sixteenth Century Lutheran Context', in *Piety, Politics, and Ethics*, ed. Carter Lindberg (Kirksville, Mo.: Sixteenth Century Journal Publishers, 1984), pp. 119–38.
68. See Kevin M. Watson, 'The Form and Power of Godliness: Wesleyan Communal Discipline as Voluntary Suffering', *Wesleyan Theological Journal* 43:1 (Spring 2008): 165–83.
69. Oden, *Systematic Theology*, 3:330.
70. Oden, *Systematic Theology*, 3:330.
71. Oden, *Systematic Theology*, 3:330, emphasis added.
72. Oden, *Systematic Theology*, 3:332.
73. Oden, *Systematic Theology*, 3:336.
74. (Grand Rapids, Mich.: Baker Press, 2008).
75. We are indebted to Craig Nash of Waco, TX, for helping us understand and evaluate the various labels.
76. Thanks to Markus Thane for relaying and translating this German expression.
77. The genesis of the emerging church, at least as known in North American post-evangelicalism and as influencing later adherents and detractors alike, is attributable to the establishment of Emergent Village (see www.emergentvillage.com).
78. See esp. Brian McLaren, *A New Kind of Christian: A Tale of Two Friends on a Spiritual Journey* (San Francisco: Jossey-Bass, 2001).
79. McLaren, 'Why I Am Emergent', in A *Generous Orthodoxy: Why I Am . . .* (El Cajon, Calif./Grand Rapids, Mich.: Zondervan, 2004), pp. 275–88.
80. See the discussion in Dan Kimball, *Emerging Worship: Creating Worship Gatherings for New Generations* (Grand Rapids, Mich.: Zondervan, 2004); and more generally on worship, see Terry W. York, *America's Worship Wars* (Peabody, Mass.: Hendrickson Publishers, 2003); and more generally on (post-)evangelicalism, see Robert Webber, *The Younger Evangelicals: Facing the Challenges of the New World* (Grand Rapids, Mich.: Baker, 2002); Dave Tomlinson, *The Post-Evangelical* (Grand Rapids, Mich.: Zondervan, 2003).

81. See Leonard I. Sweet and Andy Crouch. *The Church in Emerging Culture: Five Perspectives* (Grand Rapids, Mich.: Zondervan, 2003).
82. See Stanley J. Grenz and John R. Franke. *Beyond Foundationalism: Shaping Theology in a Postmodern Context* (Louisville, Ky.: Westminster John Knox, 2001); Carl A. Raschke, *The Next Reformation: Why Evangelicals Must Embrace Postmodernity* (Grand Rapids, Mich.: Baker, 2004); Myron B. Penner, *Christianity and the Postmodern Turn: Six Views* (Grand Rapids, Mich.: Brazos, 2005); James K. A. Smith, *Who's Afraid of Postmodernism? Taking Derrida, Lyotard, and Foucault to Church* (Grand Rapids, Mich.: Baker, 2006). For criticism of this aspect of emerging churches, see D. A. Carson, *Becoming Conversant with the Emerging Church: Understanding a Movement and Its Implications* (Grand Rapids, Mich.: Zondervan, 2005).
83. For a more sustained discussion compare the works of Mark Driscoll, *Confessions of a Reformission Rev.: Hard Lessons from an Emerging Missional Church* (The Leadership Network Innovation Series. Grand Rapids, Mich.: Zondervan, 2006); *The Radical Reformission: Reaching out without Selling Out* (Grand Rapids, Mich.: Zondervan, 2004), to those of Peter Rollins, *The Fidelity of Betrayal: Towards a Church Beyond Belief* (Brewster, Mass.: Paraclete Press, 2008); *How (Not) to Speak of God: Marks of the Emerging Church* (Brewster, Mass.: Paraclete Press, 2006).
84. Darrell L. Guder (ed.), *Missional Church: A Vision for the Sending of the Church in North America* (The Gospel and Our Culture Series. Grand Rapids, Mich.: Eerdmans, 1998); Brian D. McLaren and Anthony Campolo, *Adventures in Missing the Point: How the Culture-Controlled Church Neutered the Gospel* (El Cajon, Calif.: EmergentYS, 2003).
85. See, for example, Robert Webber, *Ancient-Future Faith: Rethinking Evangelicalism for a Postmodern World* (Grand Rapids, Mich.: Baker, 1999).
86. MacIntyre, *After Virtue*, 3rd edn (South Bend, Ind.: University of Notre Dame Press, 2007), p. 263.
87. Jonathan R. Wilson, *Living Faithfully in a Fragmented World: Lessons for the Church from MacIntyre's After Virtue* (Harrisburg, Pa.: Trinity Press, 1997). 'New Monasticism', in fact, had already been called for by Bonhoeffer; see *Testament to Freedom* (San Francisco: HarperSanFrancisco, 1997), p. 424.
88. See the collection of conference papers in Rutba House (ed.), *School(s) for Conversion: 12 Marks of a New Monasticism* (Eugene, Ore.: Cascade Books/Wipf & Stock, 2005).
89. See the appendix in Shane Claiborne, *Irresistible Revolution* (Grand Rapids, Mich.: Zondervan, 2006) and available online at http://www.newmonasticism.org/12marks/12marks.php.
90. Jonathan Wilson-Hargrove, *New Monasticism: What it Has to Say to Today's Church* (Grand Rapids, Mich.: Brazos Press, 2008), p. 69. Undoubtedly, Wilson-Hargrove and other new monastics represented by him are influenced by the thinking of Stanley M. Hauerwas and

William H. Willimon, *Resident Aliens: Life in the Christian Colony* (Nashville, Tenn.: Abingdon Press, 1989).

91. Newbigin, *Truth to Tell*, p. 85.
92. We recognize this is a charitable and hopeful reading of the emerging church's orientation to the ancient church. Many have criticized a tendency in the emerging church to an *ad hoc* appropriation of Christian tradition in which the elements of tradition are ripped out of an old context and jammed into a new context, losing much of their significance in this process of abstraction. That said, re-contextualization is both inevitable and salutary, and a flat conservatism that seeks only to repeat the elements of tradition without reference to their new context is equally mis-guided.
93. We have certainly failed to do justice to the 'theology' of emergent churches in our focus on their ecclesiology. We recommend the following: Ray S. Anderson, *An Emergent Theology for Emerging Churches* (Downers Grove, Ill.: InterVarsity Press, 2006); Eddie Gibbs and Ryan K. Bolger, *Emerging Churches: Creating Christian Community in Postmodern Cultures* (Grand Rapids, Mich.: Baker, 2005); Doug Pagitt, *Church Re-Imagined: The Spiritual Formation of People in Communities of Faith* (Grand Rapids, Mich.: Zondervan, 2005); Pagitt and Tony Jones (eds), *An Emergent Manifesto of Hope* (Grand Rapids, Mich.: Baker, 2006); Steve Taylor, *The Out of Bounds Church?: Learning to Create a Community of Faith in a Culture of Change* (Grand Rapids, Mich.: Zondervan, 2005). Also, see the insightful analysis of Jeff Keuss, 'The Emergent Church and Neo-Correlational Theology after Tillich, Schleiermacher and Browning', *Scottish Journal of Theology* 61:4 (2008): 450–61.
94. Of course this is symptomatic of the Reformation as a whole. See, for example, the essay of Tim Conder, 'The Existing Church/Emerging Church Matrix', in *An Emerging Manifesto*, eds Pagitt and Jones, pp. 97–108; and the Lutheranesque 'futuristic' ecclesiology claimed by McLaren, *Generous Orthodoxy*, p. 285.
95. A term preferable to 'global' or 'third world' Christianity, according to Lamin Sanneh, *Whose Religion is Christianity? The Gospel Beyond the West* (Grand Rapids, Mich.: Eerdmans, 2003).
96. See, for example, Gustavo Gutiérrez, *The Power of the Poor in History*, trans. Robert R. Barr (Eugene, Ore.: Wipf & Stock Publishers, 1983).
97. See the final part of Veli-Mati Kärkkäinen, *An Introduction to Ecclesiology: Ecumenical, Historical & Global Perspectives* (Downers Grove, Ill.: InterVarsity Press, 2002).

PENTECOST AND ECCLESIA

1. Earlier, in Jn. 14.26, Jesus speaks of 'the Advocate, the Holy Spirit, whom the Father will send in my name'. Whether sent by Jesus or by the Father in the name of Jesus, it is clear that the Spirit's mission follows on, and furthers, the mission of Christ.
2. James B. Torrance, 'The Place of Jesus Christ in Worship', in Ray S. Anderson (ed.), *Theological Foundations for Ministry: Selected*

Readings for a Theology of the Church in Ministry (Edinburgh: T&T Clark, 1979), p. 364 (a comment he attributes to Calvin).
3. John D. Zizioulas, *Being as Communion: Studies in Personhood and the Church* (Crestwood, N.Y.: St. Vladimir's Seminary Press, 1985), p. 130.
4. 'Christ institutes and the Spirit constitutes. The difference between two prepositions (in- and con-) can be enormous ecclesiologically. The "institution" is something presented to us as a fact, more or less a *fait-accompli*. As such, it is a provocation to our freedom. The constitution is something that involves us in its very being, something we can accept freely, because we take part in its very emergence' (Zizioulas, *Being as Communion*, 140).

CHAPTER 3 – MEDIATION

1. John Wesley, Sermon 16, 'On the Means of Grace', in *Wesley's 52 Standard Sermons* (Salem, Ohio: Schmul Publishing Company, 1988), pp. 149–62.
2. That Wesley could not have accepted such a flatly false dilemma – institution or event, form or content – is seen in his lifelong commitment to the Church of England. His attentiveness to the means of grace reflects both biblical and Anglican religion.
3. William Abraham, a Wesleyan theologian, argues that ecclesial renewal is a product of the Holy Spirit and a function of the church's return to the means of grace and its canonical heritage in all its richness, rather than a deliverance following on solutions to seemingly intractable epistemological problems. (Abraham, *The Logical of Renewal* [Grand Rapids, Mich.: Eerdmans, 2003], p. 158) Renewal, that is, is a gift. But this hopeful, epicletic model does not allow for turning our back on the church or our canonical heritage. Indeed, it is the 'displacement of the canonical heritage' and a narrowing of the work of the Spirit (to exclude that heritage) that lies at the root of the church's ills (162).
4. Wesley considers these the three 'chief' means (2.1), to which others might be added. We will also discuss baptism below, and we might add singing, fellowship, service and mission to the list.
5. Thanks to a reminder from Fred Sanders of the central importance of this characteristic of grace.
6. U2, 'Grace', *All That You Can't Leave Behind* (Island Records, 2000).
7. On these categories, and their application, see Jesse Couenhoven, 'Grace as Pardon and Power: Pictures of the Christian Life in Luther, Calvin, and Barth', *Journal of Religious Ethics* 28:1 (2000): 63–88.
8. R. Michael Allen, 'The Church and the Churches: A Dogmatic Essay on Ecclesial Invisibility', *European Journal of Theology* 16:2 (2007): 115. Allen here qualifies Thomas Aquinas' dictum that 'grace does not destroy nature but perfects it' (*Summa Theologica* 1.1.8.2); or, he at least more effectively preserves it against the misuse to which it is frequently put.
9. Alexander Schmemann, *The Eucharist: Sacrament of the Kingdom* (Crestwood, N.Y.: St. Vladimir's Seminary Press, 2000), pp. 31, 197,

142, 196. This 'scholastic reduction' can be traced to the West (46, 160 – 'our still-born, western school theology'), though it dominates the Eastern church and its manuals as well and leads to a '"pseudo-morphosis" of the Orthodox consciousness'. (46) For a parallel complaint from the West, with a detailed historical report, see de Lubac, *Corpus Mysticum*.

10. Schmemann, *The Eucharist*, pp. 162–63.
11. Alexander Schmemann, *Of Water and the Spirit: A Liturgical Study of Baptism* (Crestwood, N.Y.: St. Vladimir's Seminary Press, 1974), pp. 11, 44. An added problem is that validity is described in immanent terms. After all, it is, finally, the promising Father, the present Christ and the powerful Spirit who guarantee sacramental validity.
12. Schmemann, *Of Water and the Spirit*, p. 152.
13. Wesley, Sermon 16, 'On the Means of Grace', 5.4.
14. Schmemann, *Of Water and the Spirit*, p. 60.
15. Barth, *Church Dogmatics* I/1, p. 55.
16. 'God saves no one but sinners, He instructs no one but the foolish and stupid, He enriches none but paupers, and He makes alive only the dead; not those who merely imagine themselves to be such but those who really are this kind of people and admit it' (Luther, *Luther's Works* 25:418–19).
17. Chesterton notes that some symbols seem to arise from an ordinary human instinct's distinction between what we might call 'arbitrary' and 'fitting' symbols in G. K. Chesterton, *Heretics*, in *The Collected Works of G. K. Chesterton*, vol. 1 (San Francisco: Ignatius Press, 1986), p. 175.
18. Hunsinger, *The Eucharist and Ecumenism: Let Us Keep the Feast* (Cambridge: Cambridge University Press, 2008), pp. 162, 170.
19. See Hunsinger, *The Eucharist and Ecumenism*, p. 164.
20. Wesley, Sermon 16, 'On the Means of Grace', 5.4.
21. George, 'The Sacramentality of the Church: An Evangelical Baptist Perspective'. p. 317.
22. Consider Mk 1.16–18.
23. Bonhoeffer, *Discipleship* (Minneapolis, Minn.: Fortress Press, 2003), p. 207.
24. It is not that paedobaptists ignore this transition, as evidenced by a strong view of original sin and the ancient tradition of including an exorcism and renunciation of the devil in the baptismal liturgy. But the difficulty of imagining an infant in transition and a popular romanti-cizing of children tends to make infant baptisms a time of blessing more than transition.
25. It is because of the finality of this stark reality, because in baptism we die and are raised, that all traditions have rejected re-baptism.
26. A particularly striking illustration of this is found in the 'large baptis-mal trench or pit (perhaps intentionally similar to an open grave)' of the Racovian Bruderhof (or Polish Bruderhof of Raków, Poland). See George Huntston Williams, *The Radical Reformation* (Philadelphia:

The Westminster Press, 1962), p. 705. Thanks to Brian Brewer for this reference.

27. Water is an ambiguous symbol, gesturing toward deliverance and judgment (at the flood and the exodus), purification (e.g. Ps. 51.7), chaos (Gen. 1.2; Mk 4.35–41; cp. Rev. 21.1) and life (e.g. Ps. 36.9). Schmemann speaks of 'three essential dimensions of this symbolism' – the cosmic (water as source of life), the destructive and the purifying (*Of Water and the Spirit*, pp. 39–40).

28. John Webster, *Word and Church: Essays in Christian Dogmatics* (New York: T&T Clark, 2006), p. 124.

29. On the importance of covenantal categories for baptism, see James V. Brownson, *The Promise of Baptism: An Introduction to Baptism in Scripture and the Reformed Tradition* (Grand Rapids, Mich.: Eerdmans, 2007) and Michael Horton, *People and Place: A Covenant Ecclesiology* (Louisville, Ky.: Westminster John Knox Press, 2008), pp. 99–119, 143–44.

30. And so we can rightly say that baptism is 'a sign of the Kingdom of God and of the life of the world to come' (*Baptism, Eucharist and Ministry*, Faith and Order Paper No. 111 [Geneva: World Council of Churches, 1982], §7).

31. Bonhoeffer, *Discipleship*, p. 87. The parishioners of The Cathedral of Our Lady of the Angels in Los Angeles live in this reality from week to week as they congregate between a baptismal with a tapestry picturing John's baptism of Jesus and a tortured Christ on the cross behind the altar.

32. These idioms of dying and rising and the taking off and putting on of clothes both reflect Paul's baptismal piety and ethic. The language of clothing can better be understood when one learns that, early on, 'Christian converts were baptized naked' (Wayne A. Meeks, *The First Urban Christians: The Social World of the Apostle Paul* [New Haven, Conn.: Yale University Press, 1983], p. 151).

33. Furthermore, Gerhard Lohfink argues persuasively that this was not an innovation of the Gentile church, but an adaptation of the implicit catechumenate which was Israel's life. In other words, the immediate repentance, belief and baptism of many disciples of Jesus and in the first days of the gospel's expansion (whether Jews or 'God-fearers' – that is, Gentile proselytes) presuppose a long formation in Israel's life. In short: '*Judaism was the catechumenate of the primitive Church*'. See Lohfink, *Does God Need the Church? Toward a Theology of the People of God* (Collegeville, Minn.: The Liturgical Press, 1999), p. 268 (emphasis his).

34. See Tom Smail's description of the Spirit's empowering role in human response to Christ in *The Giving Gift: The Holy Spirit in Person* (London: Darton, Longman and Todd, 1988), pp. 70–71, 73.

35. See the fierce debate between Joachim Jeremias (*Infant Baptism in the First Four Centuries*, trans. David Cairns [Eugene, Ore.: Wipf & Stock, orig Eng 1960]) and Kurt Aland (*Did the Early Church Baptize Infants?* [trans. G. R. Beasley-Murray; Eugene, Ore.: Wipf & Stock, orig Eng

1961]), and then Jeremias again (*The Origins of Infant Baptism: A Further Study in Reply to Kurt Aland* [trans. Dorothea M. Barton; Eugene, Ore.: Wipf & Stock, orig Eng 1962]). And now see Everett Ferguson, *Baptism in the Early Church: History, Theology, and Liturgy in the First Five Centuries* (Grand Rapids, Mich.: Eerdmans, 2009).

36. The phrase, borrowed from a different context, is Auden's, in his poem 'The Fall of Rome'.

37. 1 Pet. 3.21 ('baptism . . . now saves you') must be understood instrumentally and in light of the synthetic unity of which water baptism is a part.

38. Calvin, *Institutes of the Christian Religion* 4.15.6 (trans. Battles).

39. See also the expansion of 'God the Father, Almighty, Maker of heaven and earth' in the Heidelberg Catechism, q. 26.

40. See further Hans Urs von Balthasar, *Unless You Become Like This Child* (San Francisco: Ignatius Press, 1991).

41. Luther's final words were rumoured to have been: 'Wir sind Bettler. Hoc est verum'. ['We are beggars. That is true'.]

42. James B. Torrance, *Worship, Community, and the Triune God of Grace. The Didsbury Lectures 1994* (Carlisle, England: Paternoster, 1996), p. 24. See the entire discussion on 'Worship – Unitarian or Trinitarian?', pp. 6–31.

43. Augustine, *Confessiones* 3.6.11. In Chadwick's translation: 'But you were more inward than my most inward part and higher than the highest element within me'. (p. 43)

44. Torrance, *Worship, Community, and the Triune God of Grace*, pp. 34–35.

45. Barth, *Church Dogmatics* IV/2, p. 705.

46. Brad Harper and Paul Louis Metzger, *Exploring Ecclesiology: An Evangelical and Ecumenical Introduction* (Grand Rapids, Mich.: Brazos Press, 2009), p. 33.

47. Telford Work, *Ain't Too Proud to Beg: Living through the Lord's Prayer* (Grand Rapids, Mich.: Eerdmans, 2007), pp. xviii, xiii. Calvin thought the same thing, though he too frequently restricted prayer to its effects on the one praying, to the neglect of prayer's work in the world. For an attempt to rethink prayer in terms of God's response to his people (though a rather drastic over-correction), see Clark H. Pinnock, *Most Moved Mover: A Theology of God's Openness* (Grand Rapids, Mich.: Baker, 2001). Pinnock writes, quite reasonably: 'Prayer highlights the fact that God does not choose to rule the world without our input. It also suggests that the future has not been exhaustively settled' (p. 42).

48. See Cyprian (*De Dominica oratione*), the first to exegete the Lord's Prayer in this way.

49. See Richard Foster, *Celebration of Discipline: The Path to Spiritual Growth* (San Francisco: HarperCollins, 1998).

50. Those who pray for the kingdom's coming 'desire to behold Christ the Saviour of all rising again upon the world. He will come. He will come and descend as judge, no longer in a lowly condition like us or in the

humility of human nature. He will come in glory such as becomes God, as he dwells in the unapproachable light, and with the angels as his guards' (Cyril of Alexandria, *Commentary on Luke, Homily 73*; cited in *Ancient Christian Commentary on Scripture: Luke*, ed. Arthur A. Just, Jr. [Downers Grove, Ill.: InterVarsity Press, 2003], p. 186).

51. Joachim Jeremias, *The Lord's Prayer*, trans. John Reumann (Philadelphia: Fortress Press, 1964), p. 32.

52. The food we buy at the grocery store lasts long enough, and our refrigerators are cold enough, that we can go weeks without praying for daily bread. This is probably bad for our souls.

53. Cited in Jeremias, *The Lord's Prayer*, p. 24. The final phrase is Jeremias'. Jerome is commenting on the Matthean form of the Lord's prayer.

54. John Nolland, Lk. 9.21–18.34, *Word Biblical Commentary*, vol. 35b (Dallas: Word Books, 1993), p. 621.

55. Jeremias, *The Lord's Prayer*, p. 30.

56. See Cyprian, *De Dominica oratione*.

57. Wesley, Sermon 16, 'On the Means of Grace', 2.1.

58. Augustine, *Confessiones* 1.1.1 (trans. Chadwick).

59. So Christopher Seitz advocates 'first reading the book for its own sake – what will be called a *per se* reading – and then moving forward to ask in a critical way just how this book of Hebrew Scripture becomes Old Testament when interpreted in reciprocity with the New. That is, there are two tasks confronting the Christian reader: interpreting the Old Testament *per se* and the Old *in novo receptum*, as received in the New. A key question arises at this point. How is the Old heard and reinterpreted, without obliterating or simply moving beyond the original *per se* witness?' (Seitz, *Word Without End: The Old Testament as Abiding Theological Witness* [Grand Rapids, Mich.: Eerdmans, 1998], pp. 194–95).

60. It is for reasons such as this that Aquinas insists that interpretation of the fourfold sense of scripture always be rooted in the literal sense: 'That signification whereby things signified by words have themselves also a signification is called the spiritual sense, which is based on the literal, and presupposes it' (*Summa Theologica* 1.1.10).

61. Calvin, *Institutes* 1.7.4.

62. We are again influenced here by Jean-Luc Marion, *God without Being*, 139–58. However, Marion assumes the person functioning *in persona Christi* must be a diocesan bishop in particular. For our view, see our excursus on the development of the episcopacy.

63. David Bosch suggests that the disciples recognized Christ by the nail marks in his wrists when he took, blessed, broke and gave them the bread (*Transforming Mission: Paradigm Shifts in Theology and Mission* [Maryknoll, N.Y.: Orbis, 1991], p. 59). This need not disqualify our claim that it is in fellowship that we recognize Christ, though it does serve to further qualify it by insisting that our fellowship with Christ involves our recognizing him as the crucified one.

64. Jn 5.39. See Wesley, Sermon 16, 'On the Means of Grace', 3.7.

65. Acts 17.11–12; 2 Tim. 3.15–17. See Wesley, Sermon 16, 'On the Means of Grace', 3.7–9.
66. See Irenaeus of Lyons, *On the Apostolic Preaching*, trans. John Behr (Crestwood, N.Y.: St. Vladimir's Seminary Press, 1997).
67. Even Moses 'wrote of me', says Jesus (Jn 5.46).
68. J. I. Packer, *God Has Spoken* (Grand Rapids, Mich.: Baker, 1979), p. 97, cited in Telford Work, *Living and Active: Scripture in the Economy of Salvation* (Grand Rapids, Mich.: Eerdmans, 2002), p. 25.
69. Thanks to a comment from Alan Jacobs on the Spirit's role in the transmission of the Bible.
70. See Webster, *Holy Scripture*, 86ff.; Webster, 'Resurrection and Scripture', in *Christology and Scripture: Interdisciplinary Perspectives*, eds Andrew Lincoln and Angus Paddison (New York: T&T Clark, 2008), pp. 138–55.
71. Calvin, *Institutes* 1.7.4.
72. Calvin, *Institutes* 1.9.3.
73. Calvin, *Institutes* 1.8.
74. Calvin, *Institutes* 1.7.5.
75. 'Recognition, acceptance, giving audience, devotion, a checking of distracting desire, faith, trust, a looking to Scripture for consolation: such attitudes and practices are to characterise the faithful reader of Scripture, and their absence denotes a degenerate understanding of what is involved in reading it' (John Webster, *Holy Scripture: A Dogmatic Sketch* [Cambridge: Cambridge University Press, 2003], p. 69).
76. Calvin, *Institutes* 1.4.1.
77. Calvin, *Institutes* 1.5.12, 1.11.8.
78. 'Just as old or bleary-eyed men and those with weak vision, if you thrust before them a most beautiful volume, even if they recognize it to be some sort of writing, yet can scarcely construe two words, but with the aid of spectacles will begin to read distinctly; so Scripture, gathering up the otherwise confused knowledge of God in our minds, having dispersed our dullness, clearly shows us the true God' (Calvin, *Institutes* 1.6.1). This blindness is not merely a function of our sin, though it is that; our inability to see God also reflects his utter transcendence. Calvin writes that 'the splendour of the divine countenance, which even the apostle calls "unapproachable", is for us like an inexplicable labyrinth unless we are conducted into it by the thread of the Word; so that it is better to limp along this path than to dash with all speed outside it' (*Institutes* 1.6.3).
79. Irenaeus, *Adversus Haereses* 1.8.1.
80. Note D. A. Carson's clever comment: 'A text without a context is a pre-text for a prooftext'.
81. Two accounts which acknowledge the difficulty of these conversations and yet hold out hope for a biblical account of homosexuality, see Oliver O'Donovan, *Church in Crisis: The Gay Controversy and the Anglican Communion* (Eugene, Ore.: Cascade Books, 2008); Richard B. Hays, *The Moral Vision of the New Testament: Community, Cross, New Creation: A Contemporary Introduction to New Testament Ethics* (San

Francisco: HarperSanFrancisco, 1996), pp. 379–406. For an account of the formerly (but similarly) vexing question of whether slavery is biblical, see Mark A. Noll, *The Civil War as a Theological Crisis* (Chapel Hill, N.C.: The University of North Carolina Press, 2006).

82. 'We must avoid the twin heresies that over- and underestimate the letter: that the literal sense has *nothing* to do with the letter, or that the literal sense has *only* to do with the letter. The letter is the indispensable means for performing the communicative act and for signalling the intention, but it is only a necessary, not a sufficient condition for meaning. Interpretation is "literalistic" only if one overlooks this dual parentage and reduces the literal to the sense of the letter (e.g. to *langue*). By no means do I wish to advocate literalistic reading, the hermeneutic equivalent of the cult of the body. Rather, I am arguing that literalistic reading is less than fully "literal" – that it is insufficiently and only "thinly" literal – insofar as it ignores the role of authorial intentions and communicative acts' (Kevin J. Vanhoozer, *Is There a Meaning in This Text? The Bible, the Reader, and the Morality of Literary Knowledge* [Grand Rapids, Mich.: Zondervan, 1998], p. 311).

83. Vanhoozer, *Is There a Meaning in This Text?*, p. 317. The entire discussion of scripture's perspicuity and the literal sense is especially insightful (pp. 307–17).

84. William J. Abraham, *Canon and Criterion in Christian Theology* (Oxford: Oxford University Press, 2002 [1998]), p. 471. Also see the comprehensive proposal in *Canonical Theism: A Proposal for Theology and the Church*, eds William J. Abraham, Jason E. Vickers, Natalie B. Van Kirk (Grand Rapids, Mich.: Eerdmans, 2008).

85. Abraham, *Canon and Criterion*, p. 470.

86. 'The impression given in this interpretation is that the provision of the canon of Scripture is the provision of a criterion to settle contested questions . . . . [S]uch a reductionism ignores the possibility that to have a canon of Scripture is to have a sophisticated means of grace which is related to formation in holy living in a host of ways. On this alternative reading, Scripture functions to bring one to faith, to make one wise unto salvation, to force one to wrestle with awkward questions about violence and the poor, to comfort those in sorrow, and to nourish hope for the redemption of the world. The interpretation of Scripture primarily or exclusively as an epistemic norm of morality and of theology erodes these crucial dimensions of canonical materials' (*Canon and Criterion*, 6–7).

87. See Abraham, *The Logic of Renewal*.

88. On the inversion through which modernity has come to view the Bible in light of the world rather than the world in light of the Bible, see Hans W. Frei, *The Eclipse of Biblical Narrative: A Study in Eighteenth and Nineteenth Century Hermeneutics* (London: Yale University Press, 1974).

89. Karl Barth, 'The Strange New World within the Bible', in *The Word of God and the Word of Man*, trans. Douglas Horton (London: Hodder & Stoughton, 1935), pp. 28–50.

90. Calvin, *Institutes* 1.7.2.

91. Such as that found, for instance, in neo-Scholasticism. See Avery Dulles, *Models of Revelation*, 2nd edn (Maryknoll, N.Y.: Orbis, 1992), p. 45.
92. Schmemann, *The Eucharist*, pp. 78–79. See also Ratzinger's complementary understanding of scripture and tradition cited in our chapter on Metaphor.
93. Gerhard Ebeling, 'Church History is the History of the Exposition of Scripture', in *The Word of God and Tradition* (Philadelphia: Fortress Press, 1968), pp. 11–31.
94. MacIntyre, *Whose Justice? Which Rationality?* (Notre Dame, Ind.: University of Notre Dame Press, 1988), p. 12.
95. Luther's Works, 34:286f., in the 1539 preface to the first volume of the Wittenberg edition of his German works. Cited in Oswald Bayer, *Theology the Lutheran Way*, ed. and trans. Jeffrey G. Silcock and Mark C. Mattes (Grand Rapids, Mich.: Eerdmans, 2007), p. 60. See Bayer's discussion of the three-fold pattern of listening to the word on pp. 42–64.
96. John Webster, 'Resurrection and Scripture', p. 138. Barth suggests that it is in receiving the apostles' unique witness that we receive Christ's self-witness (*Church Dogmatics* IV/1, p. 718).
97. Webster, 'Resurrection and Scripture', p. 140.
98. Webster, 'Resurrection and Scripture', p. 141.
99. On the significance of asking 'Who?' rather than 'How?', see Dietrich Bonhoeffer, *Christology*, trans. John Bowden (London: Collins, 1966), p. 36.
100. If we run the risk of belabouring the point in continuing to return to the active presence of the triune God in the church, it is only because that is just the point that discussions of ecclesiology often neglect.
101. Calvin, *Institutes* 4.17.1.
102. Calvin, *Institutes* 4.14.9.
103. The historic origin of this title for the Lord's Supper derives from the *Sursum Corda*.
104. We will use the terms interchangeably.
105. Though this is a motley bunch, the one requirement is that they come dressed for the occasion (Mt. 22.10–13; Rev. 19.7–8).
106. Remembrance as dramatic inclusion is not quite the same as re-enactment or re-presentation, however. While he may overplay the contrast, Ben Witherington helpfully writes: 'The Lord's Supper is not a *reenactment* of the Last Supper in the same way that the Passover celebration is a bringing into the present of the Passover night in Egypt . . . . In fact, *the focus of the Lord's Supper is not on "the night when Jesus was betrayed"* but on the death of Jesus and its benefits. . . . *Anamnesis*, remembering and cherishing and keeping in mind, not reenactment or re-presenting, is the characteristic of this meal according to Paul' (Ben Witherington III, *Making a Meal of It: Rethinking the Theology of the Lord's Supper* [Waco, Tex.: Baylor University Press, 2008], p. 130).
107. *m. Pesach* X. 5. Cited in Lohfink, *Does God Need the Church?*, p. 67.

108. See, for example, Mt. 26.20–25, 31–35. Michael Welker notes the significance of the betrayal motif in the eucharist, and its surprising neglect in eucharistic theology, in *What Happens in Holy Communion?*, trans. John F. Hoffmeyer (Grand Rapids, Mich.: Eerdmans, 2000), pp. 73, 103, 143–44, 171.

109. On Jesus as slave of all, see Phil. 2.5–11; Mt. 20.27–28; Mk 10.43–45. On the foot-washing, see Jn 13.1–17. The meal at which Jesus washes the disciples' feet may not have been the Passover meal (see 13.1), though even if not, the account of it is woven together with Jesus' last meal with his disciples (see 13.21ff.; cp. Mt. 26.19–35; Mk 14.17–31; Lk. 22.1–38).

110. Hunsinger, *The Eucharist and Ecumenism*, p. 145.

111. Hunsinger, *The Eucharist and Ecumenism*, p. 168.

112. Calvin again: 'a sacrament is never without a preceding promise but is joined to it as a sort of appendix, with the purpose of confirming and sealing the promise itself, and of making it more evident to us and in a sense ratifying it . . . . But as our faith is slight and feeble unless it be propped on all sides and sustained by every means, it trembles, wavers, totters, and at last gives way. Here our merciful Lord, according to his infinite kindness, so tempers himself to our capacity that, since we are creatures who always creep on the ground, cleave to the flesh, and, do not think about or even conceive of anything spiritual, he condescends to lead us to himself even by these earthly elements, and to set before us in the flesh a mirror of spiritual blessings' (4.14.3).

113. Roger Olson demonstrates the notion of mere symbolism to be unfaithful to Zwingli and the earliest (Ana)baptists; mere symbolism in turn is only found in 'folk theology' (Olson, 'The Baptist View', *The Lord's Supper: Five Views*, p. 105).

114. Alasdair I. C. Heron, *Table and Tradition: Toward an Ecumenical Understanding of the Eucharist* (Philadelphia: The Westminster Press, 1983), p. 28.

115. See Jeremy S. Begbie, *Voicing Creation's Praise: Towards a Theology of the Arts* (Edinburgh: T&T Clark, 1991); Richard Bauckham, 'Joining Creation's Praise of God', *Ecotheology* 7 (2002): 42–59. Bauckham explicitly, and vigorously, denies that humans are to be called 'priests of creation'. His point is that the non-human creation can praise God on its own, thank you very much, and does not need humanity to articulate its praise for it. Bauckham points to the language of the Psalms, but his argument also suggests a general antipathy on his part to hierarchy. While the non-human creation certainly does praise God in its own way, part of the human way of praising God includes doubling the praise of the non-human creation. That is, we praise God on our own behalf, and we also praise him on behalf of the non-human creation by repeating its praise in our words.

116. See the fine discussion by Hunsinger in *The Eucharist and Ecumenism*, pp. 21–92.

117. Calvin, *Institutes* 4.17.10 (trans. Beveridge – Battles renders it as 'analogy'); also see 4.17.3.

118. See Calvin, *Institutes* 4.17.31; also see 4.17.10. Schmemann also turns to pneumatology and a movement of ascension (see *The Eucharist*, pp. 60, 168–69, 221, 224).

119. We suggest a certain amount of compatibility with Marion's attempt to deconstruct the idol of time (*God without Being*, 161–82), which deconstructs the chronological as our discussion deconstructs the spatial.

120. Geoffrey Wainwright, *Eucharist and Eschatology* (Peterborough, England: Epworth Press, 2003 [1971]), p. 188. Wainwright describes the eucharist as a taste, sign, image and mystery of the kingdom (pp. 187–91). He summarizes the eschatological character of the eucharist. It is 'the proleptic advent of our Lord as Judge and Saviour ("Maranatha!"), granting us a foretaste of the eternal feasting of a life shared in society with God ("Antepast of Heaven"), a tangible anticipation of the time when God will be all in all ("Firstfruits of the Kingdom")' (p. 292).

121. Note the ambiguity of the reference to body here – is it referring to the risen Christ, the church or the bread? Likely, all three.

122. Witherington, *Making a Meal of It*, p. 140.

123. William T. Cavanaugh, *Torture and Eucharist: Theology, Politics, and the Body of Christ* (Malden, Mass.: Blackwell Publishing, 1998), p. 263.

124. See Ps. 98.7–9: 'Let the sea roar, and all that fills it; the world and those who live in it. Let the floods clap their hands; let the hills sing together for joy at the presence of the Lord, for he is coming to judge the earth. He will judge the world with righteousness, and the peoples with equity'.

125. George Weigel, 'Catholicism and Anglicansim: The End of an Era', in *The Washington Post* (21 October 2009); available online at http://newsweek.washingtonpost.com/onfaith/panelists/george_weigel/2009/10/catholicism_and_anglicanism_the_end_of_an_era.html).

126. For the latest Anglican statement on this issue, see Michael Nazir-Ali et al., *Women Bishops in the Church of England? A Report of the House of Bishops' Working Party on Women in the Episcopate* (London: Church House Publishing, 2004); available online at http://www.cofe.anglican.org/info/papers/womenbishops.pdf.

127. Ruth Tucker and Walter Liefield, *Daughters of the Church: Women and Ministry from New Testament Times to the Present* (Grand Rapids, Mich.: Zondervan, 1987).

128. Tucker and Liefield, *Daughters of the Church*, p. 440.

129. For a more comprehensive study, see Mary T. Malone, *Women and Christianity*, 3 vols. (Maryknoll, N.Y.: Orbis, 2003). And for a study related but not limited to Christian history, see Bonnie S. Anderson and Judith P. Zinsser, *A History of their Own: Women in Europe from Prehistory to the Present* (New York: Oxford University Press, 2000).

130. Karen Jo Torjesen, *When Women were Priests: Women's Leadership in the Early Church and the Scandal of Their Subordination in the Rise of Christianity* (San Franscisco: HarperCollins, 1993). It should be noted that the 'deaconess', while understood as a deacon's wife in the West, is

widely recognized as a distinct office in the East, one which lasted for several centuries – more on deaconesses below.

131. See Acts 12.12; Rom. 16.3–5; 1 Cor. 16.19; Col. 4.15; and Phlm. 2 – a list identified by Elizabeth A. Clark, s.v. 'Women', in *Encyclopedia of Early Christianity*, 2nd edn, ed. Everett Ferguson (New York: Routledge, 1999), p. 1181.

132. Valerie A. Karras, 'Priestesses or Priests' Wives: *Presbytera* in Early Christianity', St. *Vladimir's Theological Quarterly* 51:2–3 (2007): 321–45.

133. Karras, 'Priestesses', pp. 337–39.

134. Karras, 'Priestesses', p. 322, n. 4.

135. See Frances M. Young, 'Hermeneutical Questions: The Ordination of Women in the Light of Biblical and Patristic Typology', in *Women and Ordination in the Christian Churches: International Perspectives*, eds Ian Jones, Kristy Thorpe and Janet Wootton (London: T&T Clark, 2008), pp. 21–39.

136. For the possibilities, see Donald Hochstetler, *A Conflict of Traditions: Women in Religion in the Early Middle Ages, 500–840* (Lanham, Md.: University Press of America, 1992). For a broader treatment of women in this context, see Katharina M. Wilson and Nadia Margolis, *Women in the Middle Ages: An Encyclopedia* (Westport, Conn.: Greenwood Press, 2004); and Jennifer Lawler, *Encyclopedia of Women in the Middle Ages* (Jefferson, N.C.: McFarland & Co., 2008).

137. Gary Macy, *The Hidden History of Women's Ordination: Female Clergy in the Medieval West* (Oxford: Oxford University Press, 2008); Macy, *A History of Women and Ordination, vol. 1: The Ordination of Women in a Medieval Context*, ed. Bernard Cooke and Gary Macy (Lanham, Md.: Scarecrow, 2002); Macy, 'The Ordination of Women in the Early Middle Ages', *Theological Studies* 61:3 (September 2000): 481–507.

138. See, for example, Virginia Burrus, *Chastity as Autonomy: Women in the Stories of Apocryphal Acts* (Lewiston, N.Y.: Edwin Mellen Press, 1987).

139. Christina Harrington, *Women in a Celtic Church* (Oxford: Oxford University Press, 2002); ref. Brigit of Kildare.

140. Katherine L. French, *The Good Women of the Parish: Gender and Religion after the Black Death* (Philadelphia: University of Pennsylvania Press, 2008).

141. For an overview, see Helen M. Jewell, *Women in Late Medieval and Reformation Europe* (New York: Palgrave Macmillan, 2007), esp. chapter 7, 'Women Who Exceeded Society's Expectations'.

142. While women's roles in the Protestant Reformation are worthy of full discussion, we omit it here for the sake of space. For a complete treatment, see Tucker and Liefield, *Daughters of the Church*, 171–206, and Jewell, *Women in Late Medieval and Reformation Europe*, passim.

143. See William Webb, *Slaves, Women & Homosexuals: Exploring the Hermeneutics of Cultural Analysis* (Downers Grove, Ill.: InterVarsity Press, 2001).

144. Webb, *Slaves, Women & Homosexuals*, defends the egalitarian position as biblical, but finds homosexuality unbiblical because the Bible's

treatment of slavery and women was counterculturally liberating, while the Bible's statements about homosexuality was counterculturally restrictive. Karras, 'Priestesses', 344–45 concludes with a similar implication about women's roles.

145. For a very brief introduction to the stances taken, see Daniel Burke, 'Anglican Unity in "Grave Peril" if Gay Bans not Enforced, Williams says', *Christian Century* 125:17 (26 August 2008): 15. Also, cf. the entire issue of the North American journal *Anglican Theological Review*, 90:4 (Fall 2008). For an outsider's perspective that questions the ecclesiology of the debate, see the editorial by Reformed pastor Daniel Meeter, 'Watching the Anglicans', *Perspectives* 23:6 (June 2008): 3–4.

146. Yoder, *Karl Barth and the Problem of War* (Nashville, Tenn.: Abingdon Press, 1970).

147. See his 'Letter from a Birmingham Jail' (1963) reprint in *I Have a Dream: Writings and Speeches that Changed the World*, ed. James Melvin Washington (San Francisco: HarperOne, 1992), p. 89. This specific argument, a quote in fact, is credited to Augustine (cf. *De libero arbitrio* 1.5).

148. Hence Georges Florovsky's notion of 'the double "ecumenicity" of Christian faith – in space and time' (*Bible, Church, Tradition: An Eastern Orthodox View* [Belmont, Mass.: Nordland Publishing Company, 1972], p. 73).

149. Robert W. Jenson, *Systematic Theology. Volume 2: The Works of God* (Oxford: Oxford University Press, 1999), p. 269.

150. Luther, 'An Open Letter to Leo X', in *The Freedom of a Christian*, in *Martin Luther's Basic Theological Writings*, 2nd edn, ed. Timothy F. Lull (Minneapolis, Minn.: Augsburg Fortress, 2005), p. 392.

151. See Webster, *Word and Church*, p. 196.

152. See Mark Saucy, 'Evangelicals, Catholics, and Orthodox Together: Is the Church the Extension of the Incarnation?', *Journal of the Evangelical Theological Society* 43:2 (June 2000): 193–212. Saucy asks the question through the lens of Christ's threefold office as prophet, priest and king. While we affirm his 'no', we question his insistence that '"[h]igh" ecclesiology means "low" Christology, pneumatology, and eschatology' (212).

153. Webster, *Word and Church*, p. 226.

154. The entire *corpus* of T. F. Torrance can be read as an extended meditation on the theological implications of our lives lived 'in Christ'. For one striking example, see his 'Questioning in Christ', in *Theology in Reconstruction* (London: SCM Press, 1965), pp. 117–27. A helpful pneumatological corrective, still faithful to the matter of Torrance's theme, is Smail, *The Giving Gift*.

155. See the discussion in Pannenberg, *Systematic Theology*, vol. 3, trans. Geoffrey W. Bromiley (Grand Rapids, Mich.: Eerdmans, 1998), p. 126.

156. *The Ecclesiastical Hierarchy* 561 BC (in *Pseudo-Dionysius: The Complete Works* [New York: Paulist Press, 1987]). This is given more context in *The Divine Names* 588C.

157. Dionysius, *Ep.* 9 1113B.

158. Heb. 10.19–22.
159. See Paul Minear's remarks on the unique high priesthood of Jesus in Hebrews in his *Images of the Church in the New Testament*, pp. 98–99.
160. See Douglas Farrow's brilliant apology for the doctrine of the ascension in *Ascension and Ecclesia*.

CHAPTER 4 – MISSION

1. One of the most articulate, balanced voices coming from the 'emerging conversation' in Anglo-America is Dan Kimball. See his *They Like Jesus but Not the Church: Insights from Emerging Generations* (Grand Rapids, Mich.: Zondervan, 2007).
2. Martin Kähler, *Schriften zur Christologie und Mission* (Munich: Chr. Kaiser Verlag, 1971 [1908]), p. 190, translated and cited by Bosch, *Transforming Mission*, p. 16.
3. G. C. Berkouwer, *The Church*, trans. James E. Davison (Grand Rapids, Mich.: Eerdmans, 1976), p. 391.
4. See Bosch, *Transforming Mission*, pp. 389–93. For an argument that the Bible is to be read as a narrative of the *missio Dei*, see Christopher J. H. Wright, *The Mission of God: Unlocking the Bible's Grand Narrative* (Downers Grove, Ill.: IVP Academic, 2006). For an attempt to think through the implications of the *missio Dei* for the church in a North American context, see Darrell L. Guder (ed.), *Missional Church: A Vision for the Sending of the Church in North America* (Grand Rapids, Mich.: Eerdmans, 1998).
5. Barth, *Church Dogmatics* IV/3.2, p. 768.
6. *Ad Gentes* 2.
7. It is common to speak of two missions, but it is equally valid to refer to a twofold mission, underscoring the one *missio Dei* which encompasses scripture and human history.
8. See N. T. Wright, *The Climax of the Covenant: Christ and the Law in Pauline Theology* (Minneapolis, Minn.: Fortress Press, 1992).
9. G. K. Beale, *The Temple and the Church's Mission: A Biblical Theology of the Dwelling Place of God* (Downers Grove, Ill.: InterVarsity Press, 2004), p. 392.
10. Guder (ed.), *Missional Church*, pp. 4, 81.
11. See Bosch, *Transforming Mission*, p. 144: 'The church . . . is, as proleptic manifestation of God's reign, the beachhead of the new creation, the vanguard of God's new world, and the sign of the dawning new age in the midst of the old . . .'.
12. Lactantius, *De mortibus persecutorum* 44.4–6.
13. In this, we roughly follow O'Donovan's usage of the term in *The Desire of the Nations*.
14. Eusebius of Caesarea, *Vita Constantini* 1.31.
15. Eusebius of Caesarea, *Vita Constantini* 1.28.
16. Niebuhr, *Christ and Culture* (New York: Harper and Brothers, 1951), p. 56.

17. Carter, *Rethinking Christ and Culture: A Post-Christendom Perspective* (Grand Rapids, Mich.: Brazos Press, 2006), p. 56. Also see the scathing critique in John H. Yoder, 'How H. Richard Niebuhr Reasoned: A Critique of *Christ and* Culture', in *Authentic Transformation: A New Vision of Christ and Culture*, eds Glen H. Stassen, D. M. Yeager and John Howard Yoder (Nashville, Tenn.: Abingdon Press, 1996), pp. 31–89.

18. Philip Jenkins, *The Next Christendom: The Coming of Global Christianity* (Oxford: Oxford University Press, 2002), p. 6.

19. Jenkins, *The Next Christendom*, p. 7; ref. Harvey Cox, *Fire From Heaven: The Rise of Pentecostal Spirituality and the Reshaping of Religion in the Twenty-First Century* (Reading, Mass.: Addison-Wesley Publishing Co., 1995).

20. See his chapter 'The Next Crusade', *The Next Christendom*, pp. 163–90.

21. See John D. Caputo, *The Prayers and Tears of Jacques Derrida: Religion without Religion* (Bloomington, Ind.: Indiana University Press, 1997). Derrida of course is indebted to Bonhoeffer, but what exactly Bonhoeffer intended with the phrase 'religion without religion' was unfortunately never explicated.

22. Thurman, *Footprints of a Dream: The Story of the Church for the Fellowship of All Peoples* (New York: Harper and Brothers, 1959).

23. Taken from the church's official website: http://www.fellowshipsf.org/history.html.

24. See especially Thurman, *Footprints of a Dream*, pp. 109–30, the chapter entitled 'The Image of the Church'.

25. James Cone, *Speaking the Truth: Ecumenism, Liberation and Black Theology* (Grand Rapids, Mich.: Eerdmans Press, 1986), pp. 111–28, his chapter entitled, 'What is the Church?'

26. Cone, *Speaking the Truth*, pp. 116–17. We also commend the study of Robert E. Hood, *Begrimed and Black: Christian Traditions on Blacks and Blackness* (Minneapolis, Minn.: Fortress Press, 1994), pp. 45–71, his chapter entitled, 'Africa and the Christian Tradition', wherein he analyses the relationship between 'blackness' and the church in ancient and recent history.

27. *African Reformation: African Initiated Christianity in the Twentieth Century* (Trenton, N.J.: Africa World Press, 2000).

28. Rosino Gibellini, 'Introduction' in *Paths of African Theology* (Maryknoll, N.Y.: Orbis, 1994), p. 7; this phrase is in reference to African theology more generally but is applicable to African ecclesiology in particular.

29. Idowu, *Towards an Indigenous Church* (London: Oxford University Press, 1965).

30. Boff, *Ecclesiogenesis*.

31. An admittedly dubious point, given Boff's break with Catholicism. Nevertheless, the BCCs as a whole have remained within the bounds of the Roman Catholic Church.

32. See a discussion of other examples of 'contextual ecclesiologies' in the third part of Veli-Matti Kärkkäinen, *An Introduction to Ecclesiology: Ecumenical, Historical and Global Perspectives* (Downers Grove, Ill.: InterVarsity Press, 2002), pp. 167–230.

33. Above, in our chapter on Metaphor, we found Newbigin to exemplify just such a stance. He is certainly critical of Christendom, and yet he navigated a course within mainline and ecumenical frameworks.

34. Alfred Loisy, *The Gospel and the Church*, trans. Christopher Home (New York: Charles Scribner's Sons, 1912), p. 166. See the excursus, 'Did Jesus establish the church?', in the introduction.

35. A helpful, brief overview on this question is George Eldon Ladd, *The Gospel of the Kingdom: Scriptural Studies in the Kingdom of God* (Grand Rapids, Mich.: Eerdmans, 1959).

36. Barth, *Church Dogmatics* IV/3.2, p. 792.

37. Ladd, *The Gospel of the Kingdom*, p. 21.

38. O'Donovan, *The Desire of the Nations*, p. 93.

39. God's priestly people are thus prefigured by the landless Levites, whose inheritance was the Lord himself (Deut. 18.2). See O'Donovan, *The Desire of the Nations*, p. 45.

40. See O'Donovan, *The Desire of the Nations*, p. 162.

41. Jürgen Moltmann, *Theology of Hope: On the Ground and the Implications of a Christian Eschatology*, trans. James W. Leitch (Minneapolis, Minn.: Fortress Press, 1993).

42. O'Donovan, *The Desire of the Nations*, p. 158.

43. Guder (ed.), *Missional Church*, pp. 100–02, 221.

44. Guder (ed.), *Missional Church*, pp. 93–95. Note that this is far from a passive waiting. Instead, it is a hopeful and faithful attentiveness, an eminently active watching and praying.

45. For an extended meditation on the church's heavenly citizenship which reflects the Anabaptist witness to the basic antagonism between church and world, see Hauerwas and Willimon, *Resident Aliens*.

46. Lohfink, *Does God Need the Church?*, p. 88.

47. Karl Barth, *Church Dogmatics* IV/3.2, p. 764.

48. Karl Barth, *Church Dogmatics* IV/1, p. 725.

49. *Gaudium et Spes* §1. This 'pastoral constitution on the church in the modern world' goes on to explain from this starting point 'how it conceives of the presence and activity of the Church in the world today'. (§2)

50. See Barth, *Church Dogmatics* IV/3.2, pp. 762–95.

51. Schmemann, *For the Life of the World*, p. 68.

52. Nicholas Healy is right. 'In the simple terms: God is the solution to the problems of the world, not the church. The church, although orientated to, and governed by, the solution, still remains part of the problem' (Healy, *Church, World and Christian Life*, p. 12).

53. *Baptism, Eucharist and Ministry*, 'Eucharist', Faith and Order Paper No. 111 (Geneva: World Council of Churches, 1982), paragraph 4.

54. See Newbigin, *The Open Secret*, p. 188.

55. Barth, *Church Dogmatics* IV/3.2, p. 874.
56. Webster, *Word and Church*, p. 222. So 'human, churchly reconciling action is not only prospective but also, crucially, *retrospective*, looking *back* to a final reconciliation which – τετέλεσται – has already taken place' (218).
57. 'For what specific action of the community can ever be anything but διακονία, *ministerium*, the rendering of service?' (Barth, *Church Dogmatics* IV/3.2, p. 890; also see pp. 833–34)
58. 'The matter is too vital for us to be satisfied with the assurances of men, unless we are sure that God has appointed them and speaks to us through them'. Paul 'says that as He once suffered, so now every day He offers the fruit of His suffering to us through the gospel which He has given to the world as a sure and certain record of His completed work of reconciliation. Thus the duty of ministers is to apply to us the fruit of Christ's death' (*Calvin, The Second Epistle of Paul the Apostle to the Corinthians and the Epistles to Timothy, Titus and Philemon*, trans. T. A. Smail [Grand Rapids, Mich.: Eerdmans, 1996 (1546)], pp. 80, 79, commenting on 2 Cor. 5.19–20).
59. A model John Zizioulas (*Being as Communion*, pp. 247–60) champions as both timeless and relevant for today.
60. Newbigin, *The Open Secret*, p. 95.
61. See John M. Perkins, *With Justice for All: A Strategy for Community Development*, 3rd edn (Ventura, Calif.: Regal Books, 2007).
62. Berkouwer, *The Church*, pp. 29, 33.
63. Berkouwer, *The Church*, pp. 46–48; Bruce D. Marshall, 'The Disunity of the Church and the Credibility of the Gospel', *Theology Today* 50:1 (April 1993): 78–89.
64. Berkouwer, *The Church*, p. 36.
65. If Newbigin is right that the contemporary ecumenical movement was born in and so shaped by the churches of Western Europe and North America that '[o]nly those who have had long training in the methods of thinking, of study and research, and of argument that have been developed in Western Europe can share in its work', then ecclesial reunion in the West may be a Pyrrhic victory (Newbigin, *The Open Secret*, p. 151).
66. 'This change of heart and holiness of life, along with public and private prayer for the unity of Christians, should be regarded as the soul of the whole ecumenical movement, and merits the name, "spiritual ecumenism"' (*Unitatis Redintegratio* §8).
67. One helpful discussion of the state of things is Mark A. Noll and Carolyn Nystrom, *Is the Reformation Over? An Evangelical Assessment of Contemporary Roman Catholicism* (Grand Rapids, Mich.: Baker Academic, 2005).
68. See his *Unbaptized God: The Basic Flaw in Ecumenical Theology* (Minneapolis, Minn.: Fortress Press, 1992).
69. For the significance of this distinction, see David S. Yeago, 'The New Testament and the Nicene Dogma: A Contribution to the Recovery of Theological Exegesis', in *The Theological Interpretation of Scripture:*

Classic and Contemporary Readings, ed. Stephen E. Fowl (Oxford: Blackwell, 1997), pp. 87–100.

70. The Lutheran World Federation and The Roman Catholic Church, *Joint Declaration on the Doctrine of Justification* (Grand Rapids, Mich.: Eerdmans, 2000).

71. See her *Christian Contradictions: The Structures of Lutheran and Catholic Thought* (Cambridge: Cambridge University Press, 2001), pp. 209–22.

72. John R. Mott (1865–1955) presided in Edinburgh and was the leading figure championing the student missionary movement in his work with the Student Volunteer Movement for Foreign Missions (winning the Nobel Peace Prize in 1946 for his work with Christian students for peace). He was involved in the formation of the World Council of Churches, the leading Protestant institution of the ecumenical movement, in 1948 and was named honorary life-long President of the WCC.

73. George, 'The Sacramentality of the Church: An Evangelical Baptist Perspective', p. 310.

74. Harper and Metzger, *Exploring Ecclesiology*, p. 17.

75. Carl E. Braaten, *Mother Church: Ecclesiology and Ecumenism* (Minneapolis, Minn.: Fortress Press, 1998), p. 3.

76. George Hunsinger, *The Eucharist and Ecumenism*, p. 2.

77. What kind of unity would the Spirit create but precisely the real, patent unity of persons? This is not exhausted institutionally, and it certainly includes a oneness of belief and of spirit; furthermore, our unity with the heavenly church must be invisible this side of the *eschaton*. But the proof, as they say, is in the pudding; and any unity that is *merely* spiritual and not generative of visible forms (never mind the unity that is generated *by* and *in* visible forms) is hardly worth the name.

78. See Henri de Lubac, *The Church: Paradox and Mystery* (Staten Island, N.Y.: Alba House, 1969), pp. 4–5.

79. See, for example, Hunsinger, *The Eucharist and Ecumenism*. Hunsinger is refreshingly honest, admitting that 'what to do about those churches rooted in the anabaptist traditions, including charismatics and pentecostals, is beyond me' (11).

80. These are rough categories, and we are wary of relying too heavily on the distinction (in this case) between structure and spirit; but nonetheless, the terms name realities.

81. Vatican II gestures in this direction with its surprisingly sanguine statement that the church 'subsists in the Catholic Church . . . although many elements of sanctification and of truth are found outside of its visible structure' (*Lumen Gentium* §8). Not only is good found outside the visible structure, but sin is also found in the church, which is 'at the same time holy and always in need of being purified' (§8).

82. The Lutheran sense of the sufficiency of faithfulness to the gospel of Christ is a boon to ecumenism (Eric W. Gritsch and Robert W. Jenson, *Lutheranism: The Theological Movement and Its Confessional Writings* [Philadelphia: Fortress Press, 1976], p. 172, something explicitly declared in the Augsburg Confession – see AC 7.2–3). It is

a simple 'unity in proclamation and sacramental action' for which Augsburg calls (173). This is not even *dogmatic* unity; 'the required unity is in actual preaching of the gospel, not in confessional statements or systematic theologies' (174).

83. McLaren sponsors the phrase 'generous orthodoxy', which he picked up from Hans Frei.

84. For a wise meditation on the relation of truth and love in the modern world, see Benedict XVI's recent encyclical, *Caritas in veritate*.

85. 'The unity of the church is public and visible in character', writes Bruce Marshall, reflecting on Jn 17.20–26. It consists in a unity of faith, of mutual love and service, in a common baptism and in shared eucharistic participation. (Marshall, 'The Disunity of the Church and the Credibility of the Gospel', p. 79) He inexplicably goes on to focus his argument inordinately on the issue of eucharistic fellowship. The call to visible unity is surely right, but an equation of this with eucharistic fellowship (something which Marshall avoids, but which his tenor does little to discourage) is unnecessary.

86. Hunsinger, *The Eucharist and Ecumenism*, p. 2.

87. Karl Barth, *Ad Limina Apostolorum: An Appraisal of Vatican II*, trans. Keith R. Crim (Richmond, Va.: John Knox Press, 1968), p. 79. Note, too, Gerhard Lohfink's apposite insistence: 'The conversion that alone can heal the wounds of division would thus first of all be a re-rooting of the Church in the Old Testament and in Jewish reality'. It would then involve 'taking the New Testament seriously . . . but the *whole* New Testament' (*Does God Need the Church?*, pp. 302–03).

88. To recall Rom. 11.29. This is not to suggest an easy dismissal of the task of reunion, nor is it to negate Ephraim Radner's thesis that the Spirit has left the church in the exile of its schism (in *The End of the Church: A Pneumatology of Christian Division in the West* [Grand Rapids, Mich.: Eerdmans, 1998]). It is simply to affirm that God has reconciled his people in one body through the cross (Eph. 2.16), and that this reconciliation is accomplished irrespective of our application of it in the life of the church.

89. While we will focus on large-scale division, also germane to this discussion is the decision by an individual or family to leave their local church for another.

90. See R. R. Reno, *In the Ruins of the Church: Sustaining Faith in an Age of Diminished Christianity* (Grand Rapids, Mich.: Brazos Press, 2002), pp. 31–79. Reno exhorts Christians to live in the ruins of the church, choosing suffering intimacy rather than ironic distance. But also see R. R. Reno, 'Out of the Ruins', *First Things* 150 (February 2005): 11–16. For an argument in an evangelical rather than Reno's mainline Protestant context, see Matt Jenson, 'An Apology for Staying', *The Other Journal* 8 (November 2006), available at www.theotherjournal. com/article.php?id=210.

91. Schleiermacher, *The Christian Faith* §150.2, 682–83.

92. Schleiermacher, *The Christian Faith* §151.2, 684.

93. Recall Calvin's comment that human nature is 'a perpetual factory of idols' (*Institutes* 1.11.8).

94. On the need to cultivate practices of moral discernment in this arena, see Oliver O'Donovan, *Church in Crisis*.

95. R. Kendall Soulen, 'YHWH the Triune God', *Modern Theology* 15:1 (January 1999): 30. Soulen describes this as 'structural supersessionism'.

96. Jenson, *Systematic Theology*, vol. 2, 182.

97. Oliver O'Donovan, *The Desire of the Nations*, p. 131.

98. See Richard Bauckham, *God Crucified: Monotheism and Christology in the New Testament* (Cambridge: Eerdmans, 1999); N. T. Wright, *What Saint Paul Really Said: Was Paul of Tarsus the Real Founder of Christianity?* (Grand Rapids, Mich.: Eerdmans, 2000).

99. Soulen, 'YHWH the Triune God', p. 45.

100. Bruce Longenecker points out that supersessionism is not anti-Judaism in his 'On Israel's God and God's Israel: Assessing Supersessionism in Paul', *Journal of Theological Studies*, NS, 58:1 (April 2007): 26–44 (40).

101. Gerald Schlabach quoted in Michael G. Cartwright, 'Afterword: "If Abraham is Our Father . . .": The Problem of Christian Supersessionism *after* Yoder', in *The Jewish-Christian Schism Revisited*, eds John Howard Yoder, Michael G. Cartwright, and Peter Ochs (Grand Rapids, Mich.: Eerdmans, 2003), p. 214.

102. See Bosch, *Transforming Mission*, pp. 154–65.

103. Lohfink makes the suggestion that the feeding of the 5000 in Mk 6.34–41 is just such a moment on the way towards the eschatological gathering of Israel, as the disciples order the people into groups of hundreds and fifties, evoking the ordering of Israel's camp in the wilderness. 'Jesus is forming the crowds of people, who were wandering without purpose or orientation, like sheep without a shepherd (v. 34), into the end-time people of God' (*Does God Need the Church?*, p. 147).

104. Barth, *Church Dogmatics* IV/3.2, p. 877.

105. And so Barth can write: 'Even the modern ecumenical movement suffers more seriously from the absence of Israel than of Rome or Moscow' (*Church Dogmatics* IV/3.2, p. 878).

106. In Advent, we sing of the 'long expected Jesus'. To hear Israel's scriptures faithfully is to hear in them the slow, painful, hopeful building of expectation. It is to hear a people fumbling toward a future usually only hinted at, but occasionally emerging from the fog in visions as brilliant as they are evanescent. To jump to Jesus too quickly in reading the Old Testament is to miss the Old Testament and, ironically, to miss Jesus himself.

107. Nor does christocentrism mitigate a renewed emphasis on the fundamentally Jewish character of the Christian faith. See Thesis 2.4.1 in Soulen, 'YHWH the Triune God', 46: 'The name Jesus (Y'shua) means "YHWH saves" (cf. Mt. 1.21). The title Christ has been interpreted at least from the time of Irenaeus in a trinitarian sense, as connoting the One who anoints, the One who is anointed, and the

unction. "To address [Jesus as the Christ] is a complete profession of faith, because it clearly reveals that God anoints the Son (the Anointed One) with the unction of the Spirit" (Basil the Great, *On the Holy Spirit*, pp. 12, 28). *The name Jesus Christ may thus not unreasonably be said to contain internal reference to the name YHWH and to the triune shape of the evangelical history as this history is packed into the title Christ'* (emphasis his).

108. Were we to summarize this in thesis form, we might simply adopt Joe Jones' affirmations in *On Being the Church of Jesus Christ in Tumultuous Times* (Eugene, Ore.: Cascade Books, 2005), p. 140.

109. John Godfrey Saxe, 'The Blind Men and the Elephant', in *The Poems of John Godfrey Saxe, Complete edition* (Boston: James R. Osgood and Company, 1873), pp. 135–36. The story is a much older one and is found in various cultures. See the helpful digest at http://www.noogenesis.com/pineapple/blind_men_elephant.html.

110. *Nostra Aetate* §2.

111. *The Lausanne Covenant* 6.

112. See Lamin Sanneh, *Translating the Message: The Missionary Impact on Culture* (Maryknoll, N.Y.: Orbis, 1989).

113. Karl Barth, *The Epistle to the Romans*, 6th edn, trans. Edwyn C. Hoskyns (Oxford: Oxford University Press, 1968), p. 341. Note that Barth levels the playing field here. Christians are not in a place of privilege but come under judgment as much as adherents of any other religion. The Bible is about 'the religion of God and never once the religion of the Jews, or Christians, or heathen' (Karl Barth, 'The Strange New World within the Bible', in *The Word of God and the Word of Man*, trans. Douglas Horton [London: Hodder & Stoughton, 1935], p. 45).

114. Consider those whose cognitive abilities make 'belief' appear foreign, even unrecognizable. Can a severely mentally disabled person come to faith? For an emphatic 'yes' to this question, rooting belief in embodiment and symbolic engagement, see Amos Yong, *Theology and Down Syndrome: Reimagining Disability in Late Modernity* (Waco, Tex.: Baylor University Press, 2007), p. 208.

115. One must ask, too, what counts as sufficient proclamation? Does a bumper sticker count? What about having once tuned in to a few minutes of a televised church service? If one has been badly mistreated in a church, how would the gospel have to be communicated such that the hearer would be accountable to its proclamation to her?

116. Newbigin, *The Open Secret*, p. 173.

117. George A. Lindbeck, *The Nature of Doctrine: Religion and Theology in a Postliberal Age* (Louisville, Ky./London: Westminster John Knox Press, 1984), pp. 58–59.

118. Balthasar, *Dare We Hope 'That All Men Be Saved'? With a Short Discourse on Hell*, trans. David Kipp and Lothar Krauth (San Francisco: Ignatius Press, 1988).

119. Balthasar adamantly rejects dogmatic universalism, which is an insidious form of over-realized eschatology as guilty of speculative presumption

as those who take a Dantaic delight in assigning antagonists to the various circles of Hell.

120. For a short but comprehensive report on these issues in sympathy with Lindbeck and Balthasar, see Newbigin, *The Open Secret*, pp. 78–81; also see pp. 160–89.
121. See esp. *De unitate* 6.
122. Furthermore, what are we to make of it after the schism in which the church became the churches of East and West (or at least the church in the East and West), and the Reformation, where the Western church split – only to split again, and again, and again? We will set this pertinent issue aside, having previously discussed the problem of division and hope of ecumenism.
123. Oliver O'Donovan, 'What Kind of Community is the Church? The Richard Hooker Lectures 2005', *Ecclesiology* 3:2 (2007): 187.
124. Jones, *On Being the Church of Jesus Christ in Tumultuous Times*, pp. 47–51, 62–63.
125. Harper and Metzger, *Exploring Ecclesiology*, p. 29.
126. Harper and Metzger, *Exploring Ecclesiology*, p. 263.

PAROUSIA AND ECCLESIA

1. John Piper, *Let the Nations Be Glad! The Supremacy of God in Missions*, 2nd edn (Grand Rapids, Mich.: Baker Academic, 2003), p. 17.
2. T. S. Eliot, 'Little Gidding', *The Four Quartets*. Eliot is citing Julian of Norwich's *Revelations of Divine Love*.

SUGGESTED READING

GENERAL

Barth, Karl. *Church Dogmatics*, 13 vols (Edinburgh: T&T Clark, 1956–1975), IV/1, 2, 3.2.

Calvin, John. *Institutes of the Christian Religion*, vol. 2, ed. John T. McNeill, trans. Ford Lewis Battles (Louisville, Ky.: Westminster John Knox Press, 1959), Book IV.

Catechism of the Catholic Church, 2nd edn (Vatican City: Libreria Editrice Vaticana, 1997).

Moltmann, Jürgen. *The Church in the Power of the Spirit: A Contribution to Messianic Ecclesiology*, trans. Margaret Kohl (Minneapolis, Minn.: Fortress Press, 1993 [1975]).

Pannenberg, Wolfhart. *Systematic Theology*, vol. 3, trans. Geoffrey W. Bromiley (Grand Rapids, Mich.: Eerdmans, 1998).

Vatican II: The Conciliar and Post Conciliar Documents. Study Edition, ed. Austin Flannery, O. P. (Northport, N.Y.: Costello, 1987).

CHAPTER 1 – MODELS

Boff, Leonardo. *Ecclesiogenesis* (Maryknoll, N.Y.: Orbis, 1997 [1977]).

Doyle, Dennis M. *Communion Ecclesiology: Visions and Versions* (Maryknoll, N.Y.: Orbis Books, 2000).

Dulles, Avery. *Models of the Church*, expanded ed. (New York: Doubleday, 2002 [1974]).

Goheen, Michael W. *'As the Father Has Sent Me, I am Sending You': J.E. Lesslie Newbigin's Missionary Ecclesiology* (Zoetermeer: Uitgeverij Boekencentrum, 2000).

Healy, Nicholas M. *Church, World and Christian Life: Practical-Prophetic Ecclesiology* (Cambridge: Cambridge University Press, 2000).

Hütter, Reinhard. *Suffering Divine Things: Theology as Church Practice*, trans. Doug Stott (Grand Rapids, Mich.: Eerdmans, 2000).

Hütter, Reinhard. *Bound to Be Free: Evangelical Catholic Engagements in Ecclesiology, Ethics and Ecumenism* (Grand Rapids, Mich.: Eerdmans, 2004).

Minear, Paul S. *Images of the Church in the New Testament* (Philadelphia: Westminster Press, 1977 [1960]).

Newbigin, Lesslie. *The Household of God: Lectures on the Nature of the Church* (New York: Friendship Press, 1954).

Newbigin, Lesslie. *A Word in Season: Perspectives on Christian World Missions* (Grand Rapids, Mich.: Eerdmans, 1994).

Ratzinger, Joseph. 'A letter to the bishops of the catholic church on some aspects of the church understood as communion' (Rome: 28 May 1992; available online at http://www.vatican.va/roman_curia/congregations/cfaith/documents/rc_con_cfaith_doc_28051992_communionis-notio_en.html).

Schillebeeckx, Edward. *Church: The Human Story of God* (New York: Crossroad, 1990).

Tillard, J. M. R. *Church of Churches: The Ecclesiology of Communion*, trans. R. C. De Peaux (Collegeville, Minn.: Liturgical Press, 1992).

Volf, Miroslav. *After our Likeness: The Church as the Image of the Trinity* (Grand Rapids, Mich.: Eerdmans, 1998).

Webster, John. *Confessing God: Essays on Christian Dogmatics II* (Edinburgh: T&T Clark, 2005).

Zizioulas, John D. *Being as Communion: Studies in Personhood and the Church* (Crestwood, N.Y.: St. Vladimir's Seminary Press, 1985).

CHAPTER 2 – MARKS

Anderson, Ray S. *An Emergent Theology for Emerging Churches* (Downers Grove, Ill.: InterVarsity Press, 2006).

Calvin, John. *Institutes of the Christian Religion*, vol. 2, ed. John T. McNeill, trans. Ford Lewis Battles (Louisville, Ky.: Westminster John Knox Press, 1959).

Guder, Darrell L. (ed.), *Missional Church: A Vision for the Sending of the Church in North America* (The Gospel and Our Culture Series. Grand Rapids, Mich.: Eerdmans, 1998).

Gutiérrez, Gustavo. *The Power of the Poor in History*, trans. Robert R. Barr (Eugene, Ore.: Wipf & Stock Publishers, 1983).

von Harnack, Adolf. *The Constitution & Law of the Church in the First Two Centuries* (London: Williams & Norgate, 1910).

Kärkkäinen, Veli-Mati. *An Introduction to Ecclesiology: Ecumenical, Historical & Global Perspectives*, (Downers Grove, Ill.: InterVarsity Press, 2002).

Longenecker, Richard N. (ed.), *Community Formation in the Early Church and in the Church Today* (Peabody, Mass.: Hendrickson, 2002).

Luther, Martin. 'On the Councils and Churches', in *Luther's Works*, vol. 25, ed. Eric W. Gritsch (Philadelphia: Fortress Press, 1966 [1539]).

Marion, Jean-Luc. *God without Being: Hors-Text*, trans. Thomas A. Carlson (Chicago: University of Chicago Press, 1991 [1982]).

Moltmann, Jürgen. *The Church in the Power of the Spirit: A Contribution to Messianic Ecclesiology*, trans. Margaret Kohl (Minneapolis, Minn.: Fortress Press, 1993 [1975]).

Oden, Thomas. *Systematic Theology*, vol. 3: *Life in the Spirit* (New York: HarperSanFrancisco, 1992).

Rutba House (ed.), *School(s) for Conversion: 12 Marks of a New Monasticism* (Eugene, Ore.: Cascade Books/Wipf & Stock, 2005).
Sanneh, Lamin. *Whose Religion is Christianity? The Gospel Beyond the West* (Grand Rapids, Mich.: Eerdmans, 2003).
World Council of Churches. *The Nature and Mission of the Church* (Faith and Order Paper #198; 2005).

CHAPTER 3 – MEDIATION

Barth, Karl. 'The Strange New World within the Bible', in *The Word of God and the Word of Man*, trans. Douglas Horton (London: Hodder & Stoughton, 1935), pp. 28–50.
Cavanaugh, William T. *Torture and Eucharist: Theology, Politics, and the Body of Christ* (Malden, Mass.: Blackwell Publishing, 1998).
de Lubac, Henri. *Corpus Mysticum: The Eucharist and the Church in the Middle Ages* (Notre Dame, Ind.: University of Notre Dame Press, 2007).
Ferguson, Everett. *Baptism in the Early Church: History, Theology, and Liturgy in the First Five Centuries* (Grand Rapids, Mich.: Eerdmans, 2009).
Horton, Michael. *People and Place: A Covenant Ecclesiology* (Louisville, Ky.: Westminster John Knox Press, 2008).
Hunsinger, George. *The Eucharist and Ecumenism: Let Us Keep the Feast* (Cambridge: Cambridge University Press, 2008).
Malone, Mary T. *Women and Christianity*, 3 vols. (Maryknoll, N.Y.: Orbis, 2003).
Pannenberg, Wolfhart. *Systematic Theology*, 3 vols, trans. Geoffrey W. Bromiley (Grand Rapids, Mich.: Eerdmans, 1998).
Schmemann, Alexander. *Of Water and the Spirit: A Liturgical Study of Baptism* (Crestwood, N.Y.: St. Vladimir's Seminary Press, 1974).
Schmemann, Alexander. *The Eucharist: Sacrament of the Kingdom* (Crestwood, N.Y.: St. Vladimir's Seminary Press, 2000).
Torrance, James B. *Worship, Community, and the Triune God of Grace. The Didsbury Lectures 1994* (Carlisle, England: Paternoster, 1996).
Vanhoozer, Kevin J. *Is There a Meaning in This Text? The Bible, the Reader, and the Morality of Literary Knowledge* (Grand Rapids, Mich.: Zondervan, 1998).
Webster, John. *Holy Scripture: A Dogmatic Sketch* (Cambridge: Cambridge University Press, 2003).
Wesley, John. Sermon 16, 'On the Means of Grace', in *Wesley's 52 Standard Sermons* (Salem, Ohio: Schmul Publishing Company, 1988), pp. 149–62.
World Council of Churches. *Baptism, Eucharist and Ministry* (Faith and Order Paper No. 111, 1982).

CHAPTER 4 – MISSION

Bosch, David. *Transforming Mission: Paradigm Shifts in Theology and Mission* (Maryknoll, N.Y.: Orbis, 1991).

Braaten, Carl E. *Mother Church: Ecclesiology and Ecumenism* (Minneapolis, Minn.: Fortress Press, 1998).

Carter, Craig A. *Rethinking Christ and Culture: A Post-Christendom Perspective* (Grand Rapids, Mich.: Brazos Press, 2006).

de Lubac, Henri. *The Church: Paradox and Mystery* (Staten Island, N.Y.: Alba House, 1969).

Hauerwas, Stanley and William H. Willimon, *Resident Aliens* (Nashville, Tenn.: Abingdon Press, 1989).

Jenkins, Philip. *The Next Christendom: The Coming of Global Christianity* (Oxford: Oxford University Press, 2002).

Ladd, George Eldon. *The Gospel of the Kingdom: Scriptural Studies in the Kingdom of God* (Grand Rapids, Mich.: Eerdmans, 1959).

Lohfink, Gerhard. *Does God Need the Church? Toward a Theology of the People of God* (Collegeville, Minn.: The Litugical Press, 1999).

The Lutheran World Federation and The Roman Catholic Church, *Joint Declaration on the Doctrine of Justification* (Grand Rapids, Mich.: Eerdmans, 2000).

Newbigin, Lesslie. *The Gospel in a Pluralist Society* (Grand Rapids, Mich.: Eerdmans, 1989).

Newbigin, Lesslie. *The Open Secret: An Introduction to the Theology of Mission*, rev. ed. (Grand Rapids, Mich.: Eerdmans, 1995).

Niebuhr, H. Richard. *Christ and Culture* (New York: Harper and Brothers, 1951).

Noll, Mark A. and Carolyn Nystrom, *Is the Reformation Over? An Evangelical Assessment of Contemporary Roman Catholicism* (Grand Rapids, Mich.: Baker Academic, 2005).

O'Donovan, Oliver. *The Desire of the Nations: Rediscovering the Roots of Political Theology* (Cambridge: Cambridge University Press, 1999).

Perkins, John M. *With Justice for All: A Strategy for Community Development*, 3rd edn (Ventura, Calif.: Regal Books, 2007).

Reno, R. R. *In the Ruins of the Church: Sustaining Faith in an Age of Diminished Christianity* (Grand Rapids, Mich.: Brazos Press, 2002).

Sanneh, Lamin. *Translating the Message: The Missionary Impact on Culture* (Maryknoll, N.Y.: Orbis, 1989).

Wright, Christopher J. H. *The Mission of God: Unlocking the Bible's Grand Narrative* (Downers Grove, Ill.: IVP Academic, 2006).

AUTHOR INDEX

Abraham, William 128, 215
Aland, Kurt 218
Alberigo, Giuseppe 198
Alexander, James 207
Allen, R. Michael 215
Anderson, Bonnie S. 224
Anderson, Ray S. 214–15, 237
Aquinas, Thomas 206, 208, 215, 219
Augustine of Hippo 59, 62–5, 67, 70,
    81, 123, 207–8, 218–19, 226

Badcock, Gary 202
Balthasar, Hans Urs von 189, 218,
    234–5
Banks, Robert 200
Barth, Karl 40, 44–5, 55, 110, 120, 129,
    147, 156, 164, 171, 183, 206,
    215–16, 218, 221–2, 226–7, 229–30,
    232–4, 236, 238
Basil the Great 234
Bauckham, Richard 196, 223, 233
Bauer, Bruno 195
Bauer, Walter 27, 200
Beale, G. K. 157, 227
Begbie, Jeremy S. 223
Benedict of Nursia 89, 98, 159, 212
Berkhof, Hendrikus 204
Berkouwer, G. C. 173, 227, 230
Blumenfeld-Kosinski, Renate 210
Bockmuehl, Markus 200
Boff, Leonardo 25–6, 35, 37, 45, 51–2,
    54, 162, 199, 228, 236
Bolger, Ryan K. 214
Bonhoeffer, Dietrich 44–5, 61, 111–12,
    115, 204, 207, 213, 216–17, 222, 228
Borg, Marcus 11, 197
Bosch, David 182–3, 219, 227, 233, 238
Braaten, Carl E. 211
Brent, Allen 201
Brown, Peter 207
Brownson, James V. 217

Bultmann, Rudolph 7
Burke, Daniel 226
Burke, Patrick 200–1
Burns, J. Patout 208
Burrus, Virginia 225

Calvin, John 21, 55, 68, 91–3, 118,
    125–7, 129, 131, 136, 199, 208, 210,
    212, 215, 218–20, 222–4, 230, 233,
    235, 237
Campbell, R. Alistair 200, 204
Campenhausen, Hans von 200, 209
Campolo, Anthony 213
Caputo, John D. 228
Carson, D. A. 211, 213, 220
Carter, Craig A. 159–60, 163, 239
Cartwright, Michael G. 233
Cary, Philip 211
Catchpole, David 195
Cavanaugh, William 137, 224, 238
Chesterton, G. K. 216
Claiborne, Shane 213
Clark, Elizabeth A. 225
Coakley, Sarah 209
Conder, Tim 214
Cone, James 161–2, 228
Congar, Yves 18, 25, 200
Conniry, Charles J. 209
Couenhoven, Jesse 215
Coyle, J. Kevin 207
Crossan, John Dominic 11, 197
Crouch, Andy 213
Cyprian 29–30, 32–3, 36, 89, 189–90,
    198, 202, 203, 208, 211, 218–19
Cyril of Alexandria 219

de Lubac, Henri 18, 206, 216, 231,
    238–9
Demetry, Constas H. 210
Doherty, Earl 195
Doyle, Dennis M. 43, 199–200, 236